Also by Eric Rauchway

*Murdering McKinley: The Making of
Theodore Roosevelt's America*

*The Refuge of Affections: Family and
American Reform Politics, 1900–1920*

Blessed
Among
Nations

Blessed Among Nations

HOW THE WORLD MADE AMERICA

Eric Rauchway

HILL and WANG
A division of Farrar, Straus and Giroux
New York

Hill and Wang
A division of Farrar, Straus and Giroux
19 Union Square West, New York 10003

Distributed in Canada by Douglas & McIntyre Ltd.
Printed in the United States of America
First edition, 2006

Library of Congress Cataloging-in-Publication Data
Rauchway, Eric.
    Blessed among nations : how the world made America / Eric Rauchway.
        p.   cm.
    Includes bibliographical references and index.
    ISBN-13: 978-0-8090-5580-7 (hardcover : alk. paper)
    ISBN-10: 0-8090-5580-5 (hardcover : alk. paper)
    1. United States—Foreign relations—20th century.   2. Globalization—
    History—20th century.   3. United States—Foreign economic relations.
    4. World politics—20th century.   I. Title.

    E744.R375 2006
    973—dc22   2005029675

Designed by Debbie Glasserman

www.fsgbooks.com

10   9   8   7   6   5   4   3   2   1

For Meg, Andrew, and Jane

PRIOR: I have always depended on the kindness of strangers.

HANNAH: Well that's a stupid thing to do.

—TONY KUSHNER,
Angels in America, Part Two: Perestroika

■ Contents

Blessed
Among
Nations

Introduction

This book offers a look at American history through the lens of globalization. Like a regular optical lens you might find in a telescope or a microscope, it is meant to help you see something you wouldn't if you were simply looking with your unaided eyes. It directs your attention to the movements of money and people around the globe, and how they influenced American politics and culture.

Also like a regular optical lens, it is better at bringing some kinds of things into focus than others. Just as a telescope is terrific for marveling at the mountains on the moon but pretty poor for peering at paramecia, this book is designed to help you get an appreciation for the effects of powerful global forces, not local ones.

It's not that we don't care about the paramecia of the past. The microscopic view of history, when carefully trained on the right subject—a mad prophet, a frontier speculator, a presidential assassin—can tell us a great deal. But if we want to see large features in faraway landscapes, we need to overlook these otherwise compelling close-ups.

There is another way in which I hope this book will work like a lens. Like a lot of people, I need corrective lenses to see properly, and also like a lot of people I don't like to go to the doctor very much. So people like me will wear a pair of glasses for years without seeing an optometrist. And during that time, those glasses, which were perfectly designed to help us see when they were made, get worse and worse at their job. The lenses aren't changing, but our eyes are. We just don't notice because it happens so slowly. Then, finally, we get tired of the headaches and the blurry vision and we go to the doctor and get a properly prescribed pair of spectacles. And we put them on, and suddenly we see the world as if it were new, and we realize we've been squinting through outdated lenses for far too long. I think that much of what we see nowadays when we look at American history is like this, a picture as seen through lenses that worked fine for us once, but don't work so well now that we've changed. There's nothing intrinsically wrong with our old glasses; they were just meant for a different set of eyes, and too much of the world now looks out of focus.

When you put on your new glasses after delaying a visit to the doctor for too long, you suddenly wonder how you could ever have stood to look through the old ones. I hope this book will help us see America's place in the world with the same freshness, so that we can see the same old story with a new clarity and begin to wonder how we could ever have stood to look at the world through those quaint old spectacles, missing so much of such importance.

Specifically, using globalization as a lens brings into focus the relationship between the United States and the rest of the world in the late nineteenth century, and how this relationship shaped American political development. Capital and labor from overseas pushed American political development in noticeably unusual directions during a particularly important growth spurt. This early formative influence bequeathed the United States some peculiar and lasting habits of government. The effects of globalization helped the country become a powerful nation without developing (in comparative terms) a powerful central government. In the United States, as in some other countries, we often argue over the appropriate size and authority of national government, and usually we argue from principle: a big government is better because it can provide security; a small government is better because it can allow freedom. These arguments from principle have what to a historian seems like an unfortunately timeless quality, as if government were some uniform product, of which you can have too much or too little, but which is always the same thing. If we look at how goverment grew in the first place, we might remember that it is a set of solutions to a set of problems— not theoretical problems, but practical problems—and that, in practice, not all peoples face the same problems. During its growth into a powerful nation, the United States faced a set of problems unlike those any other nation has encountered. Americans formed their habits of government by solving a set of problems specific to their circumstances. And we know that habits often outlast the circumstances that justified them, just as we often wear prescription eyeglasses long after our eyes have changed, and sometimes with bad consequences.

The long life of American habits, which outlasted the circumstances to which they were suited, has affected not only the United States but also the rest of the world fairly dramatically. To take up a literally dramatic analogy: the fifty-year period from 1865 through 1914 is, in the history of the Western world, like the play *Hamlet*. The great actors on the international stage, set at odds by bad faith, misunderstanding, and the fateful entanglement of their interests, come ever closer to catastrophe until finally they clash, and after a gruesome bout of killing none of the major players is left standing. It's terribly moving, and we in the audience feel emotionally drained. Then, somewhat confusingly, a fellow named Fortinbras walks on and says, well, now I'm the king of Denmark. And . . . curtain. Even in Shakespeare's full script there's little indication of who Fortinbras is, or what he's been up to.[1] His story, whatever it is, must have gone on mostly separate from that of Hamlet and his family, because we've been watching them, and there's been scarcely any mention of Fortinbras. Yet he must have been, in some important way that was taking place offstage or, if you prefer, outside the principal focus of the action, connected to the characters and events of the play, because here he is, king. There is something very wrong with the end of this play; the foreseeable future seems dramatically disconnected from the immediate past as we have learned it.

The world's people must have felt much this sense of puzzlement and anxiety in 1918, when at war's end the Americans suddenly emerged as the planet's great power. Where had these Americans been, what had they been up to, and what did they think were the normal relations among nations? Most of the world's people knew little more about the United States in 1918 than theatergoers know about Fortinbras at the end of *Hamlet*, and in significant ways we know little more now than they did then, because we have been telling this history as if we've been restaging *Hamlet*, without any attention to the important offstage back story. We need now, all of us, to know not only what the American Fortinbras was doing just before he emerged from the wings, but also how his strange tale connects to the main action, if we want to understand why he has gone on to behave as he did and what it means to the world.

1

Globalization
and America

*King Edward's new policy of peace was very successful and
culminated in the Great War. . . . [Afterward] America was . . .
clearly top nation, and History came to a [full stop].*
　　　　　—W. C. Sellar and R. J. Yeatman, *1066 and All That* (1931)

The United States became the country we know today
at the end of World War I, when it took over the role of "top
nation" from Britain. The story of its rise to this position of
strength began at the end of the Civil War. After the demise
of slavery, America spread west over the plains, swiftly settling
the continent and bringing twelve new states into the union.
With the winning of the West came the transformation of the
United States into the world's largest economy. By 1917, when
the United States entered World War I, America stood out among
nations, its anomalously large economy yoked in uneven harness
to an anomalously small government with unusually few powers.
Perhaps paradoxically, the United States could not have diverged so significantly from the behavior of other countries had
other countries not involved themselves so significantly in American affairs. The globalization of the nineteenth century, in which
powerful forces reached across national boundaries to bind the
earth's people tightly together, pushed American development in
a peculiar direction. We need neither admire nor despise these
peculiarities to note them and assess how much they resulted
from the impact of international factors.[1]

From the first, European settlers in America claimed they were
making a special society in the New World, but they did not mean a

society like the powerful and peculiar nation the United States became. John Winthrop may have told his fellow Puritans in 1630 that their settlement "shall be as a Citty upon a Hill," and Ronald Reagan may have echoed him in 1989, referring to the "shining city upon a hill," but their Americas and their figures of speech, though superficially similar, differed profoundly.[2] When Winthrop spoke to his Puritan flock they had not yet landed on the Massachusetts shore. They had still to build themselves even a modest shelter from the elements, and his "Citty" stood in the far future. When he imagined the people of the world looking to America, he envisioned them critically comparing the New World's people to their godly ideals, and he shuddered to think what might happen if the Puritan project fell short of virtue in the world's sight: "wee shall open the mouthes of enemies to speake evill of the wayes of god," he warned.[3] By contrast Reagan knew his "city" shone before the people of the earth, and he spoke confidently of their opinion that the United States served as a powerful exemplar of freedom. Between Winthrop and Reagan lay more than three centuries of history and a world of difference, but the bit of history that made the most difference happened relatively recently, and indeed within Reagan's lifetime. The world into which he was born, at the start of the twentieth century, was only just awakening to what a strange success European settlement had made in America.

Even if Reagan was right about what the world thinks of the United States, the earth's people have more often envied than imitated America. At the end of World War I, the United States stood out as an empire with considerable experience of conquest but little experience of administering other peoples or indeed of administering its own affairs, which it preferred to leave to the energies of private enterprise. In the years since, American leaders have frequently repeated their hope that the world would come to follow the U.S. example. But unlike Britain, which during its reign as top nation seeded the globe not only with its governmental system so that Westminster could regard itself unblushingly as the Mother of Parliaments but also with the Anglican Church and British banking and a hundred greater and lesser cultural institutions like cricket, the United States has lent the world neither its system nor its habits of government.[4] It remains now as it was in 1917, both immune to the trends of national development that elsewhere prevail and also apparently unable to persuade other peoples to follow its lead.

Moreover, the insistence of American optimists that, the evidence of history notwithstanding, the world will naturally come around to the American way of doing things has more than once led to disaster. In the 1920s, at the close of the first modern era of globalization, American leadership preserved neither peace nor prosperity in the world. And in the early twenty-first century, after another decades-long bout of globalization, the United States still stands at the forefront of nations, still mighty, still apparently called upon to lead a world of people who do not—perhaps because they cannot—follow its example.

If today Americans wish to avoid repeating the catastrophes of the 1920s we must understand why the United States became an unfollowed leader, and why other nations are still unlikely to imitate it. Likewise, citizens of the rest of the world who wish to understand why the world's top nation remains relentlessly peculiar will need to know how it became that way. The answer is simple, if paradoxical: the United States' extensive connections to the rest of the world have created and maintained the nation's peculiar habits of government. No other nation enjoyed America's unique place within the network of worldwide forces that commentators today summarize under the term *globalization*, nor have these forces affected the development of other countries as they have America. To frame the idea as a hypothesis: globalization has reinforced American character. And like all hypotheses, particularly those that rely on the use of -*ation*s and notions like national character to sum up complexities, this one bears elaboration before we test it against the evidence.

AMERICAN CHARACTER

First, Americanness needs clearer definition. If we wish to know *why* this nation is different from all other nations, we should make sure we know *how* it is different.

Scholars dislike the suggestion that America has an unusual history. We worry that an emphasis on American difference too easily slides into a celebration of American exceptionalism, or a belief that the United States can freely defy the tedious norms that govern other nations. This is a legitimate concern. Noticing that the United States has historically enjoyed considerable success with an empire built on the cheap might well lead us to continue this tradition in circumstances where it will not succeed. Noticing that the United States has historically gotten along with a habitually half-hearted commitment to social welfare might lead us to go on supposing minimal social policies will continue to suit us in the future. Yet this legitimate concern leads scholars to make some unpersuasive arguments about the past: that America's western conquests constitute not just an empire—for that case can be made—but an empire like others; that America's limited nineteenth-century pensions policies constitute not just a kind of social insurance—for that case, too, can be made, at a stretch—but a social insurance plan like others; that these histories constitute suitable foundations for modern growth in both areas.

In this book I proceed on the assumption that whatever our hopes for the future, they will fail of fulfillment if we poorly represent the past. We need to notice and explain salient differences in American development much as a natural historian might notice and explain salient differences that define a species: not to glorify it, but simply to identify it. Noting, for example, that an elephant has a trunk, and other animals do not, does not mean praising the elephant, but it helps us understand the elephant—moreover, it helps us understand the environment in which the elephant developed. An elephant has a trunk because its DNA codes for it, but that DNA survived because it represented a fit adaptation to the elephant's circumstances. So, too, with the ideas that support America's exceptional behavior: they survived because they represent adequate adaptations to historical circumstances. If we want to understand their survival, we had better understand those circumstances.

Thus, while we might want to invoke ideas or culture to explain what makes the United States stick out, we should resist this temptation. Analysis of culture, while it tells us what Americans want, tells us little about what they actually get. Americans have long expressed a devotion to liberty, both political and economic, and a proportionate distaste for government power. This devotion explains much about American desires. But history does not always permit the expression of desires and ideals in law and customs. To employ the genetic metaphor again, we may say that the United States has the gene for liberty—but, like all genes, it needs a favorable environment for its expression.[5]

Therefore we should discuss Americanness as an outcome rather than as an input, and we should focus on the influential elements in the historical environment, and their effect on the expression of American ideals. This choice would put us in the good company of some early students of American habits who studied the material environment and the international circumstances in which Americans lived. In the early nineteenth century, the German poet and politician J. W. Goethe looked at the mineral endowments of the New World and declared, "America, you have it better."[6] Writing at about the same time, the French political thinker Alexis de Tocqueville went a step further and noted that what distinguished the United States from otherwise comparable countries was not only its location in the New World but also its close connection to the Old: "In spite of the ocean which intervenes, I cannot consent to separate America from Europe. . . . The position of the Americans is therefore exceptional, and it may be believed that no democratic people will ever be placed in a similar one." America's position in an enviable environment, sustaining a vital and dynamic connection to Europe is, more so than culture, something we can carefully and conscientiously isolate and define for study. Moreover these hard facts surely influence culture, as

Goethe and Tocqueville saw, and (for those inclined to make what the Puritans would have thought heretical guesses) they may even attest to the plans of Providence.[7]

In terms of an international ranking, we can describe American-ness as follows. The United States is today the world's largest econ-omy and the world's greatest producer and consumer of energy resources, yet it depends on the investment of capital and labor from the rest of the world to carry on its routine affairs; and its government spends a smaller proportion of its people's wealth than other rich countries' governments do.[8] These characteristics make the United States recognizably American around the world today. Yet they have not always described the United States. If these attributes define Americanness now, then the United States became American during a particular and well-defined phase in its development. Specifically, during the half century following the Civil War, stretching up to the start of World War I in Europe in 1914, the United States became the America we recognize. During this time its economy quintupled in size, with its growth account-ing for a quarter of the world's economic growth. On the eve of World War I, American productivity amounted to almost a fifth of the world's economic output, whereas five decades earlier, after the Civil War, it had measured under a tenth. This unmatched expan-sion made the United States into the power it now is: the richest country in the world, with an economy more than twice the size of the next largest. This transformation also left the United States, on the eve of its intervention in World War I, a country aloof from the rest of the world, the only major nation neither convulsed by revo-lution (as with China or Russia) nor already sunk into the war.[9]

Now, we might reasonably grant that the United States differs from other countries in these ways, and that it has done so in fairly similar ways since this great nineteenth-century transformation, while objecting that all countries differ from one another. After all, countries, like kindergarteners, are each special in their own way. In having its own distinct and definite character, then, we might say that the United States is only being normal. There are two problems with using this reasoning as an excuse for setting aside distinguishing features of the American case. First, even if we concede that each nation differs in some degree from all other nations, it is nevertheless true that in recent history no other country's own special attributes have mattered so much to the rest of the world's people. American eccentricity has mattered, and for the present continues to matter, more than that of other nations, sometimes to notably violent effect. Even if in the foreseeable future we might want to know more than we do about (let us say) Chinese, Russian, or Brazilian peculiarities, just now we have a pressing need to know more about American peculiarities.

Second, conceding that each nation possesses its own specific character slights the glaring extent to which the United States goes its own way. Even if the present era of American predominance proves fleeting, and even if when it goes, it reduces our interest in understanding American character, it presents an important historical problem with an enduring present-day relevance: during the late nineteenth century, when globalization was pushing more nations to become more like one another, the United States was becoming less like other countries. Even if all nations were in some way unique, no nation differed so much from its fellows in so many important ways as did the United States. Nor should this point hold interest only for students of history, for in the present age of globalization, as much of the rest of the world converges in standards of living, there is reason to believe that the United States is once again diverging.

If we wish to speak in terms not only of difference but of significant difference, we might try thinking about national attributes not only in words but in numbers. It is important, or anyway honest, to admit that these numbers, like all historical data, can represent only estimates, inevitably prone to error. They are best guesses about an era long before the relentless enumeration of everything came to seem practical, let alone desirable. But rough estimates can serve a good purpose by drawing attention both to differences and to degrees of difference.[10]

For example, the era in which the United States emerged as an exceptional great power saw rich nations scramble to plant their flags in pieces of Africa and Asia, and for this reason it is often

known as "the age of empire."[11] The United States, which acquired
the Philippines, Puerto Rico, Cuba, and some other extraterritorial possessions in these years, became a colonial power like
other rich countries. But it did not follow what appears to be the
colonial rule. Generally speaking, richer countries had bigger
empires—unless the country was the United States, which exhib-
ited little acquisitive instinct proportionate to its ability, at least
outside its continental borders. (See figure 1.1.)[12]

Likewise the late nineteenth century saw modernizing nations
lay the basic foundations of what would become modern welfare
states. Governments responded to the long-term and cyclical
unemployment characteristic of industrialization by transferring
private wealth to needy people for the public benefit. Germany
under Otto von Bismarck passed the first proto–welfare legislation, but the Reich soon fell behind other nations in its willingness
to tax its people for social welfare. As a general rule, richer countries paid richer benefits to their poorer citizens, although Scandinavian and Antipodean nations took more of their taxpayers'
money for the poor. And as before, the United States appears in

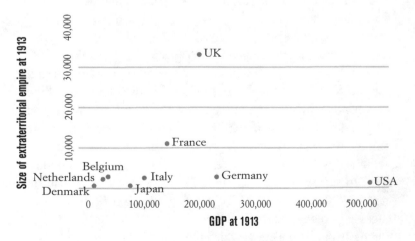

Figure 1.1 Size of extraterritorial empire in square kilometers as a function of size of
GDP in millions of 1990 international Gheary-Khamis dollars. (For further discussion, see note on page 223.)

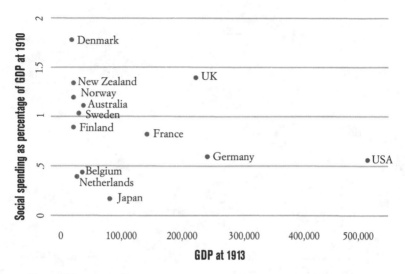

Figure 1.2 Social spending as a share of GDP, graphed as a function of GDP in millions of 1990 international Gheary-Khamis dollars. (For further discussion, see note on page 223.)

this picture as an outlier well off the beaten track of customary behavior: Unlike some developing countries that spent nothing on such policies, it did not wholly ignore social spending trends. But it did not spend on the same lines as other, more developed industrial democracies, either. (See figure 1.2.)[13]

The United States' reluctance to use state power proportionate to its economic strength extended even to matters bearing on its basic economic stability. For example, just as the nineteenth century witnessed the growth of empires and proto–welfare states, it also saw the emergence of central banks, whose designers and supporters expected them to, as editor of *The Economist* Walter Bagehot urged in 1873, "lend freely" to ease financial panics.[14] As industrial economies grew and evidence accumulated, the science of economics came to support Bagehot's intuition, and countries created central banks to lend freely in a crisis, or else they adapted older institutions to serve the purpose. Except in the United States: Congress did not create the Federal Reserve System until late in America's industrial development, and even then had no

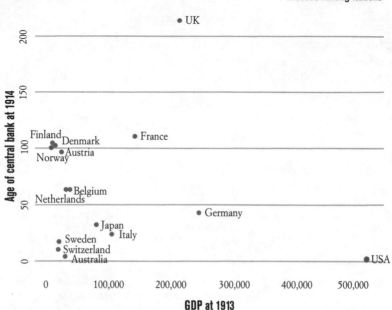

Figure 1.3 Age of central banks as a function of 1913 GDP in millions of 1990 international Gheary-Khamis dollars. (For further discussion, see note on page 223.)

intention of creating a central bank in the generally understood sense of the term. For one thing, proper central banks did not as a rule have twelve coeval and far-flung offices as the Federal Reserve did, as such a design would tend to undermine their centrality. (See figure 1.3.)[15]

Thinking about these examples, we can begin to describe how the United States stood apart from other countries in this period. We can see that while government power did grow in the United States, it grew differently than we might have expected. The three foregoing examples of major developments in the nineteenth century from which the United States notably diverged (in extraterritorial possessions, social policy status, and central banks) could accompany others. Despite having built a million-man modern army in the 1860s, by World War I the United States had a much smaller army than other major and even minor powers. (In the early 1910s, the U.S. military was about the size of Ethiopia's.) America spent less of its money through its government than other countries, and relative to the size of its economy it had a smaller government than the Netherlands. Despite its industrial development and the wage gap between its workers and its middle class, its Socialist Party was the least popular socialist or labor party in the modern nations. The United States acted differently from other industrial democracies, and also from other New World nations. A clever person might explain away any one of these peculiarities and make the United States appear more normal in one particular or another, but as the examples showing the United States as an outlier stack up, they lead to one obvious conclusion: whatever trends prevailed among other groups of nations in the nineteenth-century world, the United States went its own way.[16]

Thus we can say what we mean when we describe American character as an outcome, and we know when it became manifestly peculiar in this way. We face now the question of why it developed in this way at that time, which means we can turn to the other dense concept in our hypothesis: *globalization.*

GLOBALIZATION

Explaining the cause of an outlying case requires that we first have an idea about what caused the more ordinary behavior. Without grossly caricaturing the history of modernization and national development in the nineteenth century, we can venture a few generalizations. As nations acquired industrial methods and shifted their economic activity from agriculture to factory production, they discovered the problems of cyclical unemployment. Soon afterward they decided the state could use its taxing power to alleviate the effects of unemployment. Likewise, governments could use their military power to gain access to natural resources and markets for their finished goods. Further, as world markets became more interconnected, workers could choose to move to cities in other countries

where wages might be better, could send their savings home to support their families, and could develop an international network of
family business. Capital, too, could seek its most profitable place of
investment around the world. The combined effects of industrialization, whose costs and benefits were similar throughout much of the
world, and of global openness, which allowed markets to distribute
capital, labor, and goods more or less efficiently to the places where
they were most profitable, made the countries of the world increasingly alike. They adopted the same solutions to the same problems,
and commonly these solutions involved some increase of state power
to tax and spend in the name of improving industrial capacity.[17]

The United States struck out on its own in this otherwise
converging world because it occupied a peculiar place in the network of connections among nations that defined the nineteenth
century—or, to return to the hypothesis, because the globalization
of those years had unusual effects on America. During the years
that saw the other major powers sinking deeper and deeper into
the imperial entanglements that ultimately would stick them in
the mud of the western front, the Americans were, with the help
of investors from all over the world, sinking their resources into
the fields of their western frontier. In the years after the Civil War,
the small but vigorous frontier army of the United States waged
war against the American Indians, making way for the railroads.
As the U.S. economy quintupled in size, so did the U.S. rail network.[18] Those railroads bound the West to the East physically,
and allowed settlers and commerce to bind the West to the East
economically and culturally. By making the riches of the American interior accessible, they allowed the speedy growth of the
U.S. economy in those years.[19] And although they began their big
push across the plains with an investment from the U.S. government, those railroads could not have grown so far so fast without
the investment of overseas capital and labor that defined the
American economy in the late nineteenth century.

For, though it may seem peculiar to say so, during this period
when the United States became increasingly different from other

countries, it was most open to travelers, settlers, money, and ideas from the rest of the world. This openness was not by itself the factor that made the United States diverge from the pack. So open had the nineteenth-century world become to traffic in money and people among nations that some historians now call this period "the first great globalization boom."[20] The nations of the world had not committed themselves to controlling their borders. The construction of telegraph networks under the sea, rail lines over the land, and steamship routes across oceans made travel and communication easier, faster, and cheaper. Only war posed a serious obstacle to this motion among nations, but the supremacy of the British empire and its overall interest in a Pax Britannica prevented too many wars from slowing global motion too much. The nation of shopkeepers and shipbuilders imposed its wishes for open markets on the world to such a degree that one historian refers to the process as "Anglobalization."[21]

But if the globalization of the nineteenth century owed a great deal to the needs of the British empire, it also created the peculiar American empire. Global openness affected the United States as it affected no other nation. The United States received not only more, and more different kinds, of immigrants than any other developing nation either in the Western Hemisphere or the Antipodes, but also most of the ocean-crossing migrants who went anywhere in the late nineteenth and early twentieth century.[22] The United States also received more money from the international capital markets than any other developing nation, and more so than was the case elsewhere in the New World, this money came into the country through private banks instead of through investment in government. The private banks naturally looked after the interests of their clients, including those overseas, as they fueled the wild growth of the American West.[23] As a result of this involvement of international capital and labor in this critical phase of American development, the United States ended up with an empire and a government unlike any other country's.

EMPIRE AND THE SHAPE OF GOVERNMENT

As for the peculiar American empire, it lay west of the Mississippi, within the continent of North America, and by World War I (at which point the forty-eight contiguous states had all come into the Union) it lay entirely within the United States.[24] The newly settled West served the same purpose for America as overseas colonies served for the European powers, providing a wealth of natural resources that industrial metropoles could turn into finished goods. Just as, throughout Africa and Southeast Asia, regions rich in agricultural and mineral goods and inhabited by aboriginals unable to fight back a better-armed and often more numerous foe succumbed to imperial rule throughout the nineteenth century, so also in the American West did "an expanding metropolitan economy creating more elaborate and intimate linkages" tie itself to resource-rich territories.[25] But the United States could forge these links more cheaply than other empires. The country needed no great navy to reach its colonial hinterlands on the prairies. The navy necessary to allow Americans to proceed unmolested belonged to Britain, whose commanders kept an Atlantic peace for their own country's purposes, and in the process afforded the United States an essentially free shield behind which it could carry on its commercial affairs.[26] Nor did the United States need to fight off competing empires. Indeed, so far from threatening to settle the Great Plains if the Americans did not get there first, Canada and Mexico had to work to escape integration into the United States.

So the American empire did not entail the same costs of conquest and defense as the empires of the other great powers. But the differences between the United States and other nations do not reduce simply to cost. Even though it is true and striking that the United States spent less on government than other countries during its rise to industrial power, relatively small government does not by itself constitute the defining characteristic of American development. This quantitative difference points to an important qualitative difference. The United States did not just have a smaller or cheaper government than other nations. It had a government developed from different causes and devoted to different purposes from those of other nations.

Let us pursue this point with respect to America's inland empire by comparing it to a similar imperial effort of the same period. Ever since the middle nineteenth century, observers have compared the expansion of the United States over its prairie frontier with the expansion of Russia over its steppe frontier. When Mark Twain visited the Russian city of Odessa on the Black Sea, he exclaimed, "Look up the street or down the street, this way or that way, we saw only America!" Like the ports of Twain's beloved Mississippi, Odessa served a grassland interior that white settlers regarded as empty and begging for tillage and fertilizer. Like the grassland interior of the American West, the Russian steppes were not actually empty but were home to native peoples who resented and resisted the expansion of settlers into their territory. Like the American government, the Russian government encouraged its people to spread out over the frontier, and granted them title to homesteads, seeing in the advance of settlement the progress of the nation, which would gain access to rich natural resources. And as with Americans, Russians regarded their frontier as wild, home to dubious characters who, even if they were doing the work of civilization, were doing it violently and using methods of which urbane people would rather know less than more.[27]

But the otherwise comparable landed empires diverged significantly as to the role of government in the process of colonization. We can get a quick sense of this divergence with reference simply to the relative size of government in the colonies. In Russian Turkestan at the end of the nineteenth century, the people employed in running the colonial government amounted to maybe 2 percent of the population. In the American territories at about the same time, the people employed in running the territorial government amounted to about .8 percent of the population, for a government of less than half the size in relative terms.[28]

The Russians had a larger colonial government than the Amer-

icans not because they liked larger government or because their
culture idealized it, but because they needed it. Russian officials in
Turkestan might have admired what one colonial governor called
the "irreversible cruel expediency, calculation, and speed" with
which the United States had conquered the indigenous peoples of
the Plains and pushed them onto reservations, but they were in no
position to do the same so easily.[29] In the American territories, settlers outnumbered native inhabitants by about seventeen to one.
In Turkestan it was the other way around, as indigenous peoples
outnumbered settlers by about twenty-five to one. For the Russians, the most important colonial relationship was that between
the government and the rebellious Central Asians, and the European settlers in the region served principally as the agents of
St. Petersburg.[30] For the Americans, the most important colonial relationship was that between the colonial government and
the white settlers, who chafed at the prospect of control from
back East.[31]

To some extent this irritation manifested itself as concern
about the prominence of Washington, D.C., in local western
affairs. Although the American government in the West was small
compared to the staffing of other colonial regimes, Washington
had a greater presence in the American West than in the eastern
United States. As one historian writes, "The West . . . served as
the kindergarten of the American state."[32] In this classroom the
U.S. government mastered a limited set of skills, and fewer than
its peers among imperial powers, but it did learn to conquer and
administer aboriginal populations, and to promote and subsidize
private enterprise. More dramatically, in terms of the growth of
government power, at around the turn of the twentieth century
the U.S. government learned also how to regulate private enterprise. And the pressure to do it came substantially from western
voters themselves.

For although white westerners felt themselves to have an
"essentially 'colonial' relationship" to the East, which had more
capital and a longer history of political independence, they did
not at the turn of the century object principally to government

involvement in their affairs. Whereas in 1880 the government literally occupied the American West with soldiers, by 1900 those troops had mainly gone. You were more likely to come across an officer of the U.S. military in Rhode Island than in many of the badlands and onetime prairie battlefields.[33] During the decades around 1900, the American West contributed to the growth of government not because it needed conquering, but because its voters, wishing to regulate private enterprise, supported the increase of government power. Westerners objected more to the control exerted by private interests such as banks and railroads than to the influence of government in their lives.

Like other colonials, westerners nursed their resentment as a way of defining their politics. But unlike other colonials, they had the power to express their discontent through policy.[34] What had been Dakota Territory, ruled from Washington, could in 1889, as the new states of North and South Dakota, put four senators and three congressmen in the Capitol in Washington, whereas (for example) India had no MPs in the Parliament at Westminster.[35] Westerners in the United States did not have to resort to armed revolt, terrorism, or other forms of extra-political resistance to colonial authority.[36] They had an outlet for their frustrations in national politics. The twelve states that came into the Union between the Civil War and World War I provided one-quarter of the U.S. Senate, or twenty-four senators, who spoke for these people who felt themselves to have been recently colonized.[37] The government that Americans built for themselves in this age of modernization therefore represented in considerable measure the anger of westerners at the effects of outside forces on their condition.

When a colonial people grow angry at outside control of their affairs, they quite often chafe specifically at economic control, and they normally begin to explain how capitalism itself oppresses them. And criticism of industrial capitalism fueled the growth of state power throughout the world in the late nineteenth century. As more nations allowed more people to vote, soon enough ordinary working-class people could vote. The working class quite naturally knew a great deal about the shortcomings of industrial capitalism—especially its tendency to put large numbers of people out of work on an unpredictable basis, and its lack of provision for the sick, injured, or old. As working-class people got the vote, their governments grew proportionately more sensitive to the critique of industrial capitalism. Thus, industrial democracies adopted policies to provide unemployment insurance and pensions in response to the voting habits of laborers.[38]

But the anticapitalist sentiment of a colonial people differs from the anticapitalist sentiment of labor movements. This helps to explain why, although it is broadly true that a critique of capitalism fueled the growth of state power in America just as it did in other countries, it is more precisely true that, because the U.S. government offered a disproportionate representation to its formerly colonized West, the government grew according to the dictates of a different critique of capitalism than prevailed elsewhere. The colonial settlers of the American West resented having to borrow money at what they saw as unfavorable rates of interest, resented the conditions placed on loans, resented seeing the profits from moneylending leave the West to fund the further growth of the already rich East. They resented having to pay shipping rates to monopolist railroads to get their goods to market. And they focused their resentment on the owners of the banks and railroads, whom they saw—with some reason—as not only distant but foreign. Just as the influence of foreign capital contributed to the quick building and settlement of the West, it determined the essentially nonsocialist character of the American response to industrial capitalism, which focused its ire on the outside ownership and control of American assets.[39]

IMMIGRATION AND THE SHAPE OF GOVERNMENT

As much as foreign capital investment pushed American development into exceptional channels, another major component of the production equation—the influence of foreign labor—mattered even more. The abuse Americans heaped on foreign capital sounded positively polite compared with what they had to say about foreign labor. By the early twentieth century, the West was full of native-born, white Americans who had left the eastern cities where immigrants were landing in record numbers. For as much as the great international movements of people in the late nineteenth century flowed from east to west across Europe and the Atlantic Ocean, they continued flowing east to west within the United States. As Europeans arrived on the eastern seaboard, native-born Americans packed their bags and moved west, leaving the old cities behind.[40]

Apart from this further contribution to the peculiar character of the American West, the influx of foreign labor had two, much more significant, effects that pushed the United States onto a road that diverged from the one other nations traveled. Whereas earlier migrations in American history had consisted principally of people coming from the European countryside and seeking a place on an American homestead, immigrants who came to the United States as part of what social scientists called the "proletarian mass migration" in the late nineteenth century increasingly represented an international class of little-skilled workers seeking a better-paying part of the global job market.[41] Throughout the early twentieth century, laborers in urban areas were 40 percent foreign-born, and at any point a third of them would have come to America within the last ten years.[42] The arrival of millions of international workers in the United States pushed down the wages paid to American laborers and gave the United States a multicultural working class.

As millions of wage laborers came to the United States, increasing the supply of strong backs and hardened hands, native-born suppliers of such labor saw the demand for their work fall, and thus their wages, too. In the late nineteenth and early twentieth century, real wages for American industrial workers stagnated, dropped, or rose modestly, while those of the middle class and richer Americans rose more noticeably.[43] The perceptible gap between taxpayers and worse-off wage laborers widened. Better-off Americans, increasingly able to afford gramophones, automobiles, and exotic goods that arrived from the four corners of the earth by mail and rail, enjoyed an increasingly different standard of living than their poorer neighbors. Under such circumstances, it was easier for the ordinary taxpayer to identify with the rich than with the poor, and the taxpaying American was that much less likely to sympathize with the worker, that much less likely to think "There but for the grace of God go I," and thus less likely to support policies that would use public money to pay for social insurance.[44]

Nor was the middle-class person's distance from the working poor a matter only of money. In the early 1900s, the manufacturing industries in American cities employed a workforce that was about one third foreign-born (of whom one third had come to the United States within the previous ten years). Consider by comparison the professional workers, who were only half as likely to have come from another country.[45] (See table 1.1.) The urban

Location and Occupation of Immigrants	1900	1910	1920
Foreign-born as percentage of U.S. population	14	15	13
Foreign-born as percentage of U.S. urban population	22	23	20
—as percentage of the manufacturing workforce	35	37	31
—as percentage of the professional workforce	16	17	14
Recent immigrants as percentage of the U.S. population	3	6	3
Recent immigrants as percentage of the U.S. urban population	6	9	5
—as percentage of the manufacturing workforce	10	18	9
—as percentage of the professional workforce	3	5	3
Approximate number of resident immigrants recorded as having arrived since the last census (in millions)	2.6	5.2	3.3

Table 1.1 From the Integrated Public Use Microdata Series (IPUMS) samples. (For further discussion, see note on page 224.)

working class in the United States was visibly alien—not only foreign-born but newly arrived. This cultural difference between classes, added to the material difference, reduced the likelihood that Americans would support social policies like those of other nations, and ensured that whenever Americans thought about the problems of an industrial working class, they thought about the problems of immigration.

In having a significantly immigrant working class, the United States did not differ wildly from other developing countries that relied on migration to swell their populations and keep their growing factories well supplied with workers. What made the United States different was its profoundly polyglot immigrant population. The country not only received far and away more immigrants than any other country, it received more kinds of immigrants from a wider variety of countries. Workers who spoke different languages and worshipped at different altars were more sensitive to the cultural divisions among them and less attuned to their shared economic interests. They were also less likely to unionize or to support any kind of socialist movement. The issue of immigration, and of the ethnic and racial variety resulting from it, shaped the politics of the American labor movement and pre-vented it from lobbying for policies generous to, or even focused on, the working class.[46]

WHY AMERICAN CHARACTER AND GLOBALIZATION MATTER

With its relatively inexpensive, impermanent inland empire, its nonsocialist politics of anticapitalist protest, and its variegated, imported urban proletariat, the United States experienced few of the pressures pushing other countries to develop strong central states. European countries had to increase the size and authority of their governments to pay for welfare and warfare. It would have been surprising if the U.S. government had resembled them, given its different position in the world at the time. It would also have been surprising if the United States had turned out to look like any other New World nation: on a very brisk analysis, we must recognize that it simply had far too much money to look too much like other new societies. It looked therefore like a hybrid between the Old World and the New, with features all its own. Its habits and institutions of government, which came quickly to seem strikingly American, represented the United States' adaptations to its unique place in the world, as a peripheral state and a special beneficiary in a global system through which capital and labor moved more or less freely.

We might thus conclude that the American way is, therefore, neither a good nor a bad thing in itself but rather a better or a worse adaptation to environment. If these habits and institutions served the United States reasonably well while it developed into an industrial power in the nineteenth century, they served noticeably less well in the world after 1918, when the United States had become "top nation." We might then draw the lesson that particular circumstances call for particular policies, and that when the circumstances change, it is wise to change policies. Certainly, a tendency to cling to old adaptations in new environments can lead to disaster in the political as in the natural world.

Nor should we need the benefit of sophisticated historical hindsight to reach this conclusion. For although *globalization* and other catchwords do useful work by summarizing a vast and complex array of processes, policies, and attitudes, they hide the true subjects of history. The people who picked up and moved from one country to another, the people who saw them come and made provision for their arrival, the people who lent and borrowed money—all made decisions based on the world they knew. If in their millions their choices added to something we can now call *globalization*, in the eyes of the people who made them, these decisions represented well-reasoned or heartfelt responses to the world in which they lived. If today we experience global markets as abstractions, in the nineteenth century people saw workers hauling wires up the beaches from the ocean floors, tying one country to another. Boarding a ship for the Atlantic crossing, they could feel, as we can only assess, the risk in choosing to seek work in America instead of in Argentina. Most important, the students of America's place in the world—the businessmen, the economists, the lawyers, and the politicians—could sense in 1918, as an ominous foreboding, their world coming to an end, and could see a changed and dangerous landscape ahead. Insofar as we live in similar circumstances today, we might usefully put ourselves in the position of those who sought to shepherd the United States through this transition to a new historical era. We can see how they fared, why they succeeded, and when they failed as they tried to turn their eccentric country into the center of a new world order.

2

Capital

In the back of the *National Service Handbook*, a pocket guide to the U.S. government produced in 1917, readers could find a series of maps showing how Washington, D.C., exerted its influence over the country. Alongside maps illustrating obvious spheres of influence—the geographic responsibilities of the army or navy, for example—the handbook's editors included a more unusual map, depicting the government's ability to regulate the influence of capital on the American economy. (See figure 2.1.) The map showed the country divided into the twelve districts of the Federal Reserve System, which had then been operating for only three years. Each district had a financial capital, the city hosting its Federal Reserve Bank. But the map also showed a shadow system to the Federal Reserve, so that within the districts there appeared a second, and sometimes a third, city of economic regulation. The Federal Reserve Banks' younger siblings were the Federal Land Banks of the Federal Farm Loan system, which Congress created in 1916.[1]

For even though the Federal Reserve System already had enough capital cities so that, as one of its architects said, in case of dire emergency each of its member banks would be no more than "one night's [train] ride" away from a Federal Reserve Bank, it still had critics throughout the South and West, who viewed it as a suspiciously centralized structure. They would have preferred

Figure 2.1 Banking map of the United States.

fifty reserve banks: one in each of the then forty-eight states plus
one each for the District of Columbia and the Alaska Territory.[2]
These chronically indebted farmers wanted easy access to their
creditors. Lenders located nearby, living among and knowing
their debtors well, would have that much more sympathy for their
clients. As Congressman Robert Bulkley (Democrat of Ohio)
wrote, "agricultural interests will always feel greater confidence
in the viewpoint of their own board."[3] Farmers' preference for
consideration by "their own" led Bulkley and other sympathetic
congressmen to create the Land Bank system on the heels of
creating the Federal Reserve System. Congress meant the Land
Banks to make credit even more easily available to farmers than
the Federal Reserve System could.[4] For even in its infancy, and
despite farmers' considerable role in its creation, the Federal
Reserve System did not feel to rural Americans like their own
creature. After all, its vice-governor and major intellectual figure
was Paul M. Warburg, a member of the Wall Street firm Kuhn,
Loeb and Co. and, in the words of Congressman Joe Henry

Eagle (Democrat of Texas), "a Jew, a German, a banker and an alien."[5]

That fragmented banking map and this anger at foreign bankers reflected the long American struggle over the peculiar impact of global investment capital on the United States. Capital raced around the world through the late nineteenth century, seeking profitable occupation with a freedom unmatched before or afterward, at least until the last decades of the twentieth century.[6] Betting on countries developing industrial capacity, investors lent their savings to the engines of economic growth, which in turn pushed the frontiers of the modern world forward on all continents. The biggest bettors were the British, whose speculations accounted for more than half of the foreign investment in the world, and whose pounds sterling supported private and public enterprises in more than eighty countries.[7] By far their favorite bet was the United States, which received more than other countries of whatever blessings the world's capital markets could bestow. In the decades after the Civil War, the United States became the world's biggest debtor nation, so that by 1914, Americans had borrowed almost twice as much as anyone else.[8]

Yet it was not only the sheer quantity of U.S. involvement in the world's capital markets that made its experience of nineteenth-century globalization unusual. The character of the investment differed, too. First of all, despite seasons of disaffection, the United States always returned to the favor of British investors. Not only did it receive the most capital overall in the fifty years between the Civil War and World War I, it received the most in seven of the ten five-year periods from 1865 to 1914. Other, momentary favorites came and went: India was the darling of the British investor's eye from 1865 to 1869, but then disappeared over the next five years as the City of London lavished its affections on American ventures instead. Argentina enjoyed the top spot from 1885 to 1889, but then, blighted by bank failures and debt default, it faded from view and the United States returned to its accustomed place. Fickle though British investors could be, they never long forgot the lure of the American markets.[9]

Second, alone among the great borrowers, the United States emerged as a great lender during this period. In one of the unfairnesses characteristic of capitalist competition, the United States, which received more foreign investment than other developing countries, least needed it, having enormous resources of its own.[10] Even as it borrowed like a poor country, it lent like a rich one. At 1914, the United States had lent out about half as much as it owed.[11] In extending credit to the belligerents during the early years of World War I, America would switch almost in an instant from being the biggest debtor to the biggest creditor in the world.[12]

Third, and most important for understanding the peculiar development of the United States in this period, the foreign investment flooding into the country coursed through peculiar channels. In most developing economies, a sizable chunk of the foreign capital coming into the country passed through government hands. Governments borrowed money and invested in their countries, yielding returns for themselves and their lenders alike. In other major receivers of British investment in the late nineteenth century, between one-fifth and two-thirds of the sterling placed in a developing country went into public debt. But not in the United States, where only about 6 percent of British investment passed through the hands of public officials. More than 60 percent of British investment in America went instead through private hands and into America's privately owned railways.[13]

Taken together, these factors suggest an outline to the unusual story of the United States in the first great age of globalization. The development of the U.S. economy into the country's expansive frontier exerted an irresistible attraction on overseas investors, who poured money into the railroads then spreading over the landscape. The United States provided a relatively stable environment for the investment of foreign capital. It built up sufficient financial capacity to become a major world lender. But, unlike other developing countries, it did not do so by drawing capital into its public coffers. Instead, American financial strength depended on the abilities of men in private life, bankers whose personal and business connections spanned the oceans. These men naturally held themselves responsible to their investors, and not to voters. Yet they wielded a financial power in the United States that in other countries rested with governments. As the push and pull of globalization produced winners in America, so also did it produce losers, particularly in the remoter sections, where foreign capital mattered most. The prominence of these private barons among the winners fueled the growing conviction among the losers that foreign bankers were wicked and American bankers were foreign. But then, Americans might not have had such visible targets for their ire had they, through their elected representatives, proven more responsible with other people's money.

A NATION OF DEFAULTERS

In the beginning, sober American leadership made overseas underwriting possible. In 1790, Alexander Hamilton, as secretary of the Treasury, earned his permanent place in the pantheon of American statesmen by undertaking the unglamorous job of reorganizing the national debt. By assuming state debts incurred during the Revolutionary War and by establishing a tax policy to pay off those and other government debts, the United States established its good name in the credit markets of the world.[14]

The early American ability to pay taxes and support government debt ensured the appeal of investment in the United States. Creditors saw a government bringing in money on a steady basis and using it to pay off debt. They could make an easy contrast between the United States in this respect and, for example, Argentina. Facing foreign debt after its own early wars, and dominated by the ranching interests that preferred inflation to taxation, Argentina stooped to an unsustainable strategy of simply printing money to finance its operations. Buenos Aires could not afterward match Washington in its ability to stand behind its obligations.[15]

But in shaping the American response to nineteenth-century globalization, state irresponsibility proved as important as federal responsibility. If Alexander Hamilton won the first battle for federal financial maturity, his successors suffered a string of defeats.

In 1808, when President Thomas Jefferson's embargo policy reduced, albeit briefly, American exposure to the world's markets and encouraged the nation to look inward, Secretary of the Treasury Albert Gallatin proposed a plan for the national transportation network, budgeted and outlined for completion in ten years. Gallatin proposed that the federal government take up this project because, in his view, local and state governments lacked the necessary capital, credit, or political will. Gallatin's plan and later versions of it went down to defeat in a Congress divided, on this as on so many other issues, along sectional lines. Southerners feared the increase of power that a plan of internal improvements might bring to the federal government, and politicians of Andrew Jackson's party fed these fears. The Jacksonians argued that the federal government did not provide a forum adequate for the discussion of such issues, explained that local interests would better meet their transportation needs, promoted the virtues of "states' rights," and defeated time and again the proposal that the American people might through their national legislature make a decision on how to provide for the country's economic development. As a result, the construction of such projects fell to the states, which executed them first for better and later for worse.[16]

With the federal government out of the business of borrowing for construction, the early period of success, including New York State's Erie Canal, gave way to a more disastrous era of state funded transportation routes, and both fatefully involved foreign investment. The Erie Canal paid its way and redeemed its debts, and the perhaps seven million dollars of its bonds held by Englishmen established a seemingly happy starting point for American states to get funding on the London markets and then pay it down as their economy grew westward.[17]

The system of state financing appeared to work well enough even through the national economic panic of 1837. Though commodity prices fell and unemployment shot up in that year, British investors scrambled over one another to lend yet more money to

Americans. The immediate crisis passed, but then the Bank of the United States collapsed in 1841.[18] In the subsequent months, eight states—Arkansas, Indiana, Illinois, Louisiana, Maryland, Michigan, Mississippi, and Pennsylvania—and the territory of Florida announced that they would not be paying down their debts anytime soon or possibly ever.[19]

The defaulting states invoked various legal dodges of varying legitimacy to justify their bad faith to their creditors, but an explanation that came most easily rested on the commonly held if unpleasant principle that foreigners did not deserve repayment because they were foreign—and they were extra-foreign if they were Jewish. Governor Alexander McNutt of Mississippi claimed that the bonds on which the Magnolia State was defaulting represented debts owed to one of the Rothschilds, the prominent Jewish banking family whose firms had headquarters in European nations. McNutt did not make clear which Rothschild he meant, and for his purposes it did not much matter:

> The blood of Judas and Shylock flows in his veins, and he unites the qualities of both his countrymen. . . . He has advanced money to the Sublime Porte [i.e., the Ottoman Empire, an Islamic kingdom; this was not true], and taken as security a mortgage upon the Holy City of Jerusalem, and the Sepulchre of our Saviour. [This was not true, either, though it helped inflame anti-Semitic prejudice.] It is for the people to say whether he shall have a mortgage on our cotton fields, and make serfs of our children. Let the Baron [Rothschild] exact his pound of flesh of . . . the Bank of the United States.[20]

McNutt threatened to resign if the state legislature voted to honor its obligations, but he need not have bothered. By his rationale, it was better not to pay up, credit be damned, for who would wish to pay debts to an unchristian banking operation, even if its money had built up banks, schools, and roads? Patriotism overruled responsibility: another Mississippi defaulter declared he would prefer to "slap John Bull in the face than to quail before his power."[21] By 1842, Americans had opted out of paying almost all of the approximately $174 million they owed British investors, which represented about a quarter of all British overseas investment and about $4 billion in today's money.[22]

A little racism or at least antiforeign sentiment made it easier to shrug off a debt. Owing money to someone easily construed as a greedy, overly wealthy, foreign (ideally, for the purposes of a mainly Christian population, Jewish) investment banker gave a fine righteous feeling to one's refusal to pay. But this picture did not accurately outline the sources of overseas investment in American ventures. To be sure, richer Englishmen were more likely than poor ones to hold overseas investments—but a significant share of British investors in America were ordinary people simply seeking to save money.[23]

One of these was Sydney Smith, a writer who gave voice to British anger at irresponsible American debtors in an open letter to the U.S. Congress. Though himself an investor in Pennsylvania bonds and quite well-heeled, Smith ranked below the Rothschilds on the rich list. He was simply putting aside some of his savings, and was horrified that Pennsylvania should treat its obligations so cavalierly. Smith calculated that the state need only tax itself at a rate of about 1.5 percent to pay the interest it owed. Modern economists calculate likewise that Pennsylvania might readily have bailed itself out had it "imposed a realistic property tax in 1836."[24] But the people of Pennsylvania were not prepared to behave in a realistic fashion.

Smith concluded, therefore, that the American people were "a nation with whom no contract can be made, because none will be kept; unstable in the very foundations of social life, deficient in the elements of good faith, men who prefer any load of infamy however great, to any pressure of taxation, however light." Duff Green, an American journalist and influential Jacksonian, replied that Smith suffered from "morbid," or irrational, America-hatred. Smith disagreed, saying he denounced America not because he hated it in itself, but because Americans' irresponsible behavior with other people's money was hurting ordinary British savers who had put their confidence in the United States: "because her [America's] conduct has been predatory—because she has ruined so many helpless children, so many miserable women, so many aged men—because she has disturbed the order of the world. . . . Why is such hatred morbid? Why is it not just, inevitable, innate?"[25]

Smith predicted that the consequence of these defaults would be a friendless United States, unable to borrow from the world's great capital markets and therefore unable to wage modern war. "In the whole habitable world they cannot borrow a guinea, and they cannot draw the sword because they have not money to buy it." He hastened to explain he meant a real war, "not irruptions into Canada . . . but a long, tedious maritime war of four or five years duration."[26] To wage such a war, he reasoned, Americans would need—as every other country did—the confidence of and the ability to borrow from London, both of which they had now lost.

Smith's prediction had an element of truth, though in the short term it looked wrong. Within a short time, the United States would involve itself not only in relatively inexpensive incursions on its neighbors—including the war of 1846–1848 with Mexico, which netted for the United States what is now its Southwest— but also in a major war, with a significant maritime component, of four years' duration, which is to say, the Civil War. Yet the shadow of the defaults of the 1840s would extend over that war, and shape its influence on the politics of the United States.

TOWARD WALL STREET

In 1857, the novelist Charles Dickens was developing a name for himself in Britain as a performer of his own work, especially *A Christmas Carol*, which he read both in and out of holiday season with such "joviality" and "mirth" as to cheer even listeners who already knew the book.[27] One of Dickens's more mirthful lines came at Americans' expense. After Scrooge, the banker whose name was good as gold at the London Exchange, sees Marley's ghost, he worries that time and the calendar have stopped for him. Finding on closer examination that it is still Christmas Eve and that time is proceeding as usual, he draws a sigh of relief: "If there were no days to count by," he reflects, a check drawn on the Scrooge account would be worth no more than "a mere United States' security."[28]

After the defaults of the 1840s, the promoters of public responsibility in America tried to overcome their fellow country-men's reputations as reprobates. "Disgrace has fallen upon the people of this country in the eyes of the civilized world," an arti-cle in the highly respectable *North American Review* declared, and urged, "Let every honest man, then, . . . never rest, until the faith of his country had been redeemed, and its honor secured from reproach."[29] Barings Bank, the London bank that repre-sented the U.S. government overseas, commissioned articles like this one in the American press, gave money to sympathetic politi-cians and parties, and pressed for legislation that would restore American credit. Even these extraordinary measures brought only partial success, so that two decades after the defaults, as the U.S. Civil War was breaking out, American credit was still the stuff of Dickensian jokes.[30]

At the start of the war, the embattled U.S. government could not obtain much credit overseas, though not for lack of trying. The secretary of the Treasury, Salmon P. Chase, privately sounded out the Rothschilds, only to be turned down: "If the war should continue, it can only be carried on at a monumental expense, and loan would have to follow loan in order to provide the means."[31] To ensure that the rebellious states did not benefit-from British largesse, Robert J. Walker, representing Chase in London, did his best to keep the history of Southern state repudiations of debt fresh in English minds. Walker wrote a pamphlet, which ran through three printings, reminding British investors that Mississippi was still in default after two decades, and that a Mississippian, Jefferson Davis, now held the title of

Confederate president.[32] Would-be borrowers of the Confederate States of America suffered from the history of bad risk as long as anyone cared to exploit it.[33] As for the United States of America, it turned out the Rothschilds were right about the expense of the war and the need for further loans, but they were wrong about the American ability to gather adequate resources to pay those loans off.

Spurned on the world bourse, the U.S. government mustered support from the home front. The Philadelphia banker Jay Cooke put together a national organization, comprising thousands of salesmen, to sell government debt to American investors. Cooke's outfit sold $5 million of the U.S. government's 1861 bonds, while it took 147 other organizations to sell a further $25 million. Cooke reveled in the financial independence that the United States had forced upon itself: "We . . . had better not put a whip into the hands of foreigners to punish us," he declared, promoting instead his own ability to raise funds at home.[34] Soon after the end of the war, in 1871, Cooke replaced the British bank Barings as the American government's financial representative in London.[35]

Cooke's own success did not last long. In 1873 Jay Cooke & Company failed in a panic stirred by the same factors that had led to its rise: the lure of the West and the irresponsibility of American state debtors. Cooke had bet on the Northern Pacific Railroad, and his bank collapsed when his position proved overly optimistic. In the ensuing financial turmoil, eleven states—Alabama, Arkansas, Florida, Georgia, Louisiana, Minnesota, North Carolina, South Carolina, Tennessee, Virginia, and West Virginia—went into default on debt, stopping payment on about $130 million, or about $2 billion in twenty-first-century dollars.[36] British capital fled the United States, but only temporarily. When it returned, Cooke's firm had gone, but British investors put their money with firms like his, rather than with the incorrigible public borrowers among the American states.

Cooke's collapse in 1873 brought to a close the story that had begun with the state defaults in the 1840s and set the stage for the era of global investment that followed. Early American unwillingness to use the creditworthy federal government for funding expansion westward had produced a string of state enterprises devoted to the development of the frontier, some sturdier than others. For their own part, the states enjoyed the protection of the federal government from foreign creditors: however irritated Sydney Smith and his fellow investors might get, Britain could not use its superior military force to threaten the bad debtors of Mississippi or Pennsylvania without also threatening the United States as a whole. So, in a pinch, the states felt free to default on their debts. British creditors remembered these habits and stayed leery of American lending for the better part of the next two decades. In the 1860s, neither the United States nor the rebellious Southern states obtained as much overseas support as they would have liked. The United States proved able to turn inward, to organize and draw on its considerable domestic resources. Cooke's firm developed selling techniques to meet this need. Other firms arose to work with Cooke's and with one another, giving rise to the cluster of investment banks known collectively by their shared address, Wall Street.[37]

The demonstration of American financial strength and political resilience during the Civil War ensured that overseas investors would give the country another look once the fighting stopped, and as they did so, the importance of the unusual American experience began to show. British investors hoping to profit from the new era of frontier development sought investment in railroads around the world, just as they had backed roads and canals before. In Australia, the colonial governments owned and operated the railroads, so backing the Down Under frontier meant buying government bonds. Likewise, in Canada the dominion government stood behind railroads. In either case, the British investor had the confidence that British law protected his investment. In other countries, like Argentina, British banks directly owned and operated railroads, partly because the local population had not enough capital or experience to develop their own banks. Thus a Londoner wanting to put his pounds into the pampas could do it through a British firm. In the United States, local governments had a poor record, and the federal government had found that it could sell its debt to its own people. But for the adventurous soul seeking a berth in the American railroad industry there was now Wall Street, with its nexus of private investment banks and their overseas connections, to which the Civil War had given birth and to which the new era of globalization would lend strength. British investors putting money in America could now do so through private American firms with offices in England.[38]

TRANSATLANTIC TIES AND THE SHAPE OF THE NATION

In 1916, an American conspiracy theorist devoted to discovering the baleful influence of bankers in America wrote:

> It has been said that our government was composed of three branches: the legislative, the executive, and the judicial, in the order named. I think that five divisions would better represent our present system in actual practice, and in the following order of influence and power: The independent (?) American voting citizen, the legislative, the executive, the judiciary, and the SOVEREIGN HOUSE OF MORGAN.[39]

This description goes beyond the truth, but it brushes past the truth on its way to the lunatic fringe. Morgan and bankers like him played an administrative role in the American economy that other developing countries gave to their governments. They helped to determine the possible ways westward.

The U.S. government did take the first steps toward a rail system linking the East to the West. Lobbyists from railway companies wanted public backing for their risky private ventures in the trackless West, and with the Pacific Railroad Act of 1862, Congress acceded to their pleas. The law created the Union Pacific Railroad Company, named its directors, and gave public land for the railroad's right-of-way, and also, along the projected line of track and telegraph wire, granted land to the companies to use or sell, along with further loan subsidies.[40] Considering both land and loans, the U.S. government ended by paying perhaps a third of the cost of the Union Pacific.[41] But the role of the U.S. government was much less than that of the government in, for example, Canada. The Canadian Pacific (CP) Railway, incorporated in 1881, also received land grants and other government subsidies. These amounted to around half of its cost.[42] Moreover, through the 1880s and 1890s, the CP accounted for about 40 percent of the railway track open in Canada, whereas at about the same time total American land-grant railroad mileage accounted for around 14 percent of the track in the United States.[43] The Canadian government's efforts thus accounted for a much larger share of railway construction than the U.S. government's efforts did.[44] Potential investors saw that the Canadian government stood behind Canadian railroad securities. In America, some agency other than the government had to play the role of guarantor. Here the Morgans stepped in.[45]

The Morgans' ambition, coupled with America's unique position, made them powerful. Junius Spencer Morgan, successful in American business, moved to Britain in 1854. He lived in Hyde Park and developed a successful London bank, J. S. Morgan and Co. He died an English householder, and only for his burial did he return permanently to the land of his birth. But as he told his son at mid-century, moving to the present home of finance did not mean taking his eye off what he firmly believed would be its future. "Always be a 'bull' on America," he advised Pierpont.[46] And so Junius saw his son set up in New York with the idea that as capital found fertile soil in the United States, a Morgan would stand ready to cultivate its field, tend its growth, and reap a fair portion of the harvest.

The Morgans had both company and competition in their ocean-spanning efforts. Just as J. S. Morgan in London had an American partner in the bank of Drexel, Morgan and Co., so Brown Shipley had Brown Brothers, Morton Rose had Morton Bliss, Seligman Brothers had J. W. Seligman, and so on. The matching names in the firm rosters were of course no coincidence.

Banking depends on trust, and members of the same family know quite well whether they can trust one another. If the bond between father and son did not exist or proved unreliable, banking families ensured that marriage provided other trustworthy partners.[47] Happy weddings brought the Warburg sons, heirs to a German banking tradition, into the families of New York bankers at Kuhn, Loeb. Business went along with matrimony as a matter of course, and the Warburg boys who moved to the United States became a living link to the Old World.[48]

The physical links between the Old World and the New increased in number and decreased in length day by day through the late nineteenth century, and the world's people could see it happening. As the seasons passed, more ships came into harbors from more distant locations. News of the world found its way speedily into the broadsheet columns, pushing up commodity prices or letting them fall. And increasingly in the years after the Civil War, teams of men went irregularly and with some fanfare down the seashore and into the surf to haul thickly armored cables the last few feet up the sand, bolt them into their housings, and electrify the connection from one continent to another.

After the first successful transatlantic cable, in 1866, a web of wires began making its way over the ocean floor. (See figure 2.2.) The speedy connections between great cities made those capitals, for the purposes of sharing information, virtually the same place, a set of networked communities in constant contact.[49] Plenty of hopeful philosophers predicted that these connections would bring the peoples of the globe together in spirit and ambition. As the *Times* of London declared, "the Atlantic is dried up, and we become in reality as well as in wish one country."[50] But the harmonizing effects of this globalization were slow to realize themselves, if indeed they ever came. In the nearer term, that web of wires appealed principally to those who could make war or profit.

Men like the Morgans and the other Euro-American banking families who had members at either end of these wires represented not capital itself but the channels through which capital flowed, over which they stood guard and through which they

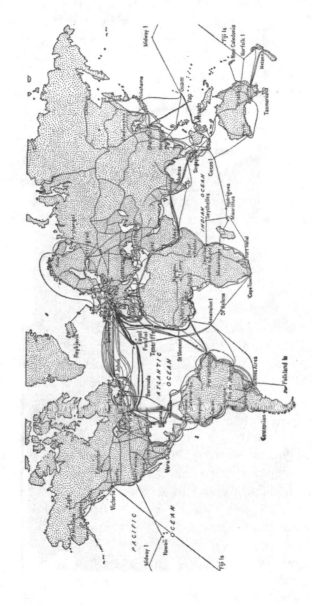

Figure 2.2 A map of the connected world, with Britain at the center: the world telegraph network after World War I.

guaranteed, as nearly as possible, its safe passage. They served their clients by providing a seal of approval for American firms. And the Morgans, in particular, did a good job of it: the presence of a Morgan partner on the board of an American firm told the market, quite confidently and accurately, that the firm was worth more than others—on average, about 15 percent more.[51]

The bankers' power to signal to investors that they should bet on one firm rather than another made them important figures indeed in directing the flow of capital into the United States. Americans at the time rightly saw their big bankers as men of the world, moving easily between nations, exerting a power that in other countries rested with governments. And when Americans grew unhappy with the capricious coming and going of investment capital, with the effects of market fluctuations on the value of their land and crops, they blamed the bankers and their foreign allegiance. To Americans frustrated by the bankers' control of their affairs, the global network of the nineteenth century looked not like threads stitching together the fabric of a common humanity, but rather like the tentacles of a monstrous foreign octopus, choking the world to get its feed. (See figure 2.3.) The picture, from a protest tract of the 1890s, illustrates the resentment that Americans, particularly those in the West, bore toward the bankers and their global combines that pushed pioneers carelessly across the continent.

For as they directed the course of investment in America, the big bankers also shaped the settlement of the American West. The prospect of greatest returns lay in the exploitation of the frontier, and so capital went first of all into railroads, but also into ranching, mining, and the other industries that made money in the one-time wilderness. Had overseas investors not bankrolled the swift growth of American railroads, the United States could not have pushed so far and so fast into the West as it did.

This frontier push did not happen smoothly. Like a fast tide flooding into a small estuary, the flow of foreign capital made waves. So promising did the American vista appear, so rapidly did the steel rails shoot for the horizon, that irrational exuberance

THE ENGLISH OCTOPUS.   It Feeds on Nothing but Gold!

Denver Road.

Figure 2.3 Another map of the connected world with Britain at the center: "The English Octopus."

occasionally prevailed over good sense. Construction booms drew rails into the prairies well ahead of anyone's desire to travel there, and as boom turned suddenly to bust, the inward flood of pounds turned with matching speed into an ebb, stranding enthusiastic pioneers at the end of a little-used line until optimism surged once more. But hope seemed always to return, and so, too, did foreigners with money to bet. (See figure 2.4.)

Observers at the time and afterward saw an irony in these cycles. Foreign investors put a tremendous amount of money into American railways, pressing them to grow. As the level of foreign investment rose, so did the construction of American railway track. It appeared that this high level of investor confidence from overseas proved too much of a good thing. Investors put in much more money than the American railway industry could profitably use in the near term. But these companies had to do something with the money, so they laid rail. It turned out they built too many railroads too quickly.[52] As the journalist (and later,

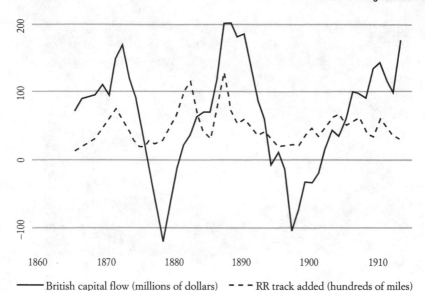

British capital flow (millions of dollars)   - - - RR track added (hundreds of miles)

Figure 2.4 Flow of British investment to and from the United States, shown along with track added to the American railway network.

railroad executive) Charles Francis Adams, Jr., wrote, "The people of the West eagerly invited foreigners to build railroads for them. . . . They found . . . the railroads of the West had been built a great deal too rapidly, and the business of the country could not support them." In the enthusiasm for investing in American railroad construction, Adams wrote, "The best and the most preposterous lines were equally built; competing line was run upon competing line between the great centres; while other lines were laid out from points where no one lived to points where no one wanted to go."[53] Such willy-nilly building led periodically to collapses, creating an unstable and unpredictable American railroad industry.

The bankers responded to the cycles of boom and bust by taking a step further into what, in other countries, was the traditional sphere of government, and moved to establish a monopoly over the railroads. Men like Morgan began consolidating firms to eliminate competition and to ensure a steadier stream of income for investors, including those international ones who might as easily put their money elsewhere. The monopolists and their admirers believed that railroads suffered from what they called "crazy competition"—the construction of railway lines to compete for the same traffic.[54] A passenger or freight-shipper might naively believe such competition to be a good thing, and not at all crazy, because railways competing for their customers' traffic might have to charge more competitive (which is to say, lower) prices than monopolist railways, which had by definition no fear of being undercut by rivals. But capitalists frankly preferred monopoly, which permitted higher rates and thus reliably higher profits; and monopoly was therefore what men like Morgan fought hard to make from the chaos of the railway business. Where monopolies proved impossible or illegal to construct, they would accept a gentlemanly understanding that railroads should solicit one another's cooperation when setting prices. The discontent of their British customers, who fretted that "the wars between the railroad kings were ruining the property of British bond and shareholders," as *The Economist* warned, spurred them to action.[55]

The desire to solve these problems and allay these fears finally drove J. Pierpont Morgan and his yacht *Corsair* onto the waters of New York Harbor on a summer day in 1885. He took aboard his ship the quarreling representatives of the competing Pennsylvania and New York Central railroads. *Corsair* did not let its bickering passengers disembark until Morgan had fully conveyed his message from the investors of the Old World to the railroad men of the New. At the behest of his British clientele, Morgan explained that he wanted to see less competition among American railway owners. Competition brought lower rates and lower profit margins and thus less joy to investors than monopoly did. If the pounds sterling were to continue coming from London, competition between railroads had to diminish, and monopoly profits had to rise. By day's end, the railroads agreed to buy out each other's interests, so far as the antimonopoly laws allowed, and beyond that to let Morgan act as intermediary to buy the remainder. The two railroads would respect each other's territorial rights, rather than compete for the same customers.[56]

The *Corsair* agreement to eliminate construction of certain competitive lines was, the *Commercial and Financial Chronicle* declared, "the embryo" of later cooperative railroad agreements, and it set Morgan on the path toward what *The Wall Street Journal* called "a general consolidation of all [rail]roads in the country."[57] Its success at reducing competition pushed Morgan to further railroad "Morganizations," as the press liked to call them. By 1898, he had Morganized about one-sixth of the railway mileage in the country.[58]

Conversely, five-sixths of the nation's mileage remained un-Morganized. Some of it belonged to another monopolist effort—that of Brown Brothers Harriman, perhaps, or of Kuhn, Loeb—but some of it enjoyed neither protection from competition nor an investment-house seal of approval, and thus remained vulnerable to the surge and ebb of finance. Even Junius Morgan could not speak for all British investment, let alone all foreign investment, nor could Pierpont Morgan speak for all the American railways or even enforce an industry-wide noncompetitive agreement, though he tried to arrange one in 1889.[59]

The problem with Morgan was one not only of the limits on his responsibility but of the limits on his power. Complaints against him and other major bankers emphasized his power to make monopolies, and his entire lack of responsibility to anyone but his investors (many of whom were foreign). But as great as the power of the private bankers might have been, it was not great enough to prevent the problems that plagued the growing West. A Morgan could certify the value of the railways he controlled, and he could effect the consolidation of lines on which he had direct influence, but unlike public monopolies in other parts of the world, he could not control the development of the American railway industry as a whole, nor could any other influential banker. In consequence, Americans who moved west along with the waves of foreign investment and railroad construction found themselves stuck at the end of a bankrupt line or a privately owned monopoly with nobody to hear their protests.

Similar protests against the influence of foreign capital appeared in other New World nations, and the reactions of such nations varied in keeping with each country's particular position in the world of international finance. In Canada, where the government played a larger role in promoting westward expansion, anger at overseas investors helped push the government to nationalize the railways. A commission chartered to recommend policy for the Canadian rail industry concluded in 1917 that "control of an important Canadian company should be in Canada. But this cannot be secured as long as [the railway] is owned by shareholders in England. . . . Therefore . . . control . . . should be surrendered into the hands of the people of Canada."[60] This move conformed to a well-established Canadian habit of promoting expansion as a government policy, pushing toward the West so that Americans would not get there first.[61] In Argentina, the government had urged foreigners to build and operate railways, and foreign-owned lines dominated the process of expansion. As foreign ownership came to seem a threat to Argentinean independence, opposition parties promoted an Argentinean nationalism that defined itself against the developmental policies of the ruling party.[62] In Brazil, foreign-owned railways competed with domestically owned lines, and politicians defused this threat to profitability with regulation that provided pricing advantages to Brazilian owners.[63] In the United States, the foreign ownership of some major railway interests had augmented the power of private monopolies and banks that were threatening the prosperity of western citizens who, owing to state representation in the Senate, had disproportionately loud voices in Washington. American politicians therefore addressed themselves to the perceived threat of foreign capital by moving to break up such monopolies, regulate their effects, and otherwise redress the specific grievances of constituents in the West.[64]

Contemplating the task of filling out the continental economy to fit the size of the railway network, the historian Henry Adams

(Charles Francis's brother) wrote, "The generation between 1865 and 1895 was already mortgaged to the railways, and no one knew it better than the generation itself."[65] Adams understated the case. His generation of Americans, and indeed America as they knew it, had to a considerable extent been created by the railways, which enabled the nation's rapid growth and spurred the peculiar politics, Populist and Progressive, of his age.

For in the American political system, growth changed the electoral map. In the years between the Civil War and the First World War, the United States filled out the map of the continental states. Congress admitted one by one to statehood these territories full of disappointed settlers, stung by boom and bust, resentful of capitalists with global interests. They attained citizenship and the ability to send legislators to Washington. They instructed these lawmakers to exert some control over the foreigners, bankers, railways, and wires that seemed now to be choking their part of the world.[66]

THE PRODUCT OF PROTEST

Failures, defaults, and monopolies pocked the whole American landscape, but they appeared with greater frequency in the economically less developed regions of the South and West. Of the eleven states defaulting in the 1870s, ten were southern. Of the $498 million in railway bonds that went into default at the same time, $216 million represented lines west of the Mississippi.[67] Given the pattern of international investment in the United States and the regional concentration of boom-and-bust effects, it would be entirely unsurprising if in the late nineteenth century an American political movement were to emerge, concentrated in the South and West, devoted to the regulation of credit and of railway transportation, opposed to the creation of private monopolies, and tinged with a significant air of antiforeign, perhaps specifically anti-British, sentiment.

Of course, just such a movement did indeed emerge. Protests against the effects of credit coming and going in the developing regions of the United States—protests styled variously the Green-back, People's Party (or Populist), Free Silver, and eventually Progressive movements—emerged to agitate for legislation enabling the federal government to regulate railroads, money, credit, and banking. Spokesmen for such movements identified the problems plaguing the South and West as those of debt, and particularly foreign debt. As the bestselling writer William Hope Harvey argued in 1899,

> Over TEN BILLION dollars of our indebtedness of FORTY BILLION is due to English money lenders. . . . Englishmen now own a majority of the stock of our railroads [this was not true of the industry overall, though it was true of some major lines]. . . . Our fields and factories are being stripped to pay interest to the money lenders of England. . . . In Egypt and India she has placed her soldiers to protect her bondholders. . . . The money lenders of America, who are advocating our present financial laws, are the soldiers of England on the soil of the United States.[68]

Harvey, and the millions of Americans who thought like him, had no admiration for Pierpont Morgan's arguably benevolent accomplishment of stabilizing certain sectors of the railroad industry. They saw that Morgan's interests as a moneylender lined up with those of other moneylenders, who were—or so they had always seemed to Americans in danger of default—not only foreign but sinister. The connected world, its filaments reaching out like beastly arms to draw wealth from the indebted prairies, posed a vision of peril to ordinary citizens in the American countryside, whose deep-rooted suspicion of bankers finally bore fruit in the early twentieth century. (See figure 2.5.)

The ungainly Federal Reserve System was one of the principal products of this suspicion. Nine months after J. P. Morgan's death in March 1913, the Federal Reserve was born. When Morgan died, the banker Frank Vanderlip wrote, "The king is dead. . . . There

OUR DEBTS LIKE A GREAT SPONGE COME WEST AND
SOAK UP THE MONEY.

Figure 2.5 The long arm of the British creditor.

are no cries of 'Long live the king,' for the general verdict seems to
be that there will be no other king; that Mr Morgan . . . can have
no successor, for we are facing other days."[69] The Federal Reserve,
a hydra-headed banking system that was neither central nor a
bank, fulfilled Vanderlip's prediction. Conceived by the Republicans who began assembling plans for a central bank after the panic
of 1907, and borne to completion by the Democrats who controlled the House after 1910 and the Senate and presidency after
1912, the Federal Reserve faithfully if unprettily represented its
mixed heritage. The infant would not get much practice standing
on its own legs. The first members of the Federal Reserve Board
took office only a week after the Great War began and the world in
which they had learned their trade changed.[70]

By the early twentieth century, almost all parties agreed on the need for some kind of federal agency with the ability to stabilize the supply of credit. The bankers and the borrowers both wanted to smooth out boom-and-bust cycles. The great debate within the United States turned on the question of how central such a system would be and what kind of people would run it. A more central system might act in a unified fashion but would respond less to local concerns. Similarly, Americans disagreed whether bankers— expert in the machinery of finance, but presumably devoted to their own private interests—would control credit, or whether politicians—subject to the will of their constituents, whatever their expertise—would do it instead.

The Federal Reserve might have got started a little sooner had Americans been able to settle these points. Because they could not, the system proved an awkward creature, late to mature. At its creation, the Federal Reserve Board had offices in a hallway at the Treasury Building, sandwiched between the offices of the secretary of the Treasury and the comptroller of the currency (both of whom served on the Federal Reserve Board)—and so one might suppose that the Fed was a creature of the Treasury Department and responsible to the president.[71] But to characterize the Fed as a government agency, controlled by political appointees and directly reporting to the Treasury, would annoy the Republicans and financiers who had worked and lobbied so hard to create a nonpolitical central bank whose members thought only in terms of economic interest and not of electoral advantage. In the minds of such men, the Federal Reserve Board did not have nearly enough independence from the politicians in Washington.

In its original form, the Federal Reserve System reflected these contradictory wishes. Its Board was central, which to bankers seemed a good thing, but consisted entirely of political appointees, which to debtors seemed a good thing. The Board stood at the top of a system of twelve regional banks (whose dispersal across the countryside favored debtors) owned and operated by bankers (which pleased bankers). The secretary of the Treasury and the comptroller of the currency were automatically members of the

Federal Reserve Board, so two regular administration officials would be on the Board at all times. The president, with the advice and consent of the Senate, would appoint the remaining six members of the Board. In theory, therefore, the banking community and its interests would have no say over the membership of the Federal Reserve Board.[72]

The most articulate spokesman for the bankers' objections to this compromise was Paul Warburg, the German-born banker who moved to America when he married into the Kuhn, Loeb firm, and quickly became a leading thinker among American financiers. Warburg objected to the secretary of the Treasury serving on the Federal Reserve Board because, as he drily put it, "men whom duty toward their party compels not to neglect the political aspect of each case should be kept away from this post." Warburg protested the decentralization of authority in the system: "a system of twelve Federal reserve banks will prove a failure." He argued vigorously for keeping the system as separate as possible from the U.S. government to avoid "political pressure addressed to Congress or to the executive for the lowering or raising of rates," which would impair the "efficient and honest management" of the economy.[73]

President Wilson acknowledged the strength of these objections by naming Warburg to serve on the first Federal Reserve Board in the summer of 1914. Better to have a critic making the compromise work than attacking it from the outside. The Senate approved three of Wilson's nominees without delay. But Warburg and another nominee, Thomas Jones, met with dissatisfaction from the Senate Banking Committee. Jones served on the board of the International Harvester Company, a monopoly created when J. P. Morgan's firm engineered a consolidation of the McCormick and Deering manufacturers of farm machinery. The resulting trust controlled about 85 percent of the market in equipment for reaping and harvesting, and its monopoly position allowed it to charge "prices quite out of line with costs," as one historian notes.[74] Jones was so closely associated not only with a private monopoly, but with one that directly did business with farmers, that he met insurmountable resistance in the Senate and could not gain approval.[75] Warburg's case proved more complex. The senators wanted to interview him. Warburg refused on the grounds that the committee had not interviewed other candidates and he did not deserve singling out.[76]

The committee chair, Gilbert Hitchcock (Democrat of Nebraska), claimed that the senators had a good reason for wanting to talk to Warburg. "All the committee knows is that Mr. Warburg came to this country from Germany, where his father is a leading banker, and that his connection with Kuhn, Loeb & Co. has enabled that firm to be so eminently successful in its European affairs."[77] Hitchcock could scarcely have concocted a collection of left-handed compliments more obviously designed to agitate western debtors. In his apparent innocence he made sure to mention that Warburg was of alien birth, connected to European banking interests, and also to Jewish banking interests that profited handsomely from foreign connections.

Warburg finally agreed to a private interview with the committee and without a stenographer, during three hours of which Senator Joseph Bristow (Republican of Kansas) grilled Warburg about Kuhn, Loeb's connection to railroad monopolies.[78] Had the erupting European crisis not filled the committee with a sense of urgency, they might never have let Warburg on the Board. Under the circumstances, his ascent did not represent a thoughtful compromise but an unspoken agreement that the U.S. government was going to have to make do in wartime with the inherent conflicts that nineteenth-century globalization had wrought in the nation. And for as much as such conflicts kept Americans from reaching a clear decision on how to deal with the international movement of capital, they mattered even more in the international movement of labor.

■ 3

Labor

Until the start of World War I, the distribution of labor within the United States depended considerably on the forces exerted by worldwide open markets for workers. Between the middle nineteenth century, when the development of steamships made transoceanic travel much cheaper, and 1914, when the outbreak of global hostilities blocked the sea-lanes, some fifty-five million Europeans crossed the ocean to the New World.[1] Some fled famine or persecution, but most set sail as a way of simply taking the next step from a continent already much in motion. Since industry came to Europe, seeding machinery throughout its countryside, it had become less and less profitable to sustain small farms. Families adapted by sending sons to cities—to work, save, and then return. When word came of better wages in farther-flung cities, emigrants went.[2]

Of the fifty-five million who left Europe, thirty-three million went to the United States.[3] Pushed from their homes by the failure of family farming, scouting the Old World cities for their chances in new industries, these Europeans found themselves drawn finally to the docks. At the quayside they might have taken ships for Argentina, Australia, Canada, or Brazil—and millions did. But far more often than not, as they placed their bets on where they might do best in the New World, they chose the

United States, which more than any of the other New World countries became a receiver of new peoples.

But as with the investment of foreign capital in the United States, what made the investment of foreign labor particularly consequential was not its quantity alone, but its character. First of all, although the U.S. labor market could offer high wages to certain kinds of workers, it did not offer the best opportunities to everyone. Immigrants came to America in such great numbers not because the United States offered, in some broad sense, greater opportunity, but because it offered specific opportunities that suited their specific needs. For example, some migrants from Italy would have enjoyed greater opportunities in Argentina than in the United States. In Argentina, Italians made up 39 percent of the foreign-born population and 12 percent of the total population, as opposed to 10 percent and 1.5 percent, respectively, in the United States. For this reason alone, Italian migrants enjoyed greater commercial, cultural, and political influence in Buenos Aires than in New York. Perhaps more important, they had a better chance of buying their own land on the Argentine pampas than on the American prairie, and they also stood better odds of establishing their own businesses in the city. Thus, Italians suited to take advantage of these entrepreneurial opportunities—mostly, these were northern Italians—were more likely to go to Argentina. By contrast, Italians from southern Italy, simply seeking a low-skilled job at a good wage with the intention of holding that job for a season and then returning home, were more likely to choose the labor market of the United States. The different opportunities available in the different American countries attracted different kinds of Italian migrants.[4]

Having noticed that the United States drew Italian immigrants who were less likely to stay than the ones that went to Argentina, we might expect the United States to look much like other English-speaking, immigrant-receiving countries in the nineteenth-century world, simply as one of many stops in a global labor market. Most migrants in the nineteenth-century world had the same plans as those southern Italians who preferred the United States to Argentina: find a job at a good wage, save some money, and return home. Knowing this, we would expect to see workers leaving immigrant-receiving countries, either when they had saved up enough to go home or when they spotted an even better opportunity elsewhere. And indeed, we do see this onward migration: best estimates suggest that around one-third of the migrants who went to the United States eventually left.[5] Even so, the United States did a better job of holding on to its migrants than other countries in the New World. Quite often, especially in the peak years of global migration around the turn of the century, more people left Australia or Canada than arrived there, their ports of entry looking more like rest stops than gateways to settlement.[6] And even if among Italians, migrants to the United States were less likely to settle than those bound for Argentina, among immigrants overall, the situation was reversed. More than half of immigrants to Argentina later returned home.[7]

The discrepancy between what Italian immigrants did and what immigrants overall did points to perhaps the most important distinguishing characteristic of immigration to the United States during this period: its profound diversity. So many different kinds of immigrants came to the United States that what one group did could easily be cancelled out by the behavior of others. Other immigrant-receiving countries looked profoundly different from the multicultural United States. For example, almost all of Argentina's immigrants in the decades around 1900 came from either Spain or Italy.[8] The decisions, cultural affinities, political inclinations, and business practices of a single immigrant nationality could, and did, shape Argentine history. In this respect, Argentina was typical of New World nations. Not so the United States: among immigrants to the United States, no single nationality dominated.

Taken together, these factors suggest an outline to the unusual story of the United States among the immigrant-receiving countries. As much as the investment of foreign capital pushed Americans farther west, faster than they otherwise would have gone, so did the investment of foreign labor. Just as capital moved more easily around the late-nineteenth-century world in response to the urgings of better profit farther afield, so too did labor move, and for much the same reasons. The development of the U.S. economy into its expansive frontier exerted an irresistible attraction on people overseas who saw in that expansion a seller's market for strong backs bent to hard labor. The United States proved a sufficiently strong attraction for people to come, and also for them to stay, mainly settled in their various island neighborhoods dotted around the country's industrial cities. There they competed for jobs with native-born Americans, who in response sometimes became migrants themselves, within their own country, and not always cheerful ones. As the market in migrants gave some people what they most wanted, it also disappointed others, some of whom came to view the newcomers as the cause of their troubles. Because many of the newcomers could vote (in some states, without even having to become citizens), the peculiar politics of a diverse and highly mobile working class pushed America onto its own peculiar political path. Whenever Americans took up the politics of working people, they were concerned overwhelmingly with the issues of migration.

HOBO SOCIOLOGY

Jack London, the American novelist, spent a season on the road as a tramp in the 1890s, moving among the hundreds of thousands of rootless men who amounted, in the uneasy opinion of most observers, to an ominous new phenomenon. Although Americans had always been a traveling people, priding themselves on their readiness to pluck up stakes when bad luck hit, at news of better luck from out of town, they liked to think of themselves as trailblazers seeking the main chance, not as migrant workers. Certainly, for much of their earlier history, Americans had moved as settlers to homesteads and ranches on the unclaimed reaches of the prairie. But in the decades around 1900, some subtle shift in the pressure to move pushed these mobile Americans in a different direction. So alarming did this shift seem that among the men seeking work, London noticed a considerable number of men studying them, carrying notebooks and recording their stories. London scorned "the average Eastern tramp investigator," these men who would believe any silly story and scarcely understood how to hop a freight.[9] But the college men on the road were busily collecting material that helped them build a picture of a people in motion, men who were mainly not the aimless tramps of London's enthusiasms. Nor did the American hoboes signify a sickness peculiar to the United States. They were an integral part of a worldwide movement of migrants who were walking away from low wages or a poor job market and looking for better luck farther down the road, ultimately along the rail lines and sea-lanes to the West.

Hobo sociology began with numbers. Even the census, which came around only once every ten years, captured the basic story of people moving. As of the 1880 count, Americans who left home to live in another state were more likely than their countrymen to stop in a rural part of the country; by 1910, these internal migrants were more likely to live in cities than the average American.[10] Migrants within America were changing from settlers to city dwellers, and the workers among them were no longer pioneers but proletarians.

This change in America's internal migrations reflected a change in the world's international migrations. The world's people, when looking for a place to settle and try their luck as landowners, had for years chosen among the settler colonies of the New World. While the American frontier featured available land, they had found their place there. But as the American landscape filled in, the character of American arrivals from the Old World began perceptibly to shift in the late nineteenth century. Tens of millions of Europeans left their countries, moving mostly from the newly industrial regions of Italy and the areas under the Austrian and Russian crowns, not because they expected to put down roots in a new land and become part of a new people, but because they were looking to get paid better for what they did than they were at home. And mostly the jobs they held at home were city jobs. Thus, in 1910, immigrants in America were significantly more likely to live in cities than the immigrants present in the United States in 1880.[11]

In 1910, the class of moving people—immigrants together with internal migrants—made up more than a third of the U.S. population, with the foreign-born at about 15 percent of the population and homegrown migrants at about 19 percent.[12] The census provided only a snapshot, a blurred photograph, of these people as they moved. Not only was it taken too infrequently to document precisely the activities of migrants, but its enumerators were less likely to find and count people with no fixed residence. More frequent measures show some of the ebb and flow of migration, and thus suggest a motive for motion. Immigrants, who had to endure some bureaucratic processing at official ports of entry, left a more copious record than internal migrants. And although each individual decision to migrate assuredly featured its own complexity— because even when millions are moving, it is rarely easy to decide to cross an ocean, possibly never to return, to start a new life and take up a job in a country whose language and laws you do not know—nevertheless, as we look back, a clear pattern emerges from the overall profile of the people who moved.

Choosing at random a page from the manifests of arriving ships, running a finger down the list of names and stopping at whim, you would have better than three chances in four of picking someone between the ages of fifteen and forty—better than half again as good as the chance of picking such a young person from the 1910 census records representing the U.S. population as a whole. Moreover, almost two times out of three you would find yourself pointing at a man's name rather than a woman's.[13] The profile of the immigrants as mainly young and male, coupled with what we generally know and can safely assume about the division of labor within families, suggests right away that the immigrants were people with little to lose and much to gain, and less to fear from the hardships of travel than other family members. Thinking about where to live and work, they would have put their fingers to the wind to test the prevailing trends in wages and the availability of jobs before they set a course across the sea.

And if this exercise in inference fails to persuade, we can consider the relation of migration to economic growth on the same measure we used to think about the coming and going of foreign capital. Setting the numbers of immigrants to the United States annually alongside the mileage of railway track constructed for each year, we can see that the peaks and valleys of the lines closely correspond. (See figure 3.1.) The lines move up and down in such close synchrony not because immigrants worked on the railroad—though some did—but because the two sets of numbers rose and fell in response to the same attractive force: the promise of economic growth, which the United States was able regularly to make and often to keep.

If you wanted to know whether the same was true of native-born Americans who moved from the place of their birth, there

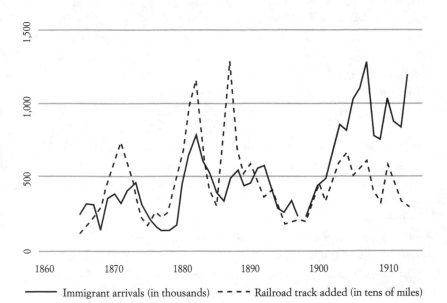

Immigrant arrivals (in thousands) ━ ━ ━ ━ Railroad track added (in tens of miles)

Figure 3.1 Immigrant arrivals to the United States, shown with track added to the U.S. railway network.

were few columns of figures available to consult. After all, Americans moving from state to state did not have to declare themselves. In the absence of a statistical overview, students of migration sought the view from beneath. Which is why the hobo sociologists hit the road; for example, in the summer of 1891, at the age of twenty-six, a young Princeton graduate and scholar of political economy named Walter Wyckoff shouldered a backpack and began hiking west away from Long Island Sound without a penny in his pocket or an idea of where he would spend the night. He thus started a year and a half on the road as a day laborer, seeking work where he could find it and keeping a job for no longer than he thought he needed it. For Wyckoff, this time constituted a period of scientific observation, an "experiment in reality," to see the moving workforce of America firsthand and document its habits.[14] For much of his journey, he followed the railroads, especially once he reached the middle section of the country, where, he wrote, "it was natural to follow the Union Pacific Railway" as the main route to the West.[15] As a young white man eager to work at the going rate and willing to travel a few miles up the road if necessary to get the pay, he looked much like any of the hundreds of thousands of mobile laborers who plied American roads in those years, following the new rail lines to the new cities, competing with the new immigrants for what work they could find.

DIVERSITY

No sooner had Wyckoff begun taking notes on his fellow workers than he hit a snag. "There has been difficulty in the way of intercourse with the men. I speak no Italian, nor any of the Scandinavian tongues, so that my acquaintance has been confined to my own countrymen, who are few in number in the gang, and to the Irishmen and negroes, and an occasional Hungarian who understands my stammering German."[16] The diversity that hampered Wyckoff's experimental observations crippled working-class politics—or so Karl Marx's coauthor Friedrich Engels, writing at about the same time, noticed. The division of American workers along cultural lines meant that there was no single American working class. The laborers of the United States, Engels wrote, sorted themselves into "the native-born and the foreigners, and the latter into (1) the Irish, (2) the Germans, (3) the many small groups, each of which understands only itself; the Czechs, Poles, Italians, Scandinavians, etc. And then the Negroes. . . . The dissimilar elements of the working class fall apart."[17] Workers who could hardly talk to one another would not spend much time debating the finer points of unionization, or industrial action. Indeed, beyond creating a difficulty of communication, the mix of cultures might well keep one part of the workforce at odds with another, as Catholics and Protestants or Poles and Prussians preferred to honor Old Country conflicts over newly shared economic interests. Diversity kept the workers from making common cause.

This diversity resulted from the peculiar pattern of migration to the United States. The mixture of peoples characterized all immigrant-receiving countries, but it characterized the United States to a greater degree. As the playwright Israel Zangwill wrote, "every country has been and is a 'Melting Pot.' But America, exhibiting the normal fusing process magnified many thousand diameters and diversified beyond all historic experience . . . is *the* 'Melting Pot.'"[18] To an extent, this suggestion might seem a paradox. After all, although the United States took the largest number of immigrants, it took a smaller number in proportion to its already large population. This observation could tempt a critic to dismiss Zangwill. For example, in the 1910 U.S. census, the total population was about 92 million, and in that year the United States received about 1 million immigrants, or a new population numbering a little over 1 percent of the resident population. Meanwhile, in the 1911 Canadian census, the total population was about 7.2 million, and in that year, Canada received 331,000 immigrants—in absolute terms, only a third as many as the United States, but in terms of its impact on Canada, an influx amounting to nearly 5 percent of the total population.[19] This might lead us to think that immigration ought to have mattered five times as much in Canada as in the United States, and that, contrary to Zangwill, in truth the True North was *the* Melting Pot.

But what Zangwill noticed, along with Engels and Wyckoff, was that American diversity began before the ships docked in New York. In Zangwill's slightly unflattering phrase, the people coming down the gangplanks into American ports constituted "a hodge-podge of simultaneous hordes."[20] In this respect, migration to America differed dramatically from that to other New World nations. Among the immigrants to the United States in the decades around 1900 were some of all kinds, and of a few kinds there were a great many—Italy accounted for almost one-quarter of the total, Russia and Austria for almost one-fifth each, and the British Isles for a little over one-tenth—but no one people held a majority. By contrast, immigrants to Australia and Canada came most noticeably from the British Isles. Immigrants to Argentina came principally from Spain and Italy, to Brazil from Portugal and Italy. In each case the New World nations remained, demographically speaking, colonies of their Old World parents, while the United States became a new kind of hybrid. (See figure 3.2.)

This hybrid vigor filled some observers, such as Zangwill (and indeed, in later years, most Americans), with respect for America's plentiful origins. The immigrants brought with them cultural traditions that inspired hopeful Americans with a sense of their nation's continuing vitality. As Randolph Bourne wrote in 1916, "We have needed the new peoples—the order of the German and the Scandinavian, the turbulence of the Slav and Hun—to save us from our own stagnation."[21] But to the new immigrants themselves, and to many Americans who saw them come, the diversity of immigrants mattered less for its effect on culture than for its effect on the job market. Just like the investors of capital who looked around the world and decided that the investment of their money in the United States would pay the highest returns, the workers who looked around the world figured, more often than not, that investment of their sweat in the United States would yield the highest wages. Even if American employers did take

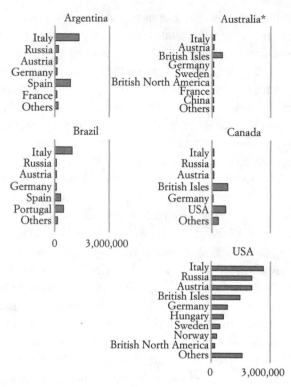

Figure 3.2 Volume and variety of immigrants as reported by receiving country for 1891–1910, *except for* Australia (indicated by asterisk), for which data is for 1901–1910, only half the period reported by the other countries. (For further discussion, see note on page 225.)

advantage of them, by paying the immigrants less than they paid native-born American workers, the immigrants were still going to earn more in the United States than they would have earned at home.[22] And American employers delighted in the diversity of the immigrant population, but not because businessmen believed in cultural outreach: it allowed them to lower the cost of labor significantly.

When American manufacturers and foremen looked at Zangwill's "simultaneous hordes," they saw just what Engels saw, and they believed that it gave them two great advantages. First, the more workers there were, the less they had to pay each worker—

that was the simplest arithmetic, and enough to make any paymaster cheerful on seeing the shiploads of people sail past the Statue of Liberty. Increased supply meant reduced demand, and thus lower prices: it was as if the factory owner suddenly had lower bills for coal or water, a situation that increased the profit he could draw from his factory. But sheer volume did not provide the only, or possibly even the most valuable, advantage to employers. What mattered was variety. The multiplicity of languages and cultural traditions among the immigrants allowed thoughtful managers to sign up a workforce from a selection of nations whose people had never heard much about one another, and possibly what little they knew they did not like. From the sugar plantations of Hawaii to the steel mills of Ohio, American employers promoted cultural diversity because it meant weaker unions and higher returns to capital.[23]

In predictable response, American-born laborers tended to oppose immigration for the same twin reasons: in its quantity it drove down wages, and in its quality it weakened unions. The American Federation of Labor, the nation's major organizer and representative of unions from the late 1880s onward, restricted its membership to skilled crafts in which there were few new immigrants. From 1897, the AFL lobbied for the restriction of immigration.[24] AFL leader Samuel Gompers put workingmen's sense of culture clash clearly when he wrote a pamphlet entitled *Meat vs. Rice: American Manhood vs. Asiatic Coolieism: Which Shall Survive?*[25] Henry George, a popular philosopher of American labor radicalism, watched the new workers with dismay:

Coming not individually, but in squads and bodies, speaking strange languages, herded together, in a style much below even the not very high standard of the [native-born] Pennsylvania miner; and believed to be imported, or at least induced to come, for the express purpose of reducing wages and making employers independent of their men, these new-comers have naturally been regarded with dislike and dread.[26]

Competition for wages reinforced and expanded upon existing intolerance, George believed. "Forced . . . into competition with him . . . laborers in California have learned to dread and hate the Chinese," he wrote, and so too would "laborers in Pennsylvania [compete with and hate] the Poles and Hungarians."[27] Whatever the principle and morality of the immigration issue, the lines of conflict had become clear by 1910. So, too, had the effects of immigration on the American workforce.

The 1910 census found that almost 15 percent of Americans had been born in another country. But if you were to walk down the streets of a city in that year and stop at random a workingman heading home for dinner, the chances you would find yourself speaking to someone from another country at least doubled, to around 30 percent. If you were in one of the major industrial cities, like Chicago, Detroit, or New York, the chances improved to around fifty-fifty. Some industries employed an especially large proportion of new immigrants. If you chanced to stop a man that year who had come to the United States to work in a steel mill, the odds were much better than even that he had come to the country within the last two decades, among the new group of mostly urban, industrial immigrants, against whom the unions most deeply wished to defend their workers' interests.[28]

In short, the forces fighting to stop immigration were failing, and its effects shaped some industries more than others. Consider the steel industry, a major muscle of American manufacturing might. Between the 1880 and 1910 censuses, not only had the proportion of foreign-born steelworkers increased, but the vast majority among those foreign-born at the mills in 1910 had come to the United States after 1890. (Another way of thinking about the scope of the change is to say that for every native-born worker added to the steel industry, two foreign-born workers were added.) (See figure 3.3.) And within the industry, the foreign-born and the native-born divided along class lines. Almost all of the white-collar jobs, such as salesman, manager, and clerk, and almost all of the more-skilled jobs, such as foreman, electrician, draftsman, and machinist, belonged to native-born Americans. By

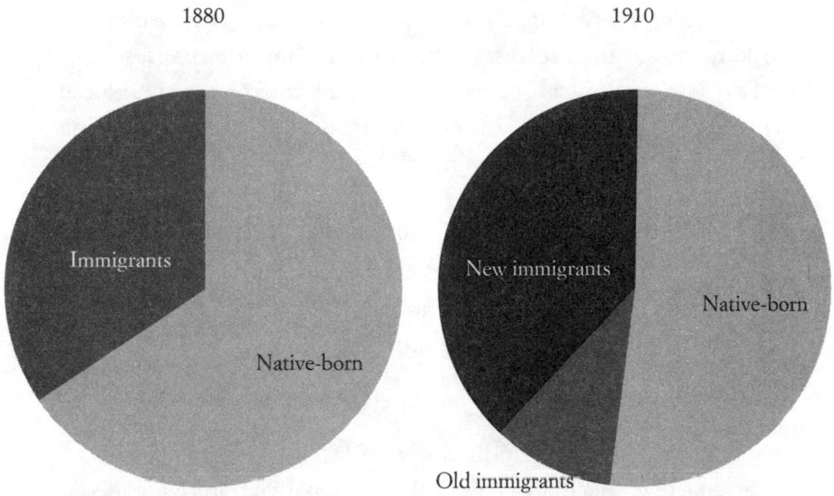

1880   1910

Figure 3.3 Nativity of workers in the iron and steel industries according to the 1880 and 1910 census samples in IPUMS. (For further discussion, see note on page 225.)

contrast, the general laborers, the furnace men, smelters, and pourers, the truck and tractor drivers were more likely than not to be immigrants. Almost 40 percent of the immigrants in the industry came from Austria-Hungary, 16 percent came from Russia, 12 percent from Italy, 10 percent from Germany, and the rest from two dozen assorted other countries.[29] The promoters of cultural diversity among the American working class were getting their way.

In the early twenty-first century, American workers would learn to complain that their jobs had been outsourced overseas—that they had lost their jobs because their employers had found it profitable to shut down a factory in the United States and open one in a country where labor cost less. In the early twentieth century, American workers saw outsourcing happen at home: instead of factories packing up and moving to other countries, people from other countries packed up and came to work in American factories. In either case, the global market in labor changed the lives of American workers. In the earlier era, in response to movement of people into the country, some native-born American workers moved themselves, farther into the nation's interior.

The workers knew they were moving along as part of a global marketplace. As Walter Wyckoff noticed while he was packing mowing machines into shipping crates in a Chicago factory, the goods they boxed bore labels sending them "to distant ports, some to Russia, and others as far off even as Australian and New Zealand towns."[30] And the workingmen who gathered on early mornings at the factory gates moved along the same lines and across the same distances as the shipping crates:

> Most of them were Irishmen, I think, and there were certainly Italians and Scandinavians and some Welshmen, and even a few Polish Jews, [as well as two] native born. Not all of them could have been in the homeless plight in which we were, and there was scarcely a case of insufficient clothing among them, while many seemed to be habitual workmen who knew the decencies of home and some home comfort. But there were not wanting men who, like us, were evidently upon the streets.[31]

Students of the workers tried to honor the distinction Wyckoff drew between the more and less stable classes of migrants. The investigators classified those fortunate laborers who remained consistently and satisfactorily employed as nonmigratory workers, and alongside them the researchers placed the regular supply of migratory workers: hoboes offered up by the roads into town. Members of this class, even temporary ones like Wyckoff, felt strongly that they were distinct from tramps, who were migratory nonworkers (and who in turn comprised a category distinct from nonmigratory nonworkers, known to specialists as "bums").[32] But Americans who were not themselves scholars of vagrancy easily lost track of these distinctions among the members of the unending and plainly miserable procession of people up and down the roads. The reduction of workingmen to the despised status of outcasts could easily breed anger and resentment. Looking around at the alien influences in their lives, they found a ready target for their ire.

Over much of the nineteenth century, the movement of Americans from state to state did not add up to a clear nationwide pattern. People were always crossing the borders from one state to another, particularly among the states of the Mississippi River Valley, and a stream of migrants kept flowing along the route that would become the Union Pacific's highway through the nation's midsection to California. But as the number and variety of immigrants from outside the country swelled, the movement of Americans within the country gained force and focus. (See figure 3.4.)

About forty native-born Americans left their home city for every hundred foreign immigrants who arrived in the years from 1880 to 1910. Perhaps, in keeping with the strong though not wholly respectable American tradition of nativism, these internal migrants simply did not like foreigners, and sought a less cosmopolitan section of the country. One might speculate that the increasing crowdedness of the cities was all by itself driving Americans to the countryside as, in the tradition of Daniel Boone, they sought their elbow room—but this would not explain why so many Americans moved on to other cities when they moved west. Ultimately the explanation that makes the most sense is that the arrival of millions of immigrant workers drove down wages, and also drove a proportionate number of native-born Americans to seek work and luck in another city with a labor market less saturated by incoming migration.[33]

This channel of internal migration for disaffected workers did not act like the mythical "safety valve" of which historian Frederick Jackson Turner had once spoken, dissipating the pressures of industrialization in the open spaces of the West. Rather, it funneled workers into the industrial labor markets in the new cities of the West, where they often remained just as discontented with the forces that pushed them around as they had been back East. Indeed, instead of diffusing such sentiments, this migration concentrated them in western city centers. And if indeed the internal migrants were seeking escape in the West from foreign immigrants, like so many optimistic pioneers, they were bound for disappointment. In some of the new cities of the West, foreign immigrants competed for jobs in numbers matching those of their fellow countrymen back East.[34]

Even if most of the internal migrants knew where they were going and what they were getting into, so many fell on hard times that authorities felt compelled to provide for them. In the nineteenth century the task of providing temporary public lodging for the homeless fell to police stations in American cities, and by the turn of the twentieth century, 4 percent of American men had found themselves sleeping on the police station floor at one time or another. For most of them it was a short phase, and one they endured early in life. In 1891–1892—when Wyckoff was on the road—95 percent of those police-floor lodgers had been traveling for less than a year. The majority of them were under forty, and unmarried.[35] In sum, these internal migrants looked very much like the immigrants with whom they were competing for work—young, single men moving along alone not because they liked the

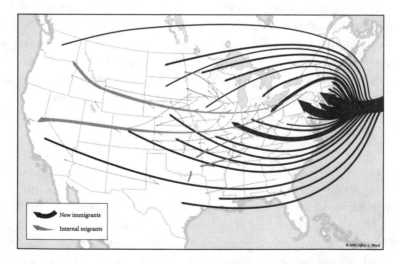

Figure 3.4 Arrows show the approximate volume and direction of immigration of "new immigrants" from Europe and of movements of native-born white internal migrants within the United States over the decade 1901–1910.

idea of traveling but because they were looking for a job at acceptable pay, and when they found it they would settle. The native-born American internal migrants among the American laborers comprised yet another mobile ethnic minority among a highly diverse working class.

The arrival of European labor on American shores thus had the same effect as the arrival of European capital: both pushed Americans to move west much faster and less gently than they otherwise would have.[36] Just as the uncertainties of railroad construction and the western economy created boom-and-bust cycles of foreign capital that made credit easy to get one day and difficult the next, so these factors affected the labor market, bringing immigrants to American shores in greater numbers during boom years and in lesser numbers during lean ones. Capital pressed west, seeking opportunity; so did labor. And just as the disappointments of the capital market generated a backlash against foreign investment, so did the disappointments of the labor market.

The principal political difference between the effects of capital and those of labor lay in the matter of liquidity. Although we often use liquid metaphors to refer to the new immigration of the late nineteenth century, speaking of a "flood" of people, a "wave," or at least of "streams," human capital is less easily liquidated than money.[37] In hard times, foreign capital easily left. But foreign labor usually stayed and could be confronted. As Americans filed into the new cities and states of the American West, believing that unrestricted immigration, encouraged by factory owners looking to cut wages, had put them out of work and pushed them away from their home towns, the subject of foreign influence on American life grew ever more important.

GEOGRAPHY

At the end of his westward journey, Walter Wyckoff climbed the last slope between him and the Pacific shore and saw the ocean before him for the first time in the three thousand miles since he had turned his back on Long Island Sound. He shouted in joy, "Thalassa! Thalassa!" (The sea! The sea!) echoing the soldiers of the general Xenophon, who crested a rise in Trebizond to see again the sea after trekking across Persia.[38] Like those relieved Greeks, Wyckoff knew his hard travels had come to a close. His experiment was over, and he could return to ordinary life. And surely many who likewise climbed out of the last California valley to the ridge of the last sierra foothill felt just as happy before the Pacific expanse, because they had reached the place they meant to settle. But surely many others among the wanderers who were not merely experimenting looked bitterly on that saltwater, knowing that it meant they had run through the full course of opportunities the continent could offer, and that the best they could hope for was better luck as they turned back to tramp eastward. Those of them who had left because immigrant labor came to their home towns knew whom to blame.

As the great migrations of the age filled the West with new settlers, Congress admitted the new territories as states—twelve came into the Union between the Civil War and World War I, six of them in 1889–1890 alone, so that by 1912 the continental forty-eight had been admitted. Because the U.S. Constitution gives to each state, however empty, two senators, this process of admission gave a powerful voice to the comparatively few westerners, to the people who believed themselves unduly pushed around by global movements of capital and labor. As the admission of new states gave voice to the internal migrants, so too did the processes of immigration and naturalization give voice to the international migrants. In the decades that followed, the uneasy conjunctions and occasional clashes between these two groups would give the politics of American industrialization its peculiar character.

These profound divisions among the diverse American working class made American politics complex enough, but they did not account for all the strangeness characterizing Washington. For as much as the custom of state representation gave the West a louder voice than its population warranted, it did the same for the South. And if westerners worried they had suffered too much from exposure to the global market in labor, southerners had hardly been exposed at all. In 1910, only 3.5 percent of the immigrants who had come to the United States since 1890 lived in the eleven states of the former Confederacy, while 8.5 percent of them lived in the twelve new states.[39] In eight states of the old South, fewer than one person in a hundred was a new immigrant. More important, the recent immigrants to the southern states were not, ethnically speaking, the same "new immigrants" who gave the rest of the nation so much to think about. Whereas the recent immigrant population to the United States in 1910 came mainly from Eastern and Southern Europe, almost 40 percent of the recent immigrants to the southern states came from Mexico.[40]

The great push of people west across the oceans and west again across the continent passed the South by. Its people lived in an eddy of the global flow that entered the country at New York (where almost a quarter of the new immigrants stayed) and sluiced along the rail lines to California. Indeed, in the wash of this passing current, the South was losing its own labor force, more swiftly each year, as black workers left their homes looking for the better chances they had heard about in the North and West. Of those who left the South, the largest part (about 40 percent) went to the industrial states of New York, New Jersey, Pennsylvania, and Illinois, where by 1910 more than a third of the African American population were migrants from the South.[41] For the decades around 1900, the South remained a bemused witness to the shifting patterns of international influence on American life even as, in the Congress, it held the political power to shift those patterns.

The geography of globalization's effects on America—hitting the North and West hard, the South hardly at all—explained the country's peculiar approach to immigration law, which only became stranger the longer the era of migration lasted. What began as a fairly traditional, racist approach to identifying white people as the most eligible for American citizenship became, under the pressure of migration, a policy "to give . . . protection to American labor."[42]

American immigration restriction began when the United States followed the racist trail blazed by the Australians in the middle nineteenth century. Beginning in the 1850s, the various Australian settlements passed laws to keep out the Chinese. In 1855, the legislature of Victoria adopted a law restricting the number of immigrants traveling on ships to one for every ten tons of cargo, and charging the ship's master ten pounds for every immigrant aboard. To make perfectly clear what it meant by "certain immigrants," the Victorian legislature explained: "And the word 'Immigrant' shall mean any male adult native of China or its dependencies or of any islands in the Chinese Seas or any person born of Chinese parents."[43] Through the 1860s and 1870s the other Australian parliaments adopted similar laws. Despite pressure from elements of the community who believed the laws "lower our prestige as an intelligent and civilized people," by 1887 all the Australian legislatures had Chinese exclusion acts on their books. In 1897 the government in Queensland brokered a "gentleman's agreement" with Japan to restrict immigration, an informal arrangement that prefigured similar deals later done by Canada and the United States.[44]

Following the Australian example, the United States barred immigration from China beginning with the Chinese Exclusion Act of 1882 and from Japan beginning with its own gentlemen's agreement of 1907. The racial exclusion of Asians from America achieved a dispassionate respectability in 1917, when Congress adopted a law ratifying and extending these earlier restrictions, drawing an "Asiatic barred zone" on the world map. South of latitude 50° north, west of longitude 110° east, natives of the Indian subcontinent, Indochina, and Central Asia fell under the restrictive bracket and joined China and Japan among the excluded nations. Congressmen had decided that blocking out exclusionary lines of latitude and longitude would cause less diplomatic offense than naming unwelcome peoples.[45] But they made their purpose clear. As Anthony Caminetti, the U.S. commissioner general of immigration, explained in his official report for 1917, the exclusionary zone "recognizes the impossibility that this country shall ever consent to the settlement here of thousands of orientals who inherently (and this is not said in a spirit of criticism at all, but merely as a statement of fact) are incapable of assimilation into the body politic of a Nation the population of which is of occidental origin."[46] Even though some racial literalists thought that people from India descended from Aryan people and speaking Aryan languages might count as Aryan, and therefore white, congressmen dispensed swiftly with this idea. As Senator Thomas Hardwick (Democrat of Georgia) explained to one of his colleagues, "even if they are technically white people they are not the sort of white people the Senator wants to come in."[47]

In adopting laws to exclude immigrants based on their race, the United States closely followed the example of other peoples who nurtured a fantasy of being, and remaining, predominantly white, and who worried that immigration might darken their national complexion. The United States did not stand out as an exception in the field of racial exclusion. Even in its squeamishness about writing racist language into law it only followed the Australian example of the middle nineteenth century. But the more important, and more controversial, part of American restriction law worked differently and served a different purpose.

Between 1897, when Congress first voted on the use of a literacy test to restrict immigration, and 1917, when it passed a literacy test law over President Wilson's veto, the prospect of excluding illiterates from entry warmed the hearts of immigration's opponents. Wilson vetoed the law because, he said, "the literacy test constitutes a radical change in the policy of the Nation."[48] He was right, insofar as the test was not nearly racist enough to fit with the established tradition of immigration restriction in the United States and in other countries. It came about for other reasons.

Americans had been using literacy tests for racially exclusive purposes since at least 1890, when southern states began using them to keep black citizens from voting. Beginning with Mississippi, the white South had adopted what one newspaper called the "transparent fraud" of a literacy test that exempted citizens who could, without reading, demonstrate an "understanding" of a portion from the state constitution. Lawmakers, registrars of voters, and citizens alike understood that the discretionary element of the "understanding" clause would allow white illiterates to vote and that it would prove curiously difficult for black citizens to demonstrate either literacy or understanding.[49] This practice persisted into the twentieth century, and its mechanism was well understood.

By the time immigration's opponents in America took up the literacy test, such transparent frauds had become the custom in other immigrant-receiving countries. Within the British empire, parliaments began using literacy tests to restrict immigration in 1897. Legislators in Natal, South Africa, devised a literacy test in which newcomers had to demonstrate their competence in a European language. As the prime minister of Natal said, "It never occurred to me for a minute that [the act] should ever be applied to English immigrants. . . . The object of the bill is to deal with Asiatic immigrants."[50] Similarly, the Australian "dictation test," adopted in 1901, allowed an immigration official, at his discretion, to require a migrant to write fifty words "in an [sic] European language directed by the officer." Sample passages included the practical "As nobody had been able to discover the actual history of the eel, people sought a miraculous explanation."[51]

In light of the Mississippi and Natal precedents, the apparently genuine effort to render the 1917 literacy test racially neutral stands out even more clearly. Congress provided for the exclusion of "all aliens over sixteen years of age, physically capable of reading, who can not read the English language, or some other language or dialect, including Hebrew or Yiddish." The law further specified that the literacy test comprise

slips of uniform size prepared under the direction of the Secretary of Labor, each containing not less than thirty nor more than forty words in ordinary use, printed in plainly legible type in some of the various dialects or languages of immigrants. Each alien may designate the particular language or dialect in which he desires the examination to be made, and shall be required to read the words printed on the slip in such language or dialect.[52]

Unlike the Natal formula, the 1917 literacy test did not require Asiatic immigrants to read in a European language, and unlike the Mississippi formula, it did not depend on a discretionary exemption. It required immigrants to read in the language of their own choice because, as President Wilson pointed out, "it is . . . merely a penalty for lack of opportunity."[53] Or, as *The New York Times* put it, the architects of the literacy test act had clearly meant to design a "labor exclusion bill."[54]

Where workers' wages were depressed and there were foreigners to blame for it, congressmen voted to restrict immigration by using the literacy test. They argued, as Congressmen John Adair (Democrat of Indiana) did, that

> we already have a surplus of unskilled labor; that American workmen of both native and foreign birth are being driven out of employment by the influx of thousands of illiterates from southern Europe, who are willing to live and do live in box cars or under the crudest kind of shelter, at an expense of 10 or 15 cents per day, and who, as a matter of course, eventually lower the standard of American wages and the standard of American living.

Adair went on to note that the test, "because it only requires them to read in the language or dialect of the country from which they came," would exclude few immigrants. "In fact, practically all who will be excluded under this bill are a few of the Sicillians [*sic*] and some of the Italians from southern Italy."[55] Census data bore out Adair's suggestion. By the numbers, among immigrants who had arrived after 1890, only the Italians had a literacy rate below that of the native-born American population.[56] (See table 3.1.) The literacy test as designed would have excluded the minority of immigrants who competed for the least-skilled positions in the

Literacy Rate	Percentage	Number in Sample
Among native-born	**69**	**311,576**
White	72	270,657
Black/Negro	46	30,832
Mulatto	56	8,209
American Indian	37	1,155
Chinese	65	105
Among immigrants	**83**	**54,663**
Up through 1890	92	22,710
1891–1910	77	31,953
Among selected nationalities of new immigrants:		
ITALY	60	4,785
AUSTRIA	72	3,435
HUNGARY	82	1,818
RUSSIA	70	5,525
GERMANY	93	9,674

Table 3.1 Literacy rate of immigrants.

American labor market, and the support for the literacy test among congressmen reflected their constituents' enthusiasm for limiting that competition.[57]

Likewise, the congressmen who most opposed the literacy test were those who had the most immigrants in their constituency. As Congressman James Thomas Heflin (Democrat of Alabama) colorfully said, "In some places, if enough foreigners locate to open a banana stand, sell hot tamales, or turn the crank of a street hand organ, straightway the Member from that district becomes a staunch advocate of unrestricted immigration."[58] On the final vote that established the literacy test as law in 1917, the opposition came almost exclusively from the northeastern states where immigrant populations were highest, and the higher the immigrant population, the higher the percentage of a state's congressmen who voted against the test.[59]

During this fight between the West, so many of whose people felt themselves hurt by immigration, and the North, so many of whose people were there as a result of immigration, the section of the country holding the balance was the South. And for the earlier part of the fight, the South's representatives favored immigration, believing "development in the black belt is at a standstill because of the worthlessness of the black and the difficulty of getting more white labor." The *Atlanta Constitution* declared in 1905 that "the employing farmers of the South are clamoring for immigrants, and no line is being drawn on their nationality."[60] Southern opposition was critical in keeping the literacy test law unpassed for the twenty years between 1897 and 1917, years during which the flow of immigrants continued unvexed and waxing to American shores, creating immigrant communities in eastern cities and anti-immigrant coalitions in the West.[61] As immigration continued, it grew clear that Europeans were unlikely to settle in the lower-wage South, whose racial animosity sometimes extended beyond blacks to darker-skinned Europeans, and so southern congressmen switched their vote on the literacy test, letting it at long last pass.

Thus the geography of immigration and internal migration, coupled with the American habit of representing states in the government, shaped the peculiar American response to migration, which resulted in a literacy test for exclusion based on class rather than race. Whether they supported or opposed the test, Americans in the age of globalization assumed that a literacy test would thin the flow of immigrants automatically, without the need for bureaucratic discretion or significant expansion of government authority. They supposed that excluding the least-skilled immigrants would ease pressures on the least-skilled workers, and that the labor needs of the country would sort themselves out. Nobody supposed that almost immediately after the literacy test law had passed it would become almost wholly irrelevant. But as

the commissioner general of immigration reported in 1919, the
global currents of labor had shifted:

> Owing to the extremely small transoceanic migration, the
> so-called illiteracy test has never yet been given a full
> opportunity to show the benefits anticipated at the time of
> its adoption as a part of our immigration law. It has found
> the greatest part of its application on the land bound-
> aries . . . [but] the exceptions made to the illiteracy test (as
> a war measure) in favor of laborers coming from Mexico
> have so modified conditions on the southern border that a
> fair estimate can hardly be made as to what the effect of the
> test would have been there under normal conditions.[62]

By the time the United States had developed a peculiar response
tailored to its unusual place in the international system, its circumstances had changed. But the era that had now passed left its
unmistakable and lasting marks on the institutions with which
Americans governed and defended themselves.

■ 4
Welfare

During the decades around 1900, the world's industrial democracies began spending their citizens' money on policies meant to soften the impact of modern factory production. Recognizing that even when industrial economies operate normally, they move people around and create unemployment, governments drafted laws for unemployment relief, for public health, for old-age pensions, and for subsidized housing. To this general rule the United States stood out as a significant exception. Although American spending on some such policies did indeed grow during this period, it grew less than in other countries. Moreover, the strange direction, as well as the modest size, of this growth reflected America's peculiar place in the global economy of the late nineteenth century. Americans channeled their relatively small amount of social spending to the people and places that needed relief not from industrial capitalism alone, but from the effects of globalization.

In other countries, the growth of social-spending programs in the late nineteenth century contributed significantly to the development of modern forms of government. Originating in the efforts of conservative politicians responding to radical pressure, these policies aimed at retaining the loyalty of citizens who might otherwise have joined subversive socialist parties. As such policies struck roots in the political institutions of a people, this collection of protections grew into coherent welfare states. People learned to look to the state for protection from the incidental, ordinary injuries of industrial economies—except in the United States, where politicians felt pressure to provide protection more from the buffeting of global markets than from the industrial economy itself.

In the common understanding of modern scholars, public spending on general welfare provides "government-protected minimum standards of income, nutrition, health, housing and education, assured to every citizen as a practical right, not charity."[1] In the crusading words of olden-day advocates, these benefits comprised a plan of

> attack upon five giant evils: upon the physical Want with which it is directly concerned, upon Disease which often causes that Want and brings many other troubles in its train, upon Ignorance which no democracy can afford among its citizens, upon the Squalor which arises mainly through haphazard distribution of industry and population, and upon the Idleness which destroys wealth and corrupts men.[2]

—thus Sir William Beveridge, whose 1942 report on a comprehensive plan of social benefits for Britain met with scorn from those Americans who looked down on their poverty-stricken, war-ravaged, and "shabby" ally for needing plans to ensure its social health.[3] So far as such Americans were concerned, the welfare state was and always would be a program for the poor people of poor nations, a cure for a disease to which Americans enjoyed a natural immunity.

To employ a different metaphor: in a fertile field, fed by river and rainfall, a farmer might have to send the natural flow of water into new sluices to prevent flood, but he would need little infrastructure to ensure his crops got their moisture. By contrast an arid field might bear as much produce if only it were similarly wet, but to get it wet took dams, ditches, reservoirs, and filters, as well as compensating additives to correct mineral imbalance. Irrigation, like other redistributive projects, also often requires significant government involvement (as westerners of the early 1900s, lobbying for federal reclamation legislation, well knew). In arid country irrigated by artificial methods, farmers learn familiarity with the mechanical and political apparatus necessary to keep them in business, while farmers in naturally watered lands might find such structures not only needless but even alien and threatening. Even if their climate should happen to shift, drying up the rainfall and the creek beds, they might prefer their old ways and prove unable to adjust their habits in time.

In the preceding two chapters, we saw enough of the history of globalization to suggest that the United States in the late nineteenth century was just such a fertile field, metaphorically wetted (and occasionally eroded) by currents of capital and labor whose headwaters lay in distant lands. Having observed this relationship between the United States and the world economy, we can put the observation and the metaphor to a test: if globalization affected the United States in a historically significant way, we should find that Americans might occasionally have felt a need for the political equivalent of a few sluice gates to divert streams of labor, or a regulator valve to smooth out the ebb and flow of capital, but that they rarely supposed they needed the redistributive structures that characterized other countries. To dispose of the metaphor, we should find that the state they developed for themselves reflected their particular circumstances. Instead of developing the governmental institutions or political habits other nations used to manage their economies, Americans adopted policies suited to their particular place in the fluid world of the late nineteenth century.

WHY THERE WAS A LITTLE SOCIALISM IN THE UNITED STATES

The political consequences of America's unique place in the nineteenth-century world normally crop up whenever we look at the problem of American socialism.[4] Socialism is usually supposed to have played an important role in the creation of modern social-insurance policies, not because socialists wanted more powerful central governments, but because conservative politicians, concerned at socialism's increasing popularity among voters, created social policies to defuse the attraction of radical movements. The relative weakness of socialism in the United States therefore plays an important role in explanations of why Americans did not have a far-reaching social program sooner than the New Deal.[5] The failure of socialism to attract supporters in the United States is usually attributed, at least in part, to one effect of globalization, because the large and diverse streams of immigration weakened the solidarity of the American working class. But if, as we have supposed, the pressure on the American working class came not only, or not chiefly, from capitalism itself but from the dislocations and rough treatment of the fluid global economy, we should also find that the United States had not only less socialism, but socialism of a different character—socialism specifically tailored to respond to the effects of globalization.

Elsewhere, socialism's appeal to the working class prompted the creation of social-insurance programs. The first nearly comprehensive social program that, in the imagination of its creator, German chancellor Otto von Bismarck, might someday cover "every German," appeared before the Reichstag in 1881 as a set of proposals. Legislators spooked by the specter of revolutionary and terrorist anarchism, communism, and (even as they debated a pension bill) a strike of historic magnitude, saw the merit of this strategy and enacted it by 1889.[6] The forces behind Germany's pioneering effort at social insurance pressed also upon the other industrial economies. Thus to greater or lesser degrees, other countries' early social-spending efforts resembled Bismarck's canny plan to short-circuit socialism.[7] But the effects of these pressures as they pushed through peculiar American channels drove the United States down its own path.

In no other industrial democracy was the Socialist Party as unpopular as in the United States. At around World War I, when socialist and labor parties throughout the modern world gained

popularity and became electoral contenders, the Socialist Party of
the United States actually lost support, falling to almost half of
what proved to be its peak appeal of about 6 percent of the
national vote in the 1912 presidential election. (See figure 4.1.)

Not only was the American socialist party unusually unpopular, it drew its slight popularity from peculiarly American sources.
In principle, socialism appealed to workers because they were
workers—which is to say because they were a class of people who
shared a common interest defined by the conditions of their employment. If they banded together they might make a revolution—
if not in the streets, then at the polls, by putting in office
lawmakers more beholden to wage earners than to paymasters. A
socialist party had first and foremost to represent a united working class. To a limited extent, this appeal succeeded in America:
in places where more workers joined an industrial union and
banded together in long strikes, the Socialist Party won more
votes at the polls than it did elsewhere. As the Socialist leader

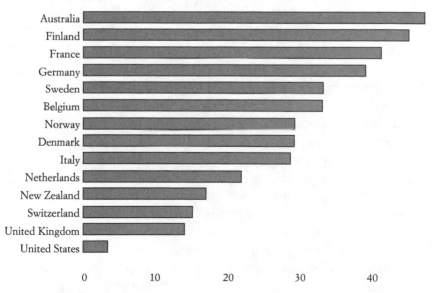

Figure 4.1 Percentage of national vote that went to a socialist or labor party in industrial democracies around the time of World War I, as averaged between prewar and
postwar elections.

Eugene V. Debs suggested, American workers, "once united in one great industrial union will vote a united working class ticket."[8]

But such successes failed to pepper the electoral map, even at socialism's peak popularity, in large measure because the American working class simply would not unite. Passionate socialist leaders, such as William "Big Bill" Haywood, might insist that "there is no foreigner here except the capitalists," but the presence and effect of foreign arrivals among the American working class mattered more than Haywood's or Debs's appeals for worker unity.[9] Just as Engels and other radicals had feared, and just as the factory managers had hoped, the arrival of new immigrants split the American working class and prevented its uniting behind the Socialist ticket for at least two reasons.

First, even though anti-immigrant spokesmen claimed otherwise, immigrants had as many reasons to oppose socialism as to support it. Native-born Americans fearful of the red menace, such as Congressman Albert Johnson (Republican of Washington), might warn that "the newly arrived alien labor is organizing," and they trembled at "the riot it must produce in time."[10] But even if this fear reflected some element of truth—and to be sure, there were radical immigrants in America—it failed to materialize in most cases. Immigrants who came all the way to the United States to earn better wages had more reason than their native-born counterparts to view the country as already offering them the best deal in the world. Immigrants who planned to leave the United States after a few years of saving money had little stake in American politics at all, let alone in the country's revolutionary transformation. In the late nineteenth century, congressional districts that were home to more immigrants were more likely to have Republican congressmen.[11] In all, we have reason to suspect that the influence of immigrants on American politics pushed debate to the right.[12]

Second, the indirect impact of immigration also inhibited American socialism by pushing the Socialist Party, despite the entreaties of idealists like Debs, to define itself as an antiglobalization party rather than a unified working-class organization. In

1910 the Socialist Party of the United States adopted a resolution favoring the restriction of immigration. Debs condemned the resolution as "utterly unsocialistic, reactionary, and in truth outrageous."[13] But, in truth, it looked like a highly shrewd move: in the two years that followed this policy shift, the Socialists enjoyed their greatest electoral successes. The party's target voters were not especially well versed in the theory of the proletarian revolution or the dynamics of Marxist progress; rather, as one socialist wrote, "I would not call the large vote polled . . . a victory for Socialist principles because there isn't fifty in the town that understand the Socialist principles. . . . The people are tired of being humbugged by the Democratic and Republican parties [and that] is the real cause of the Socialist success."[14] To be a socialist, one voter argued, "all a fellow needs to know . . . is that he is robbed."[15] And the working Americans of the era knew quite well who the robbers were: the immigrants who came to America and took local jobs at lower pay, and the absent capitalists whose distant interests drew their attention away from local conditions. One discreet report, omitting the proper names to protect the identity of the accused, quoted a Socialist candidate as exclaiming, "We are owned by the capitalists in ——— and ruled by the capitalists in ———. We do not have home rule."[16]

In short, the pattern of American socialism's very limited success makes the party look less like a workers' party per se and more like a party peddling a modestly appealing protest against the effects of globalization.[17] American socialism offered the possibility of combining a typically socialist protest against international capitalism with a less-typical protest against international labor. Socialists won their highest share of votes not in the major manufacturing cities of the northeastern United States, but in the middle-size cities and farm communities of the West, where the movement of international capital and labor hit harder. Socialists won larger shares of the vote in states with larger shares of white internal migrants—native-born Americans who had come from another part of the United States. (See figure 4.2.) Many of these white, native-born Americans moving around the United States in the early twentieth century were leaving places that had received large numbers of the new immigrants and thus they had clear reasons to feel themselves pushed around by the international labor market.

But we should remember also that even if the Socialist Party amassed support from voters who disliked the dislocating effects of the global economy, it did not amass much. At its peak, the party accrued slightly fewer than a million votes, for around 6 percent of the vote cast in the presidential election of 1912. Americans had other, more popular and more successful ways of dealing with globalization than simply declaring that it should stop. Even if the impact of immigration on American cities caused some native-born Americans to flee, settle in the West, and vote against the system, others stayed put and built a new system, one specially designed to deflect the pressures of the world economy.

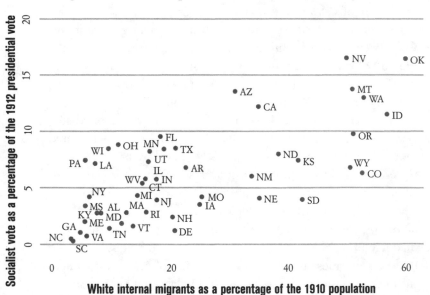

Figure 4.2 Percentage of the presidential vote for the Socialist Party in 1912 as a function of the percentage of native-born white Americans who had come to each state from elsewhere, according to the 1910 census.

WHY AND WHERE SOCIAL SPENDING INCREASED
A LITTLE IN THE UNITED STATES

After Germany set the pattern of early social spending, other countries set the pace. Denmark soon became the most aggressive spender of its citizens' resources, accompanied by other Northwest European countries. Looking at the Western world as a whole, it is possible to discern some basic guidelines governing how much countries were likely to spend on their social-welfare policies. As a general, internationally applicable rule, wealth, age, and democracy drove social spending upward. Governments spent more on the welfare of their people if their citizens were richer and had more to spare; if they were older and could more easily see the use of public pensions for the needy; and if they had the right to vote and could make their voices heard. Other things being equal, religion, low electoral turnout, and income inequality kept social spending down. Protestant countries spent more than Catholic ones.[18] Places where people had the vote, but did not use it, spent less. And however paradoxically, the greater the inequality—the greater, it would seem, the need for some sort of social safety net—the less likely a country was to see that need.[19]

If relative youth, Catholicism, and income inequality tended to depress social spending in the early twentieth century, then we would expect the United States, despite its relative wealth among nations, to spend less on its proto–welfare state than other industrial countries. Americans were younger, with a smaller share of their population over sixty-five than in any other modern industrial country except Australia or New Zealand.[20] The United States had as high a percentage of Catholics as any country without an established Catholic Church.[21] And income inequality in the United States rose over the decades between the Civil War and World War I.[22] Social scientists assessing the correlation of these factors with the strength of a people's devotion to social spending can therefore say that, other things being equal, the

United States should have spent less than other nations on programs to help the poor and unfortunate. And indeed it did.[23]

But our attention to these common factors equally at work among nations—age, religion, and inequality—obscures the root cause of these factors in particular nations. For France to have a lot of Catholics meant that France had an ancient and established Catholic Church. For the United States to have a lot of Catholics meant that the United States had a recent, and to many Protestant Americans an unsettling, trend of Catholic immigration. Likewise the newcomers, mostly young and willing to work for low wages, contributed to the comparative youth and inequality of the United States.

And indeed, because earlier-arrived Americans did not always react eagerly to their new fellow countrymen, the response to immigration made the United States less democratic than it had been, thus adding another to the list of immigration's depressing effects on American social spending. Through the late nineteenth century, immigrants quite easily became citizens and voters in the United States. Indeed, in seventeen American states at 1891, immigrants did not even have to become citizens in order to vote.[24] But as immigration continued and anti-immigrant sentiment swelled, American states began narrowing the breadth of their franchises. By the mid-1920s they had all withdrawn laws allowing noncitizens to vote. States began requiring naturalized immigrants to acquire their citizenship well before an election, and demanded the presentation of naturalization papers at the polls.[25]

On closer examination, then, we would suppose that the effects that appear to make the United States follow the rule of other countries might actually have set it apart. And indeed they did. Behind the various effects of American youth, income inequality, religious variety, and a decrease in voter participation we can see the pressure of immigration reshaping American attitudes toward the working poor, and thus diminishing American interest in policies that might aid the working poor. We also find thoughtful Americans of the period—and not only people who wanted simply to cut off immigration—expressing their concerns about American industry in terms of the peculiar place of the United States in the global economy.

In the decades around 1900, American students of industrialization paid keen attention to the other modern countries around the globe. They watched as the other industrial democracies debated new policies, moved away from socialism on the left and from laissez-faire conservatism on the right, and converged on a middle way of using the power of national government to insure society against the worst effects of capitalist economies.[26] And they watched too as the United States, despite its position as the richest and most powerful of such economies, despite its experience of wrenching depression and prolonged double-digit employment in the 1890s, resisted these political innovations. Dismayed at the feeling that the Old World was passing the New, they worried that, as one reformer put it, their country had been "unaccountably slow" to involve itself in "a world-wide movement toward juster social conditions."[27] This language—the language of a global procession, with the United States bringing up the rear—suggested that reformers saw the United States as suffering from the same problems as other countries, and simply acting slowly to take up the same solutions.[28] But it was not the only, and perhaps not the most important, way in which American reformers thought about how modern industry affected the United States.

The more astute of these reformers knew that the bare evidence of suffering, even when combined with the rebuke of knowing that Europeans had already developed policies for curing that suffering, would not move Americans to support a program of increased social spending. Simply identifying the existence of problems—say, an unconscionably high death rate among the residents of crowded city blocks—would not suffice. "A mere high mortality due to congestion will not seriously disturb a nation that complacently slaughters more people on its railways and in its factories and mines than any other country in the world," the political scientist Charles Beard wrote in 1912. He suggested that reformers should use less moral, and more urgent, arguments—

arguments that played less on the conscience of American voters and more on their prejudice.[29]

One of the most powerful observations Beard could make was to emphasize the extent to which American cities differed from other industrial towns around the world, and why. "In addition to the unhappy working and living conditions which characterize modern urban centers generally, the American city has special problems of its own on account of the large percentage of foreigners embraced in its population," Beard wrote. "Our larger cities are in fact foreign colonies."[30]

We might reasonably suppose, as the American working class appeared visibly to consist of people from other countries, that the average taxpaying American, however much he read about the high death rates in tenements or the disfiguring injuries in factories or the common injustices of sweatshops, would nevertheless feel that such problems afflicted an alien people whose problems did not properly concern him.[31] Industrial ailments afflicting an alien people who happened, for now, to live on American shores might move him no more than bloody news of foreign wars. But our hypothetical jaded taxpayer might respond differently if he suddenly realized that certain social ills could prove literally contagious.

Although the United States did not develop an ambitious plan of national social insurance on the Bismarck model, nor did its spending grow to the degree that other rich nations' did, it did increase its spending noticeably in one particular area and at one particular level of government. In each of the first two decades of the twentieth century, American cities tripled their budgets for the conservation of health and sanitation, and began for the first time to spend more on public health than on assistance to the local poor.[32] Beard noticed this trend, writing that "collective action is easier to obtain in the name of public health than in any other way. It is in this branch of government that the American armor of self-righteousness and *laissez-faire* is most vulnerable."[33] But what Beard called "the American armor" proved more vulnerable in some places than in others, and the pattern of American cities' spending on public health suggests that Americans harbored concerns not about health alone but also about the effect of globalization on health.[34]

Even though by 1866 the New York City Metropolitan Board of Health had proven that certain measures could prevent the spread of cholera, and knowledgeable public health officials had discovered that they could lobby for sewer systems by claiming that "[g]ood privies are far higher signs of civilization than grand palaces and fine arts galleries," Americans still had to learn, almost by accident, how effectively public spending could combat disease.[35] The city of Memphis, Tennessee, in response to the yellow fever epidemic of 1878 (which killed maybe 12 percent of Memphians) began construction of a sewerage system on the assumption that unsanitary conditions had caused the malady. Inadvertently, they managed to reduce by half the mortality rate among the city's people, principally by reducing the incidence of cholera, typhoid, and diarrhea—the diseases commonly spread by unsanitary conditions. Deadly bacteria that could quite easily work their way from a sewage ditch into the groundwater were contained by the confines of a simple waste pipe. With basic public plumbing, life improved and lengthened for Americans, irrespective of their race or color.[36]

Over the next decades, other major American cities undertook similar programs. Scientists embraced and preached the germ theory of disease. "The filth theory is dead," one proclaimed; "we know dirt is very rarely the *direct* cause of sickness."[37] Medical men urged cities to attack the germs directly, and municipal governments responded. They taxed their citizens to build works for purifying and filtering water and to lay pipes for carrying sewage safely away. They provided for the collection of garbage and the cleaning of streets. As they did, the death rate among city-dwelling Americans suffering waterborne diseases plummeted by 88 percent.[38] And as a result, American cities became for the first time in history healthier places than the American countryside.[39] The construction of waterworks and the overall improvement in public sanitation in the early twentieth century proved one of the great public health successes of all time.

Despite the apparent clarity of this lesson, it spread more

slowly than observers thought it should. In 1907, the periodical *Engineering News* expressed the characteristic concern of the age when it noted that one might expect more American cities to adopt water-filtration systems, "as generally as have for some decades the cities of Great Britain and Germany."[40] Even the experience of a waterborne disease outbreak did not necessarily spur a city to take preventive action.[41] The advance of science, even coupled with the lessons of experience, did not suffice. As in the early case of Memphis, other, not necessarily scientific, factors were at work.

Looking at the wide variation among American cities in their commitment to the use of government, Beard wrote in 1912 that "when all the several factors—number of inhabitants, races, industries, and location—are taken into consideration, it is evident that the cities must vary among themselves in the character of the governmental matters which they are required to take up."[42] After all, Beard had already assumed that rationality alone could not get Americans to open their hearts (and wallets) to the growth of social policies. Nonrational appeals addressing the variations among these demographic factors might therefore carry the day.

Beard's factor of "location" mattered significantly. Traditionally in American politics, geographical section markedly influenced political behavior, and it influenced the spending of public money on health, too, although in nontraditional ways. Normally southerners spent less on important public policies than did their fellow countrymen. With a large black population, historically kept illiterate to reinforce the institution of slavery, and with a hierarchical society that placed no premium on social mobility, southerners had little tradition of public education. On average, for example, a southern city spent only a little more than half what a non-southern city might spend on its schools.[43] But southern cities, with their longer, wetter warm seasons and their consequently greater susceptibility to certain kinds of disease, responded readily to the argument that municipal health systems might save them, spending on average 18 percent more per capita than their non-southern fellow Americans.[44]

The relative willingness of taxpaying southerners to fund public health projects raises another factor that Beard invoked: the composition of cities by "races." Returning to the early example of Memphis, we note that it, like other southern cities, contained a good many African Americans. White southerners have traditionally perceived African Americans as significantly racially different from themselves and have proved reluctant to pass laws even to protect blacks from lynching, let alone to aid them through the public purse. Yet Memphis's original public investment and ongoing appropriations for health and sanitation benefited African Americans as much or more than whites: over time, the difference between white and black mortality rates substantially diminished.[45]

The logic behind such apparent generosity might seem obvious, but it is worth pointing out that white southerners, however bigoted, had come to learn that germs did not respect racial distinctions. Whatever improvements a system of pumps, filters, and sewers might provide, it did no good if it served whites alone, especially as American cities of the late nineteenth century were not as racially segregated as they later became. Although southern states began using their laws to take the vote away from African Americans in the late 1880s, they did not begin passing segregation laws until the early twentieth century.[46] Living patterns followed suit, and American cities became more segregated through the following decades.[47] In the late nineteenth century, even in southern cities, whites and blacks lived sufficiently close together that providing public sanitation services for some meant providing them for all. And even residential segregation would not turn the two races into separate disease pools, so long as blacks worked in such close contact with whites. The most racist southerners had still to acknowledge that, even were segregation rigorously enforced, "from that segregated district, negro nurses would still emerge from diseased homes, to come into our homes and hold our children in their arms; negro cooks would still bring bacilli from the segregated district into the homes of the poor and the rich; . . . negro chauffeurs, negro butlers, negro laborers would . . . scatter disease. . . . Into that district would go the clothes of white families, to be laundered in environments possibly reeking with filth and disease."[48] As near to whites as the black population lived and worked, the public interest in their health could not be ignored.

The same principle applied throughout America's cities. Although the great migration of African Americans to northern and western cities had not yet reached the levels it would in the 1920s, already by the 1890s many blacks had begun to leave the South. And in the rest of the country, as in the South, almost two-thirds of black Americans in major cities worked in jobs that put them in close contact with the wider public. (See table 4.1.) They worked as domestic servants—and thus in the very home of their employers—or as porters, waiters, or elevator operators. When black Americans lived in a city, white people saw them and moved among them on a regular basis. In the years before the early-twentieth-century adoption of segregated streetcar railways, whites and blacks traveled together on public transportation.[49] Inasmuch as whites might have feared that someone of another race and unfamiliar cultural habits would be more likely to bear disease, they had that much more motive to spend money on keeping a clean environment for everyone.

Moreover, this principle applied just as well to people of different nationalities as it did to Americans of different skin tones. On average, a city with more foreign-born residents would spend more on health and sanitation.[50] Americans rightly associated migration with disease—germs had to move into the population somehow, and they could move around the world with the same ease and speed as their hosts. But Americans also quite easily, and less justly, accused racially different, long-resident immigrant populations of being the peculiar source of such diseases. During the San Francisco smallpox outbreak of 1887, the city's *Municipal Reports* declared of the long-established Chinese that "they are a constant source of danger to the health and prosperity of the entire community."[51] As servants and laundrymen, as residents of a community hard by the city's port and financial district, the

African Americans

Occupation	Percentage
Private household workers	22.7
Laborers	20.9
Laundresses, private household	13.7
Porters	4.1
Waiters and waitresses	3.8
Total in top five jobs	65.2

New Immigrants

Occupation	Percentage
Laborers	27.4
Operative and kindred workers	21.8
Managers, officials, and proprietors	9.2
Tailors and tailoresses	4.9
Private household workers	4.3
Total in top five jobs	67.6

Native-Born Whites

Occupation	Percentage
Operative and kindred workers	13.2
Salesmen and sales clerks	8.9
Managers, officials, and proprietors	7.8
Laborers	5.9
Clerical workers	5.2
Total in top five jobs	41.0

Table 4.1 Percentage of given population in the top jobs for that population, 1910, for African Americans, new immigrants, and native-born whites in American cities with populations over 30,000. (For further discussion, see note on page 227.)

Chinese moved among other San Franciscans as African Americans moved among whites in other cities, and occasioned the same response: an increased level of public attention to and spending on health and sanitation.[52] Charged with monitoring San Francisco's sanitary conditions, city officials devoted themselves to chronicling the poor conditions among the city's Chinese and its European immigrants, describing their neighborhoods as "cesspools reeking with fermenting and putrefying animal and vegetable matter."[53] By identifying Chinese and other immigrants as the particular source of problems that affected the whole city, such officials were able to argue for an increased public role in preserving the general welfare.

The exceptions to this rule provide a useful test of its power to help us understand how native-born Americans reacted to the presence of foreigners among them: while the presence of immigrants increased the likelihood that an American city would spend its money on public health, the presence of *new* immigrants in a city (other things being equal) reduced that likelihood.[54] The immigrants who arrived in the United States after 1890 came mostly from Italy, Austria-Hungary, and Russia. They made a marked contrast to the earlier migrants, who came principally from Germany and the British Isles. This perception of difference was not lost on these earlier-arrived Americans, who with their native-born counterparts expressed increasing concern about the ability of the newcomers to assimilate. Like the San Francisco Chinese or the African Americans, the new immigrants loomed large in the fearful imaginations of other Americans as bearers of disease. Yet they did not inspire the same generosity born of distaste as other racial or ethnic minorities, and indeed on balance their presence depressed a city's public health spending.

The clue to solving this puzzle may lie in a pattern we can also see with respect to African Americans. Cities with a large number of black residents spent money on public health, and not, it bears repeating, out of altruism. As the *Atlanta Constitution* noted in 1914, "To purge the negro of disease is not so much a kindness to the negro himself as it is a matter of sheer self-preservation of the

white man. Philanthropy doesn't enter into this battle of life and death; grim, primitive self-interest, the conservation of the health of the white race is the controlling factor."[55] Exceptions to this rule occurred when the black population seemed—rationally or not— less likely to come into contact with whites. When the city of Memphis responded to the threat of disease by installing municipal plumbing, the neighborhood it neglected was Chelsea, a majority-black area. In other, more segregated cities, such delays in providing services to black areas were equally pronounced.[56]

Populations of America's new immigrants lived in similarly segregated communities. On average they were even more isolated from their neighbors than African Americans, and also more isolated than older immigrant groups.[57] One Jewish immigrant pictured his New York neighborhood as sealed off from the city with "massive portals."[58]

The new immigrants not only lived in isolated neighborhoods, but they tended, unlike African Americans, to work in occupations that did not bring them into regular contact with other city dwellers. (See table 4.1.) They were most likely to work as general laborers or operatives in factories.[59] Sometimes the segregated ghettos of tenement apartments stood next to factories set apart from downtowns, constituting an island of newly arrived Southern and Eastern Europeans, whose inhabitants had neither the means nor the motive to leave their communities, while native-born whites had little incentive to visit their densely settled city blocks.[60] When immigrants seemed set apart, as when blacks seemed set apart, their health problems might have troubled other Americans less, providing less impetus toward an increased role for government in preserving public health.[61]

Moreover, the new immigrants, like African Americans, were not always politically integrated into their cities. If they had been, they might have supported greater public spending on health and sanitation; as the reformer Jane Addams wrote in 1907, the new immigrants tended to work and live among neighbors who were "unlike each other in all save the universal characteristics of man," and so found themselves acutely aware of the universal vulnerability of man to diseases.[62] But cities that received large numbers of new immigrants tended to be cities that had once received large numbers of old immigrants, too. A generation before, political parties on the outs realized if they could woo those old immigrants, especially the Irish, they might gain power. Good party men roamed the old ethnic neighborhoods with favors to ask, and to give, and thus built new political machines. But these Irish machines, now secure in their power, showed little interest in recruiting the new immigrants or spending public money to benefit them.[63]

In the long run, the white ethnic populations did not remain as concentrated as they began. The children of immigrants clambered up the professional ladder and out of the ghetto. Ethnic concentration, unlike racial concentration, lasted a relatively short time. Thus cities quickly receiving a large number of new immigrants would respond less energetically to the newcomers' presence, as the island populations of immigrants eroded under the effects of geographic and social mobility.[64]

Overall, Beard's first category—"number of inhabitants"—proved most important in understanding the pattern of spending on public health. To a point, America's larger cities spent more, per capita, on public health and sanitation than smaller ones. For American city dwellers of the era, many of them recently arrived from the countryside, the problem of disease was a product of, in the word of the day, "congestion." Too many people in one place led to the spread of disease. So larger cities, and richer cities, irrespective of whether they were home to particularly diverse populations, spent more on the costly infrastructure and operation of plumbing to keep their densely populated blocks clean.

Thus did American willingness to spend on at least one kind of social welfare grow. Contemplating his countrymen's relative responsiveness in this area, Beard wrote that "all things conspire to make public hygiene the gateway to revolutionary changes in the living and working conditions in the United States."[65] Certainly in other countries, public health looked like a natural avenue to an increased governmental role in community planning and the prevention of pollution. "The powers which primarily affect the environment of the individual cannot logically be separated from those which affect the individual as such," argued a British report on the role of the government of the United Kingdom in maintaining public health.[66] Elsewhere, spending on public health increased hand in hand with plans for old-age pensions and other social insurance. But, as routinely proved the case, the United States did not follow suit. Concern over public health remained the principal exception to Americans' lack of interest in supporting proto–welfare policies, and it was an exception that did not portend a new rule. The driving interest in it came from the local level, which in the early twentieth century was the level at which American government most markedly grew.[67] And that interest varied notably in intensity, depending on the extent to which any given city seemed, in Beard's phrase, a "foreign colony."

Even while Americans were scoring successes with public programs for health and sanitation in the cities, they were setting limits on this commitment. In keeping with the 1910 report by Abraham Flexner, *Medical Education in the United States and Canada*, the American Medical Association established itself as the accrediting agency for medical schools, and thus the gateway to the medical profession in the United States. As a result, the quality of medical schools in the country increased, while their quantity—and their accessibility to the poor—decreased. In particular, the availability of medical education to African Americans fell.[68] Americans' newly discovered interest in keeping the poor healthy did not extend to ensuring access to physicians. As with the simultaneous increase in money spent on public education, the augmented expenditures on public health responded specifically to the challenges posed by increased migration and mobility.[69] Both made it easier and safer for workers to move into and around America, but neither made other kinds of social spending more likely.

In sum, the relatively minor interest that Americans showed in increasing the ability of their governments to improve social circumstances represented a response not to the perceived excesses of capitalism or the conditions of a working class, but to the presence of migrants among them. And the increase of public expenditure on health and sanitation, as materially successful as it proved in saving lives for citizens of all races and nationalities, did not lead to more, or more kinds, of public spending. As a reaction to the visible presence of foreigners and other racially different people as an integral part of the home and work life of a city, it constituted no more than a minimum necessary commitment to accommodating them. The limited amount, and peculiar shape, of the American state owed more to the position of the United States within the global economy than to the stage of capitalism Americans had reached. And little as the federal government grew, it responded likewise to these circumstances.

THE SHAPE OF THE NATIONAL STATE

In 1917, the *National Service Handbook* outlined for the American people what their nation's government would do in war, but it began by emphasizing "the achievements of peace," which included principally the growth of government in recent decades:

> For the last generation, in our legislation, in our education, and in our social and philanthropic work, we have been trying increasingly to make the Nation make the most of itself. We have been bettering the conditions of labor and of living; by law and by private effort we have succeeded in maintaining an increasingly high standard of health and efficiency. We have been experimenting in education, adapting our school machinery and methods to the newer industrial conditions and the modes of living and earning a living that they were forcing upon our children. Our bureaus of public health, our labor laws, and our charitable organizations have combined to reduce the ravages of disease, fatigue, and unhealthful surroundings both in the home and working life of the poor.[70]

As we have seen, the growth of government spending on these causes occurred, when it did, chiefly at the local level. Yet on behalf of the federal government, the Committee on Public Information wanted to reassure American citizens that even in the midst of a major war, such advances "must be preserved."[71] To make its point that the federal government had come to involve itself usefully in the lives of all Americans, the committee included a foldout diagram, the size of a small poster, of the U.S. government and its functions. (See figure 4.3.)

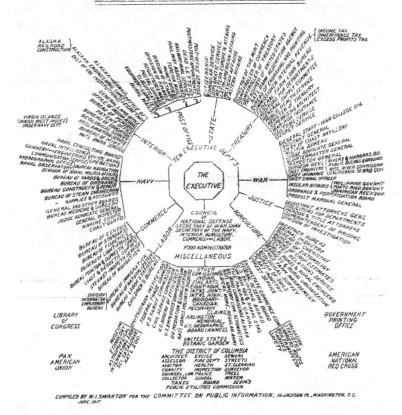

Figure 4.3 A schematic diagram of the U.S. government in 1917.

An unconventional organizational chart, the diagram showed
the White House and its reporting agencies as a sunburst whose
rays shone on almost every aspect of American life. The ambitions
and omissions of this informal coat of arms for the American
republic showed just how far the United States had lately come
toward creating a more European-style state, and also how far it
fell short. The author of the sunburst model of the U.S. government, Walter Irving Swanton, was a career compiler, a professional collector and arranger of information. He had begun by
compiling opinions on progressive Republican president Theodore
Roosevelt, whose dictum that "the Executive is the steward of the
public welfare" encapsulated the case for the expansion of federal
power in the first decades of the twentieth century.[72] The idea
was, as Roosevelt explained, that the president alone among the
officers of the federal government had a national constituency
and, at least in time of crisis, was "bound to assume that he has
the legal right to do whatever the needs of the people demand,
unless the Constitution or the laws explicitly forbid him to do
it."[73] This Rooseveltian doctrine of the public welfare came to be
known as "the New Nationalism," and the sunburst model showed
both the extent and limits of this new nationalism.

Although Roosevelt supported this idea more vigorously than
his fellow Americans, he did not uphold it alone. He borrowed
the phrase "the New Nationalism" from the author Herbert
Croly, who in his 1909 book *The Promise of American Life* argued
that "every popular government should in the end, and after a
necessarily prolonged deliberation, possess the power of taking
any action, which, in the opinion of a decisive majority of the people, is demanded by the public welfare."[74] Roosevelt's presidency
represented a major step in that process of deliberation and new
action. As Croly wrote, "He was the first political leader of the
American people to identify the national principle with an ideal of
reform."[75] As for what *reform* meant, it was then and remains now
a vague concept full of "immense suggestiveness," as Charles
Beard wrote in 1914.[76] But if we turn away from the dense clouds

of political prose and look instead at the sunburst diagram, we may more easily see what the years of reform, for which Roosevelt was only the most prominent of major proponents, provided.

Almost the entire bottom half of the executive sunburst did not exist before the Civil War. The Department of Commerce and Labor (created in 1903), the Department of Agriculture (created in 1862 and made a cabinet appointment in 1889), and the Department of Justice (1870) had all debuted within the fifty years prior to Woodrow Wilson's election. (By comparison, the preceding fifty years had seen the creation of only two cabinet positions—the Post Office [1829] and the Interior [1849].) The Council of National Defense, which would soon swell to include the new wartime agencies, had come into existence only in 1916. With a few exceptions—the U.S. Botanic Garden (1842), the Smithsonian Institution (1846), and the U.S. Soldiers' Home (1859)—the spreading "Miscellaneous" rays had been established after the Civil War.[77]

But the period of most rapid growth had come more recently. Of all the agencies listed in the diagram, more than 40 percent had come into existence since 1900. During the early years of the twentieth century, Roosevelt wielded his doctrine of executive steward-ship to pry these agencies out of a reluctant Republican Congress, or else he created them by presidential order. Later, a Democratic Congress approved them faster than President Woodrow Wilson wanted them. The twentieth-century additions to the diagram represented a sudden new effulgence of the executive sun in its ability to reach the farther corners of the American republic.

Not all of these additions corresponded to altogether new executive powers. About a third of the bureaus, divisions, or other agencies on the sunburst testified to the homely enthusiasm for better organization in government. In the early twentieth century, presidents and Congresses, when inspired to do a little political housekeeping, occasionally roused themselves to sort existing federal powers into definite pigeonholes, giving them names, putting people in charge, and holding them accountable for specific jobs.

So, for example, the Forest Service (1906) took on work previously done in the Department of the Interior's Forestry Division
and the Department of Agriculture's Bureau of Forestry. Such
redundancies often appeared across federal departments. Consequently, Roosevelt became the first of many presidents to
appoint a commission to make sense of the workings of the federal government, looking for duplication of work and recom-
mending possible efficiencies. So, too, did Roosevelt, despite a
few organizational successes, become the first of many presidents
to discover that although such a commission might make valuable
recommendations, its work would ultimately attract more dust
than congressional attention. Congress did not welcome what
Senator Thomas H. Carter (Republican of Montana) called
"executive encroachment on the sphere of congressional
action."[78] Even though Congress created the optimistically titled
Bureau of Efficiency in 1916, which had the specific chore of
eliminating redundant statistical work being done in government,
it had made little headway by the time the government drew up
this diagram.[79]

Whether the new government agencies stood for efficient
organization or for novel assertions of executive authority, they
fulfilled a variety of purposes. Scholars of the machinery of government began developing taxonomies of public functions in the
1910s, displaying a Linnaean tenacity as they tried to explain just
what it was the equipment of the state had been designed to do
(and often, what it did anyway, irrespective of design). Applying
one such scheme to the sunburst diagram, we can get a sense of
what kind of national government the Americans of the early
twentieth century were building for themselves, and also what
kind of government they had no interest in building.[80] (See tables
4.2 and 4.2a.)

Apart from the military agencies, many of which had sprung up to
answer the needs of the impending war, the new agencies most commonly served the purposes of gathering information and framing regulation. Indeed these activities bore close relation to one another.

Research itself was rarely innocent: all of the government's information-gathering efforts hinted at possible regulatory action. The Department of Agriculture collected and published useful information on the occurrence of nutrients in soils, and the Department of the Interior collected and published useful information on the occurrence of commercially valuable ores in the American earth. This knowledge had clear economic consequences, giving rise to the question of how the American land could be best exploited. More controversial still, the government began looking into the question of workers' wages and duration of employment. If the government were to testify officially as to the frequency and length of jobless periods for American workers, it might raise the question of public unemployment insurance. Likewise, once Americans knew what railroads were actually charging, they supported the use of federal power to even out the rates. [81]

So the U.S. government moved cautiously in establishing such fact-finding agencies, tying Labor and Commerce together in a single department in 1903, lest they be seen as opposing interests. Even the collection of information on American children, a near-universal interest, threatened to provoke controversy. After all, once the U.S. government began publicizing infant mortality rates among immigrants or the poor, reasonable Americans might draw the conclusion that their government ought to legislate minimum wages or maximum hours to ensure the health of families.[82]

Controversy notwithstanding, the investigative agencies proliferated and the regulatory agencies followed. If we consider the closely related activities of research and regulation as belonging in a single category, we see that they represent the major state-building effort of the early twentieth century. Thus fully a third of the new agencies on the sunburst diagram contributed to a single purpose: the development of a federal government whose researchers could say, with some precision, how the U.S. economy was running, and whose regulators could, if necessary, do something about it. They might order the readjustment of railway freight rates, or the price of borrowed money. And with the new revenue

Arm of Government	Year Created	Primary Purpose
Bureau of Standards	1901	Regulatory
Bureau of Chemistry	1901	Information
Bureau of Soils	1901	Information
Chief of Coast Artillery	1901	Defense
Bureau of Plant Industry	1901	Information
Bureau of the Census	1902	Information
Reclamation Service	1902	Development
Insular Affairs	1902	International
Board of Engineers for Rivers and Harbors	1902	Regulatory
Department of Commerce	1903	Regulatory
General Staff, War College	1903	Defense
Militia Bureau	1903	Defense
Board of Road Commissioners, Alaska	1905	Development
American National Red Cross	1905	Defense
Bureau of Entomology	1905	Information
Office of Farm Management	1905	Information
Forest Service	1905	Regulatory
Boundary Commission—Canadian	1906	International
Bureau of Naturalization	1906	Police
Superintendent of Prisons	1907	Police
Division of Investigation	1909	Police
International Joint Commission	1909	International
Commission of Fine Arts	1910	Regulatory
Bureau of Mines	1910	Information
(State Department) Western European Affairs	1910	International
(State Department) Latin American Affairs	1910	International
(State Department) Mexican Affairs	1910	International
(State Department) Eastern Affairs	1910	International
Postal Savings	1911	Social Insurance
Bureau of Foreign and Domestic Commerce	1912	Development
Children's Bureau	1912	Information

Table 4.2 The new agencies on figure 4.3. (For further discussion, see note on page 227.)

Arm of Government	Year Created	Primary Purpose
(Navy) Communication Service	1912	Defense
Board of Mediation and Conciliation	1913	Regulatory
Federal Reserve Board	1913	Regulatory
Arlington Memorial Bridge Commission	1913	Civic
Markets and Rural Organization	1913	Information
Income Tax	1913	Revenue
Division of Naval Militia Affairs	1914	Defense
Federal Trade Commission	1914	Regulatory
Panama Canal	1914	Development
Bureau of Crop Estimates	1914	Information
War Risk Insurance	1914	Defense
National Advisory Committee for Aeronautics	1915	Development
International High Commission	1915	International
States Relations Service	1915	Development
Alaska Engineering Commission	1915	Development
Chief of Naval Operations	1915	Defense
Coast Guard	1915	Defense
Pecuniary Claims	1916	International
U.S. Tariff Commission	1916	Regulatory
Bureau of Efficiency	1916	Regulatory
U.S. Employees' Compensation Commission	1916	Social insurance
Shipping Board	1916	Defense
Com. Navy Yards and Naval Stations	1916	Defense
Eight-Hour Commission	1916	Regulatory
Council of National Defense	1916	Defense
National Park Service	1916	Civic
Inheritance Tax	1916	Revenue
Excess Profits Tax	1916	Revenue
Federal Farm Loan Bureau	1916	Development
Naval Consulting Board	1916	Defense
Food Administrator	1917	Defense
Provost Marshal General	1917	Defense

Purpose	Total
Civic	2
Defense	15
Development	8
Information	10
International	9
Police	3
Regulatory	11
Revenue	3
Social insurance	2
Total	63

Table 4.2a A summary of the functions of the new agencies. (See table 4.2.)

measures of the 1910s—an income tax, an inheritance tax, an excess-profits tax—the government had an adequate means to pay for such powers.[83]

Conspicuous by their almost total absence, social-welfare programs did not form a major part of the American state. The U.S. government simply had not entered the business of taxing its wealthier citizens to support its poorer ones. On the few occasions when the United States took even a modest step in that direction, constitutional limits ordinarily let it cover only its own employees (as was the case with the Workmen's Compensation Law of 1916) or, at most, reach workers in interstate commerce (as was the case with the Employers' Liability Law of 1906). And even though the provision of workmen's compensation barely qualified as welfare—requiring an employer to pay a claim to an injured worker simply applied the existing common-law principle of individual liability to workplaces—the Supreme Court stood ready to check Congress if it looked as though it might get too generous with other people's money. In 1908 the Court struck down the employers' liability law of 1906, which held firms engaged in interstate commerce liable for employees hurt on the job. The Court found that such a requirement lay "wholly outside the power of Congress to regulate commerce."[84] To pass the Court's scrutiny, Congress had to narrow the law to hold firms engaged in interstate commerce liable for employees hurt on the job only if the work in which they were engaged while injured constituted interstate commerce. No wonder, then, that conservatives regarded the Court as their protector and gratefully believed, in the words of one Wall Street analyst, that "the Supreme Court . . . entirely prevents communistic legislation," while reformers like Theodore Roosevelt saw it as an obstacle to progress.[85] No wonder, too, that more interventionist welfare programs, like those adopted in European states that guaranteed old-age pensions or income assistance during periods of unemployment, remained entirely outside the purview of the U.S. government.[86]

But the intransigent Supreme Court did not pose the only, or perhaps even the most important, obstacle to the establishment of European social policies in the United States. Rather, the constituency for such policies mostly did not exist in America, or where it did exist, it did not wield sufficient political clout. Proto–welfare states, as they developed in other capitalist nations, existed to make the lives of industrial workers more nearly bearable, given the frequent unemployment and high risk of injury in modern factory work. Nobody realized this need more quickly than the workers themselves, and in industrial countries where the workers could vote, welfare policies predictably sprouted.[87] Which is to say, they sprouted everywhere in predictable patterns except in the United States, and for at least two reasons.

First, the Senate and the Electoral College gave Americans who lived in rural areas a disproportionately louder voice in the federal government. No matter that Nevada or Wyoming had populations that under the usual rules of apportionment would not qualify them for congressional representation; the Constitution allocated them two senators each, neither more nor less than it gave New York or California.[88] Rural Americans in the new states had their grievances: they felt pushed west and preyed upon by international capital, and found themselves living at the end of monopolistic railroad lines. But they did not suffer from the same problems as industrial workers and did not have the same interest in supporting welfare policies as industrial workers. They wanted regulation of railroads and banks but not, particularly, unemployment insurance or spending on public health.[89]

Second, as we have seen, even in those areas where industrial workers did have a significant political say, they did not speak with one voice because they did not speak the same language—which is to say, they came from many different countries. In the cities of the United States, and especially in their poorer sections, as Jacob Riis wrote in 1890, "one may find for the asking an Italian, a German, a French, African, Spanish, Bohemian, Russian, Scandinavian, Jewish, and Chinese colony," but, he noted, "not a native-born individual."[90] It was impossible to think of an American working class without also thinking of it as an immigrant working class.

In combination, these two factors, which defined the extent to which globalization shaped America, likewise shaped the U.S. government. Rural Americans, aggrieved by the role they believed foreign capital had played in pushing them to the far ends of civilization and stranding them there without adequate connections to markets, wanted government to assist them. Americans who worried about the effects of immigration wanted government to regulate the flow of foreign labor. The national state that American politicians made in the early twentieth century emerged logically from their concern over rural life and immigrant populations. Instead of adopting social-insurance policies, they passed regulatory laws to help their agrarian constituents, and they worked through the early decades of the century to pass laws regulating immigration. When they did pass laws that provided some form of social insurance, even when they adapted such laws from European nations, the laws also reflected their peculiar American concerns. Such was the case with the major social legislation in the sunburst diagram. It appeared under the perhaps unlikely heading of the Post Office Department.

A STATE CONTAINING MANY NATIONS

Congressmen supporting a postal savings system in 1910 meant to provide, as Representative Gilbert M. Hitchcock (Democrat of Nebraska) said, "the assistance of law among the poor."[91] Almost every other country in the world with even the frailest claim to economic modernity already had a postal savings system for this purpose. A simple logic supported such systems. Banks had little interest in attracting the business of poorer people. Working people in their modest clothes, clutching their modest savings, felt unwelcome—as they were meant to—in the glittering lobbies and offices of banks. Postal savings systems let people who had only a little to save put their money somewhere safe. National governments guaranteed post office deposits and set rates of interest, ensured that withdrawals and deposits were easy to make, and sometimes discouraged larger depositors by reducing the rate of interest (sometimes to zero) as the amount on deposit rose. By requiring the postal savings system to invest deposits in government bonds, they financed national debt. Even the U.S. dependency of the Philippines had such a system as of 1906. But not the United States itself, where opponents of the system, such as Representative George N. Southwick (Republican of New York) declared that "the only demand for the bill came from socialists."[92]

To pass the U.S. Congress, the bill for a postal savings system had to appeal to rural interests and address the problems of immigrants, rather than simply offer a government service to the poor. When the bill came up for debate in the House of Representatives, its backers had to make the case that it would attract people "whose earnings were so small that the banks do not care to bother with them," and work for "the hundreds of thousands of people throughout the country who have no ready banking facilities" nearby, and for "foreigners and uneducated people who are not accustomed to our banking system," as Representative Edward T. Taylor (Democrat of Colorado) argued.[93]

Serving immigrants would work to the advantage of the United States overall, congressmen explained. Where Americans tended to be "wasteful," hard-working immigrants already had thrifty habits, partly because they knew they could save up their money and profitably deposit it in postal systems in their own countries. An American postal savings system might teach native-born workers to save like immigrants, and might capture foreign capital that otherwise went overseas. In 1907, "Italians in this country [sent] $9,000,000 . . . out of this country across the water," Representative John A. Maguire (Democrat of Nebraska) warned. If the United States had a postal savings system, it might keep that foreign capital in the New World.[94]

A policy that might benefit rural Americans while simultaneously integrating immigrants into the American economy had an evident appeal. The postal savings system became law in 1910. And it attracted the constituencies it aimed for, proving most appealing in western states and among immigrants. (See figure 4.4.) Indeed, although American lawmakers studied more than thirty other postal savings systems before legislating their own, inventing almost none of it themselves and borrowing its provisions from the laws of other countries, the American system ultimately looked like none other.[95] In the United States, as in no other country, the working-class depositors of the postal savings system were largely immigrants who came from a wide variety of nations. But then, it was truer in the United States than in any other country that the working class included a significant share of immigrants who came from a wide variety of nations.[96]

For Americans who spent their time thinking about developing a proper national government, such peculiarities loomed large. Studying governments in the rest of the world might open one's eyes and mind to new possibilities, but none of those other governments faced quite the same situation as the United States, whose Constitution ensured the outsize influence of rural regions

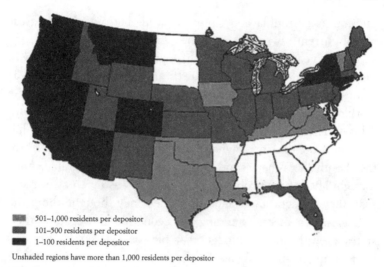

501–1,000 residents per depositor
101–500 residents per depositor
1–100 residents per depositor
Unshaded regions have more than 1,000 residents per depositor

Figure 4.4 Uptake of the postal savings system.

and whose openness to immigration meant its industrial working class looked like none other. In 1887, when Woodrow Wilson was still only a professor of politics and not yet a participant, he identified these problems as paramount. One could, Wilson allowed, study other countries profitably, but one could not hope to borrow much from them, let alone "transplant foreign systems into this country. . . . They simply would not grow here. . . . Our duty is, to supply the best possible life to a *federal* organization, to systems within systems."[97] It was well enough to study the other nations of the world, but one had also to remember that the other nations of the world teemed through American life. "To know the public mind of this country, one must know the mind, not of Americans of the older stocks only, but also of Irishmen, of Germans, of negroes."[98] Here, of course, Wilson stumbled slightly, as "negroes" did indeed belong to one of the oldest of American stocks. But this misstep reveals a further clue as to the peculiar state over which he presided at the start of World War I.

When Wilson came to Washington as president in 1913, the ideas and airs of his native Virginia did not fit most of the rest of the country. Virginia and the Old South lay outside the great global currents sweeping over the United States. Foreign labor and foreign capital did not flow through the southern economy as they did through that of the North and West. For as much as Jacob Riis searched in vain for a native-born American among the working class of New York, the opposite held true of the South. "It is apparently our lot to be a federation of cultures," Randolph Bourne wrote of America in 1916, adding "with the exception of the South."[99] When southerners thought of migrants, they thought about race problems and "negroes" as much as or more than they thought about labor.[100] When they thought about the federal government extending its economic power into their states, even through so innocuous a plan as a system for protecting working people's savings through post offices, they saw "one of the most revolutionary [laws] proposed in forty years; dangerous for the sections of the country remote from the financial centers," as Representative William G. Brantley (Democrat of Georgia) declared.[101] Brantley's figure of forty years revealed as much as Wilson's slip about "negroes." Forty years earlier, the last of the seceded southern states (including Brantley's) had finally reentered the Union after undergoing the process of Reconstruction, during which Congress required southern legislatures to pass laws protecting voting rights and acknowledging federal supremacy. Southerners still smarting from the national government's long-ago effort to dictate their local affairs chafed at any augmentation of the federal executive that might give it the authority once more to enter into the economic and social life of the South.

The federalist structure of the U.S. Constitution ensured that peculiar regions like the South and the West, even if they were sparsely settled, could lobby for their peculiar interests. In the late nineteenth century, the local interests of these sections mirrored their positions in the new global economy, with the people of the South mainly bypassed by the great global currents, and those of the West awash in their effects. The peculiar character of the federal executive in the United States, as depicted in the *National Service Handbook*, reflected the outsize influence in America of constituencies left out of, or lost in, the modern global economy. These people did not want a strong central state to get them an empire or provide welfare for the poor. They wanted government to regulate the effects of foreign capital and foreign labor, and little else. They spent their decades-long transition to an industrial economy fighting over such regulations, and the national state they made showed the scars of those struggles. In this light it was not surprising that the U.S. government looked little like the other imperial powers, and was thus unready to wage a total war. It was the product of wholly different experiences, and it produced a wholly different empire.

■ 5
Warfare

When the Great War came to Washington, a new city grew suddenly within the capital. Clustered on the grass of the mall, its buildings housed people from all over the country. Day and night it shook as if the artillery of the western front were pounding it from across the ocean. But it was not the bark of shot and shell pummeling the settlement from without; rather, vigorous activity was making it quiver from within.

Inside the hastily constructed new buildings, warping floorboards of flimsy hallways shivered to the rattle of roller skates worn by a corps of messenger boys whose course through the corridors showed the flow of information from one office to the next. Thin walls thumped to the metallic beat of machinery manned— or, rather, operated: the controllers were far more likely to be women than men—by an army of stenographers recording information and storing it for ease of use. Over these sounds rose the hum of men's voices dictating, deciding, debating whether it might not just be possible, just this once, to get the United States of America properly organized and fully in possession, at one place and one time, of all the vital information on which modern governments thrive.

Ambitious citizens looked at the throngs purposefully swarming the Washington streets and thought, "America has a real capital at last."[1] In their trim suits (wartime meant saving fabric), the

civilian war workers looked almost like a uniformed army themselves, come to fight a behind-the-lines battle against tradition to
make a new nation. The men and women peopling this vital and
fragile new center of government within government believed that
their presence in the capital represented a crisis, and not just the
crisis of war mobilization. The demands of readying for war were
real enough, but they paled in comparison with what the ambitious new Washingtonians had in mind. When they looked at their
exhausted colleagues and the maze of temporary offices, they saw
more than just an urgent answer to wartime needs. They saw the
foundations of a new national government that the United States
desperately needed in the changing world. In the world after the
war, they thought, the United States would finally have to begin
supporting a great capital on the order of London or Paris, an
administrative center equipped to manage the affairs of a world-
shaking nation so that, as one reporter wrote, the United States
could become "at last definitely part of the great world."[2] For as
proud as the members of the civilian army were of their work, they
suffered more than a little embarrassment that their country had
such urgent need of them for such mundane chores.[3]

The new Washingtonians comprised the United States' wartime brain. Thousands of them came, crowding boarding houses
so that travelers could scarcely find a floor to sleep on, filling
offices that blighted the view of the Lincoln Memorial before it
had even finished going up. Had they not gone about their business in plain sight they might have qualified as a shadow government, for they were there at the president's behest to do what the
regular government of the United States did not have the resources,
authority, or will to do for itself.

LACK OF PREPAREDNESS

President Woodrow Wilson summoned the businessmen, economists, lawyers, and other professional processors of information to provide Washington with a crash course in how to field a

million-man army, and as a necessary first step, to create a government capable of assembling, equipping, moving, feeding, and
communicating with such an army. This government needed to
find able-bodied men of fighting age, which meant they needed
to define "able-bodied" and "fighting age," and think up procedures for deciding who qualified as each. More than this, they
needed ammunition, boots, helmets, rifles, and uniforms; trucks,
airplanes, guns, and shells; paper, pencils, and paint; food—
which meant they needed to identify supplies and suppliers, and
to count and price the goods that the army would need. They estimated demand and availability of cement and rubber, varnish and
lumber, beef and oysters. They thought about the number of
hides that might be necessary to provide for an army's shoe
leather. They found sources of goods within the United States,
and they collected information about the availability of those vital
items that Americans themselves neither grew nor made. Even
setting aside the war's special requirements for weaponry, they
still had to ask that the American economy speed up tremen-
dously. They figured that soldiers wore out shoes and clothing
about five times as fast as civilians, and they needed production to
match these new levels of consumption.[4]

Their work went beyond knowing what the United States
needed, and it extended to organizing that knowledge and making it widely available and comprehensible to a voting citizenry
who would have to accept and act in keeping with those needs. In
short, it extended to organizing the nation. This much larger and
more demanding project of re-creating the United States developed naturally from the smaller task of mobilization for war, and
the new Washingtonians soon saw the need for it. Almost as soon,
they ran into problems: the government they took over made poor
material for the edifice they wished to build.

In the *National Service Handbook*, the organizers tried to
explain themselves to their fellow citizens. "Perhaps the most
important military lesson we can learn from the allies' three years
of warfare," the *Handbook*'s "item 1" began, "is that the battles of
this war will be won, in a large part, behind the lines. . . . With an

organized country behind the army, we are literally mobilizing a force of a hundred million for victory."[5] Watching the new Washingtonians at their work, it was easy to believe that they had realized their goal of an organized country. Rushing back and forth in their established routines, solving problems efficiently, they gave the impression of waging what one observer called a "stenographers' war," one that was altogether "clear, clean, straight-cut."[6] But the haste with which they had come, the mess they had to make to bring only a little order in their wake, cast doubt on the straightforwardness of what they were doing. By the time they got to Washington, the war was already, as the *National Service Handbook* confessed, three years old. Yet the country had blundered into mobilization, however heroically, as if its leaders had never thought about it before.

This lack of preparedness had impressed itself on some Americans well before Germany's unrestricted submarine warfare drew the United States into the conflict early in 1917. These Americans lamented the easygoing national character that shunned the discipline of war. But the absence of a war-making state was not, or certainly not only, the product of innate American qualities. It was the product of decisions made in keeping with the circumstances of the age. For within the memory of Americans then still living, their country had fought a highly modern, bureaucratic, and bloody organized war, one that prefigured the western front in its brutal lesson that industrial powers can, and often must, win wars by attrition. The Civil War left the United States with an army feared and admired by the British, French, and Prussians. Yet after the Civil War, the United States had dismantled its defense establishment and, over the subsequent decades, grew powerful without much of an organized or organizing state.[7]

By contrast, as soon as the European fighting began in 1914, tales of efficient mobilization already filled the war lore of the principal belligerents. These stories told how nations had within days or even hours shifted gears so that industrial engines mighty in peacetime capacity could, without a hitch, switch from production to destruction, driving an entire people toward war. The trains snaking in and out of Paris and Berlin, full ordinarily of workers and commercial freight, carried soldiers now and munitions, too, assembling divisions and conveying them to ships or the front. And, admirers said, it happened so smoothly because the statesmen had planned it all in advance. In the fateful summer of 1914 the hawkish generals and ministers of the nearly belligerent powers insisted that once the mobilization started it must continue, not stopping until it arrived at the final destination of war. They said they could not pause, because if they did they might lose their place in the train schedules, and then fall behind the enemy as he massed his troops according to *his* agenda. The generals had, as they explained patiently, plans. The plans rested on years of experience, observations of imperial diplomacy and military maneuver, and of course on a systematic understanding of the railway timetables. As the chief of the German general staff, Helmuth Johann Ludwig von Moltke, wrote, "The advance of armies of millions of men . . . was the result of years of painstaking work. Once planned, it could not possibly be changed."[8]

The existence, elegance, and execution of the great plans for war filled ordinary Europeans with pride and delight. Although politicians foresaw revolutions rising from the chaos of fighting and businessmen hedged their bets against inflation and debt, citizens who had been pressed into a service larger than themselves thrilled to their role in a great undertaking. The news of war meant they could put aside their peacetime cares and submit themselves to a cause. Infamously, the crowds celebrating the declarations of war included Adolf Hitler, who in Vienna "sank to my knees and thanked heaven from an overflowing heart that it had granted me the good fortune to be alive at such a time." Nor was it only proto-Nazis who rejoiced, as historian Hew Strachan notes; Stefan Zweig, a Vienna Jew and later an exile from Hitler's regime, joined the same crowds in a "rushing feeling of fraternity. . . . Each individual experienced an exaltation of his ego . . . he was part of the people."[9] Similar scenes played out in other nations. In France, "complete strangers could be heard addressing one another in a bizarre fashion, as if Parisians had all at once become . . . dates in a new sort of calendar. 'What day are you?' And, before the other could get in an answer, 'I am on the first' (as if to suggest, 'beat that'). . . . 'I am the eleventh' ('You'll never make Berlin at that rate')."[10]

Mobilization stories in the United States sounded rather different, despite the three years' head start Americans had, during which they might have gotten used to the idea of war. The increasingly ominous involvement of American banking interests in funding the fighting could have spurred planners to action. But as to plans, the commander of the American Expeditionary Force, John J. Pershing, claimed that when he sent his staff to fetch the army's plans for a European invasion, "the pigeon-hole was empty."[11] American military strategists had planned for a war with Japan, with whom they expected to struggle over the U.S. colony in the Philippines. They had planned for a German invasion of the Americas, either in the Indies or on the mainland of the United States. They thought it quite likely they would lose in both cases. Geography and the lack of an adequate American military presence in the Western Pacific meant Japan would have plenty of time to invade and fortify the Philippines before U.S. reinforcements could arrive there. Indeed, war games for the Japanese scenario ended up with the enemy army occupying the West Coast.[12] As for the Atlantic scenario, the U.S. defensive capability might simply not match up to the German offensive capability, or so the planners thought. More hopefully, on the centennial of the last big American war with Canada, they had thought about turning their weapons northward once more.[13] But they had not planned for a million-man army in Europe, let alone for the reorganization of the United States that would be necessary to sustain it.

As for American mobilization, Canadian prime minister Robert Borden wrote, "The Government of the United States in its various departments and activities made about all the mistakes that had been observable in the war preparedness of each of the allied nations, and probably added a few of its own."[14] If Borden showed a neighborly acidity, his critique nevertheless rightly pointed out

that the Americans had examples to follow and time to follow
them. The war had in 1914 caught the British on the wrong foot,
but they had set a pattern for how to catch up.[15] Britain began
regulating economic output in August 1915. British representatives visited the United States in May 1917 and discussed the augmentation of state power that they had found necessary to manage
the wartime economy. They explained the workings of the British
mobilization system, providing the U.S. government with information and procedures they had used, which the Americans duti-
fully filed.[16] And yet when the United States entered the war, the
government soon overtaxed the economy in its frenzy to mobilize
an army: "two-score Government agencies [were] bidding and
scheming against each other, each obsessed with a mad determination to achieve his own goal. . . . Even the capillaries of industry
were congested, and confusion arose in the most remote and
unexpected parts of the industrial body. Serious shortages arose
at the same time that the greatest industrial community in the
world was headed for asphyxiation in its own product."[17]

The European powers' plans called citizens and subjects away
from their ordinary places in feuding political parties and clashing
economic classes to the service of their country. They made individual people into numbers and the numbers went forward in
good order and at speed to the trenches. The plans of a European
power testified to the existence, age, and effectiveness of a national
government, or state; the zeal with which European citizens submitted to mobilization for war testified to their feeling part of a
singular people, or nation. The two things thrived off each other;
a large and unified nation needed a state to organize its activities,
and an organized state needed the cooperation of a people who
felt themselves bound together by belonging to a great nation. For
decades, the European nation-states had been advancing together
in tandem. As states grew in their power to care for citizens at
home through social-insurance programs, they made their citizens feel part of a shared national responsibility. As states grew
in their power to represent their people abroad in conquest or
competition for resources, they made their citizens proud to feel

part of a strong nation. Neither nation nor state in this sense existed in America, though the new Washingtonians wanted to use the demands of war as an opportunity to create both.

When the war came, the information processors realized that the government would soon call on them for help. As economist Allyn A. Young said, "War has come to be a conflict of directed masses,—of aggregates. Men, money, munitions, food, railways, shipping, raw materials, and manufactured products of great variety are pressed into the service of the nation. The problems of the effective control and use for war purposes of these various national resources is intimately dependent on a knowledge of their quantities."[18] The men and women who were good with quantities went to Washington when the war started so they could assemble what the U.S. government knew, by way of preparing to get what the U.S. military needed.

What they found dismayed them. The economist Wesley Clair Mitchell reported that when he got to Washington, American leaders knew neither how to field an army nor what they needed to know to do so, nor could they even begin to identify what remained unknown. They had, Mitchell wrote, "to find out that they needed statistics, what statistics they needed, and how to get them."[19] Mitchell and his colleagues worked feverishly, did a considerable amount of what he called "tall guessing," and routinely came up with usable data where before there had been none.[20] They adopted as their informal motto "It can't be done? But here it is."[21] Cheerful and tireless as they were, they worried. The need for their speedy work meant that their country had poorly prepared itself not just for war, but for the postwar world. The great empires were falling apart under the pressure of war and revolution. The balance of forces in the world was shifting—the information processors could see it happening in the figures that flowed through the columns in their ledgers, pooling in charts and tables. The new empires were going to matter more now, and the United States was going to matter the most. And yet the U.S. government had not prepared itself for this postwar role.

For as much as military might mattered, it counted little unless
it accompanied administrative talent. A strong sword arm might
win an empire, but it took a filing cabinet to keep one. The scram-
bling around, the duplication of effort, and the false starts the
United States made while getting ready for war alarmed the ana-
lysts new to Washington. As Mitchell wrote, American mobilization "made an admirable exhibition of national energy and
patriotism, but not a good exhibition of national intelligence."[22]
And empires needed intelligence. A sufficiently energetic barbar-
ian horde might, on any given day, ride out and defeat its neighbors. But to hold on to and gain from conquest, in short to act like
civilized people rather than savages, took forethought and planning. No serious government, certainly not the government of the
richest country in the world, should have to flail about, hastily
inventing new bureaucracies, just to find out how much it ought
to pay for soap. It should know this, as a matter of routine competence, and the U.S. government did not.[23]

Such routine competence simply did not lie within the experience of Americans who had relied for years on an incidentally
benevolent world to take care of them. So much had come so easily that they had not prepared for the world to turn suddenly hostile and make such different demands.

ABANDONING A MODERN ARMY

The debate over outfitting the U.S. Army to meet the needs of
an imperial America had roots deep in the nineteenth century.
In his 1883 report to Congress at the end of his stint as commanding general of the army, William Tecumseh Sherman tried
to declare his tenure a success by saying, "The recent completion
of the last of the four great transcontinental lines of railway
has settled forever the Indian question, the Army question, and
many others which have hitherto troubled the country."[24] Sherman's assessment proved overly optimistic. The Indian Wars
would continue into the next decade. The "Indian question"

would remain indefinitely on the national agenda. And until sometime after World War I, the proposed answers to the Indian question limited the possible answers to the army question.

The army Sherman left in 1883 was, paradoxically, less modern than the army he helped lead to victory twenty years before. In the autumn of 1864, he took about sixty thousand soldiers on foot through Georgia from Atlanta to the sea. The march served, Sherman said, as a "big raid,"[25] a demonstration that the U.S. Army could not only go wherever it liked, whenever it liked, but also that it could spare sixty thousand troops from the fighting to make a point. Using thousands of armed men to make a profound psychological impression—a message written in blood and ashes, an argument about the futility of resisting an army comprising battle-hardened soldiers led by ruthless, organization-minded men in its officer corps—was a distinctly modern device, one that anticipated later total wars.[26] American officers of the Civil War could claim world-class expertise in the field, as when General Philip Sheridan lectured the Germans on how to wage total war on the French.[27] And the army they had commanded posed a threat to any nation of the earth. A million men strong, tested in four years of brutal battle, prepared to make war on civilians when necessary, outfitted with high-grade weaponry and other modern materiel, the U.S. Army had no peers. Had any significant part of it been deployed to occupy the defeated South, it might have made a success of Reconstruction by serving as a continuing reminder of the military might of the United States of America and a deterrent to white insurgents devoted to their lost cause. Had any significant part of it been deployed to occupy the as-yet-undefeated West, it might have prevented twenty-five years' worth of Indian Wars by serving as a constant reminder of the government's willingness to keep order among its peoples.[28]

But it was not in American habits, either military or civilian, to keep a modern army. Within a year of the war's end, the entire U.S Army included fewer soldiers than had marched with Sherman to the sea, and the ranks of the regulars shrank to half that number by 1871.[29]

The speedy demobilization occurred despite the two massive military projects the nation faced, one each in the South and the West. The army, such as it was, dominated the process of Reconstruction in the South, overseeing elections, ensuring the safe passage of the mail, and policing vice districts as well as chasing down the Ku Klux Klan and other rebellious elements.[30] But for all the army's essential role, it had no strategy or doctrine of occupation, nor did the government give it one.[31] Military men wanted to fight a war, not police a peace, and Congress did not want to spend its time, money, or political capital on waging a bitter war against elements of its own citizenry who by 1870 had their own representatives in the Capitol.

And despite the critical importance of Reconstruction to the nation's political and economic unity, by 1868 the army already had more troops in the West than in the South. By 1872—well before the supposed end of Reconstruction—soldiers in the West outnumbered those in the South by a factor of four to one.[32] Judging by the allocation of force alone, the major American military endeavor of the late 1860s and early 1870s was not Reconstruction at all, but the Indian Wars. Yet even the military winning of the West, critically important as it was for settling the territories and tying them to the East, won little enthusiasm or strategic attention from Congress, or even from the soldiers who fought its battles.

The professional soldiers who preferred Indian fighting to Reconstruction complained that in the occupied South "you have not only to be a soldier, but must play the politician, a part . . . not only difficult but disagreeable."[33] But they soon found that western duty entailed the same combination of military and political skills. The blue-clad clusters of soldiers dotted about the prairies stood as a pacific bulwark between the tireless and unpredictable advance of white settlers and the truculent retreat of ill-served American Indians. "You will find," General George Crook told West Point graduates in 1884, "that the Indian has no rights which our people are compelled to respect. . . . Even the Courts are closed to him, and to secure him common justice and protect him from outrage will frequently require all your intelligence, courage, and energy."[34] As Sheridan explained to Congress in 1885, the speed of progress westward put the army in a difficult and poorly defined position. "On account of the rapid growth of our Western settlements, the Army is obliged, in some places, to protect white people from Indians, while in other places it is protecting Indians in their persons and property from the whites."[35]

The army found itself having to balance awkwardly between the settler whites and indigenous Indians, and to keep on its toes for an indefinite period. Western settlement proceeded at inconsistent speed and in unforeseeable directions, under the powerful but haphazard pressure of free enterprise and individual settler initiative, so the officers never knew when the friction that accompanied frontier progress might light the fires of rebellion. The administration of Indian reservations lay under the control of civilian or nongovernmental agencies, which soldiers believed—with some evidence—were rife with corruption, to the point that they starved their Indian charges, thus sparking raids on white settlements. "The Army cannot foresee or prevent these wars," Sherman told Congress. "All it can do is, after the Indians break out, steal, plunder, and kill some harmless farmers, to pursue, scatter, and capture them in detail after infinite toll; then conduct them back to their reservations and turn them loose to repeat the same game *ad infinitum*."[36]

Despite the army's near-constant activity and its commanding generals' perennial complaints to Congress, it policed the frontier largely outside of ordinary Americans' awareness and perforce without much support. As one civilian innocently exclaimed on meeting an officer in 1885, "Why, I supposed the Army was all disbanded at the close of the [Civil] war!"[37] No matter how often Sherman and Sheridan went before Congress to ask for more troops and more administrative authority to make and keep peace in the West, the army stayed small throughout the late nineteenth century. In part, it suffered from the vengefulness of southern Democrats, who on their return to Congress rather enjoyed the prospect of playing the rebels in a new field of battle against the

U.S. Army. And in part, the army suffered from the rage for smaller, cheaper, more efficient government that prevailed among both major parties in the late 1860s and early 1870s, as Americans wished to realize the dividends that came with war's end. Over both these factors hung musty rhetoric dating from the revolution, which called for the diminution of the army because, as Congressman Fernando Wood (Democrat of New York) said, it "performs none of the legitimate functions of our Government in time of peace. It is inappropriate to such a period."[38]

Perhaps more surprisingly, career army officers tended in their own way to agree that their beloved institution served no useful peacetime function. As General Winfield Scott Hancock told Congress in 1876, "A *large* standing army is against the policy of the nation." He went on to say that the only real purpose of the "small standing army" was "to keep pace with the progress of the [military] profession," and to serve in time of war as "a nucleus for the raw levies," the new recruits who would form the bulk of the U.S. Army in wartime.[39] Frontier warfare, as Sheridan said of the army's job in guarding Indian territory, was "very active, laborious, and annoying."[40] So far as the professional soldiers among the officer corps were concerned, Indian fighting was, as Hancock said, "an incidental duty for part of the Army . . . of secondary importance, and . . . comparatively temporary in nature."[41]

As bloody and distressing as the occasional incident in the Indian Wars sometimes proved, these battles were never bad enough for long enough to seize the passionate attention of either military or civilian America. The minimal army did a minimal job, using half its strength and half its mind—but half was enough. Had the army fared worse or done worse against its opponents more often—had there been many Little Big Horns or Wounded Knees—the commanders might have had to devote themselves sincerely to developing a doctrine of guerrilla warfare and occupation. But they did not, dreaming instead that they might try themselves someday at what they thought of as their real job, a war against a European power.

And because those European powers remained so distant, because the Indian Wars did not count as proper wars in the minds either of military or civilian Americans, the army remained an appendix of normal politics rather than becoming the central strategic arm of a new empire. The disposition of bases in the West had little to do with military considerations, and much to do with the desires of local merchants for a sense of safety and a local posting of reliable customers.[42] No matter how often Sherman complained that so many of the army's forts "are now absolutely of no use, present or prospective, and should be disposed of," they stayed, vestigial protections for abandoned westward routes, because the people who had been likewise abandoned along the lines wanted some proof, however small, that their government had not forgotten them.[43]

In consequence, a small and poorly equipped army presided over an ill-settled peace in the South and West alike. The project of settling the West in particular had long been left to the booms and busts of private finance, whose coming and going sketched routes across the landscape, some of which flourished while others withered, but all of which required the army's attention whether the tracery of paths corresponded to strategic logic or not. When he hung up his campaigner's hat in 1883, Sherman hoped the completion of the major rail routes had settled this issue, saying that the final construction of the main railways could "account fully for the peace and good order . . . and for the extraordinary prosperity which now prevails in the land. A vast domain, equal to two-thirds of the whole surface of the United States, has thus been made accessible to the immigrant, and, in a military sense, our troops may be assembled at strategic points and sent promptly to the places of disturbance, checking disorders in the bud."[44] But in truth, another era of willy-nilly expansion lay just ahead in the late 1880s, followed by a bust more severe than those before. The final throes of the Indian insurgency in the early 1890s led to a crisis in a different aspect of military policing in the West, a project that corresponded no more readily than frontier war to the educated soldiers' strategic expectations or orderly habits.

A NEW ARMY FOR A NEW EMPIRE

In the summer of 1894, in the depths of the depression of the 1890s, Eugene V. Debs led the American Railway Union into a strike against the Pullman Company near Chicago. The strike spread around the country, slowing the business of the nation to a crawl. President Grover Cleveland ordered the army to get rail traffic moving again, whatever the wishes of the workers. The president justified the use of troops by noting that stopping the railways also stopped the passage of the U.S. mail, for whose safe delivery the federal government bore responsibility. The army, under the command now of General John M. Schofield, dispatched such companies as it could spare and restored the flow of railway traffic.

As Schofield noted in his subsequent report to Congress, the crisis brought to light once more the new phase of what Sherman had called "the Army question." Sherman's "Indian question" seemed answered, if not at the time of his report then certainly by the end of the Ghost Dance movement and the quelling of the Sioux uprising in 1891, although it would shortly rise again on the Pacific frontier. But even the continental West was not, it appeared, yet won. If the Indians had been kept to their reservations, a new set of even greater western threats loomed. In the decade or so between Sherman's retirement and Schofield's report, the army had marched about seventeen times to put down strikes or demonstrations of the unemployed, using perhaps 8,200 troops a year to quell unionism.[45] As Schofield claimed, "more than once in the last summer an infuriated mob in a single city was twice as formidable and capable of doing vastly greater injury to life and property than the most formidable combination of Indian warriors that ever confronted the Army in this country." Surveying the events of 1894, Schofield urged Americans to "be proud of their little Army, so thoroughly devoted to the public interests," while noting that "the present strength of the Army is not adequate" to the job of policing the newly urban West.[46] The problems of the western frontier had faded, but they left the West no more tranquil or settled. Industrial now, radicalized, and full of immigrants as well as people angry at them, the West still needed winning.

It was easy and indeed inevitable for Americans on both sides of the 1894 strikes to associate them with immigration into America and especially into the West. The unions themselves, and people sympathetic to them, noted that the arrival of immigrant workers drove down American wages, that wage cuts had provoked the strike, and that therefore the strike was the immigrants' fault. Reports soon surfaced that "newly-arrived immigrants had been sent West to replace strikers," and unions moved to investigate the possibility.[47] So convenient a scapegoat were the immigrants that the opponents of labor activism blamed them for the strikes as well. A U.S. Immigration official sent to report on a strike in western Pennsylvania concluded that "the Italians in the region are a bad lot."[48] A Staten Island minister claimed, "Our strikes are the direct result of our immigration. Our strikers are nearly all foreigners."[49] A preacher at the other end of the country, in Long Beach, California, explained, "We have, however, enough foreigners. The immigrants of later years have been of a lower, baser order. . . . They breed anarchy."[50] Ironically, the strike and the depression that spawned it persuaded many immigrants they might as well go home again, and railroads adopted a special immigrant rate for travel from Chicago eastward to New York, "to take advantage of the homeward movement of immigrants who are now out of work in the West."[51] The *Los Angeles Times* knew how to read this atypically eastward movement of international workers: the newspaper applauded, concluding that once a "great many more" had likewise left, "it would be a good idea to frame some law that will prevent all of them from coming back again."[52]

The strikes of 1894 not only offered Americans a chance to

vent their anxieties about the disorder created by rapid westward expansion and the role of international influences in it, they put the army in the role of cleaning up the disorder. To this end, the army needed to look different than it had in its Indian-fighting heyday. As Joseph Breckinridge, the army's inspector general, declared, its recruiters had "to guard against filling the army with waifs and strays."[53] Breckinridge hoped to see the army's enlistment practices reformed, "to make recruits more fairly representative of the nation."[54] One useful step in this direction would be to limit new enlistments to U.S. citizens, a step Congress contemplated throughout 1894 and adopted after the summer of strikes.

The army that fought the Indians included a greater share of immigrants than the U.S. population in general. Between the Civil War and the strike summer of 1894, about 40 percent of the soldiers of the United States were foreign-born, a vastly higher percentage than in the population as a whole, which hovered at around 14 percent. (See table 5.1.) And in these hard depression years, Congressmen began to see the nonnative troops as cause for alarm. In January of 1894 the Senate Committee on Military Affairs reported that "no consideration appears to justify the enlistment of soldiers in the permanent Army of the United States who may owe allegiance to some foreign and possibly unfriendly power."[55] Foreign-born members of the armed services were more likely than foreign-born members of the general population to have become citizens, but the congressmen wanted to make sure they could limit the armed forces to "persons whose allegiance is wholly and absolutely due to the U.S. government."[56] In August 1894, the new recruiting law went into effect, allowing the enlistment of "no person (except an Indian) who is not a citizen of the United States, or who has not made legal declaration of his intention to become a citizen of the United States."[57] And over the ensuing decades, the army did indeed become more fully Americanized, as to both birth and citizenship, than the general population.

The determination of Congress to make the army more fully American, following on the deployment of the army against the strikes of 1894—which in the public imagination were tied to the

	Percentage Foreign-Born		Percentage Foreign-Born Who Were Citizens	
	Military	Population	Military	Population
1870	46	14	58	30
1880	35	13	n/a	n/a
1900	13	14	58	32
1910	15	15	65	26

Table 5.1 Nativity of the army and of the population. (For further discussion, see note on page 227.)

influence of foreign labor—corresponded to a new era in which considerations of ethnicity shaped the U.S. Army's mission. Ethnic diversity had always contributed to friction, and sometimes to war scares—the lynching of eleven Italian Americans in Louisiana in 1891 created one such fever, and Irish Americans were always happy to point out why the United States should go to war with the British crown.[58] But as the United States became more visibly a nation of immigrants, these scares produced formal policy responses. In the wake of the San Francisco earthquake of 1906, anti-immigrant violence targeting the Japanese led to anti-Japanese legislation in California and a diplomatic crisis that spurred the army to begin thinking about plans for a war with Japan.[59] Concern over relations with the Japanese and, after the revolution of 1910 began to destabilize the border, with the Mexicans, led army intelligence officials to begin asking Congress to authorize the army to conduct domestic military surveillance of possible agents of foreign powers.[60]

This army, adapted by happenstance to the occasional and relatively minor security needs of the internal American empire, proved largely immune to the principled arguments of reformers who had seen the rest of the world and its military might. Just as the world of the late nineteenth century saw an ideal model of the proto–welfare state emerge—a model of which Americans were aware, about which American reformers talked with enthusiasm, and to which the United States remained resistant because its peculiar circumstances seemed to render such a state unnecessary—so also did the era see an ideal model of the modern warfare state emerge: a model of which Americans were aware, about which American reformers talked with enthusiasm, and to which the nation remained resistant because its peculiar circumstances seemed to render such a state unnecessary. In the spring of 1898, Lieutenant George B. Duncan made a case that the newly globalized world required a new American army: "Time and space are being rapidly annihilated. The wind and waves of the ocean do not disturb the path of steam navigation. . . . The rise and fall of the money market in London finds its echo in New York. . . . Commercial activity pays no attention to geographical boundaries. . . . Foreign capital owns or controls a very large portion of our business interests." If what Americans wanted of their army in such an interconnected and unpredictable world was "'to conquer an honorable, advantageous, and lasting peace,'" Duncan wrote, then the United States needed a bigger army, fitted for permanent, deterrent peacekeeping deployments, prepared perhaps for the occasional offensive operation.[61] Ever since Sherman sent General Emory Upton to study the armies of Asia and Europe in 1875, military reformers had been arguing for an American army commensurate with those of the rest of the world.[62] But these arguments for reform produced as little response as those arguing that the United States ought to have a social-insurance program commensurate with those of the rest of the world. Whatever benefits Americans might have derived from building a bigger government capacity in either arena, the circumstances did not seem to compel such a swelling of the state.

Because the United States had been able to conquer its inland empire with an army so small as easily to be ignored, it continued through the age of empires to regard a permanent and sizable military establishment as unnecessary and distasteful. Even the country that most nearly shared Americans' civic republican tradition did not enjoy such a luxury; France learned early in its history that it needed as a matter of routine to assume the costs of a professional army as a normal price of its national ambitions. (See figure 5.1.) This difference in national commitment to warfare showed itself in the two countries' military pension systems.

When in the middle of the Civil War the United States began considering legislation to compensate the wounded and the widows of the struggle for the Union, reformers surveyed other nations' pension systems and singled out that of the French as the most comprehensive and, if not generous, then adequate. The comparatively liberal regime of Louis Philippe had in 1831 established a military pension that calculated a disability pension as a prorated retirement pension. The guiding principle was that the soldier would under more fortunate circumstances have survived to retirement and earned a pension, so having been disabled in the service he deserved from the state the support he might ordinarily have earned in wages and retirement benefits. The French

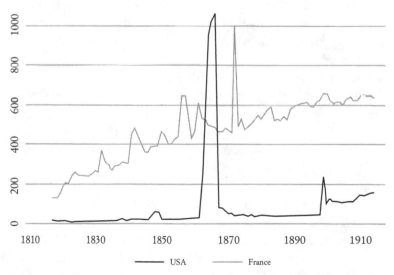

Figure 5.1 Number of military personnel in the United States and France from 1816 to 1913, in thousands of men.

system comprised both disability and retirement benefits as part of a package owed to citizen-soldiers.[63]

By contrast the Americans, up through the Civil War, considered the pensions they paid citizen-soldiers as a protection against the embarrassment of the republic's defenders falling into penury. The small regular army paid its professional soldiers their pensions as part of the regular payroll, not as part of the larger pension bureau, which handled the benefits due to veterans inevitably generated by the repeated necessity of volunteer enlistments in the country's wars. These citizen-soldiers received nothing as a matter of course; Congress had to decide on a war-by-war basis whether and how to compensate them.[64] As Congressman Philip Johnson (Democrat of Pennsylvania) argued during the debate over pensions in 1862, American pensions had traditionally been paid "for the purpose of guarding against the reduction to want of those who had been wounded in the service of their country, and were disabled from maintaining themselves and their families. Nothing more, nothing less. It never was intended to compensate them for losses sustained."[65]

The Civil War Pension Law partly abandoned this tradition in favor of "a new principle" of compensation, though it did not go quite so far as the French law.[66] The new pensions recognized that soldiers who had lost their lives or livelihoods in the country's service had earned a pension scaled to the size of that loss. But because Americans still regarded their citizen-soldiers as emergency incidental expenses, not as normal costs of doing business as an empire, they did not consider such soldiers ordinarily entitled to a retirement pension. Thus even the revised U.S. system did not quite embrace the vision of full support that the French system did.

This difference in principle accompanied a difference in the level of compensation. Although outlays for veterans took up a large chunk of the federal budget—veterans' benefits after the Civil War were as great a share of federal expenditures as veterans' benefits after World War II—they were not necessarily generous on an individual basis.[67] Even after several postwar expansions of the American benefits system—the biggest one came in 1890, when pensions became available to almost anyone who had served in the war—a U.S. military pension remained a less generous source of state support than a French one. We can render these pensions paid in different currencies comparable if we consider how large a share they represent of each country's available wealth per person. On this comparison, between 1890 and World War I, French military pensions ranged on average between 80 and 90 percent of French GDP per adult, while U.S. military pensions ranged on average between 30 and 50 percent of U.S. GDP per adult. (See table 5.2.)

The expense of French military pensions did not prevent France from developing alongside them an old-age pension system for citizens who had never been soldiers and had simply grown old. By 1910 the French were paying about .4 percent of their national wealth to .4 percent of their population who were military pensioners and another .3 percent of their national wealth to 1.5 percent of their population who were old-age pensioners.[68] At the same time, the United States was paying about .5 percent

Year	France Average Pension (francs)	GDP Per Adult (francs)	Average Pension as Percentage of GDP Per Adult	U.S. Average Pension (dollars)	GDP Per Adult (dollars)	Average Pension as Percentage of GDP Per Adult
1891	876.73	1,042.81	84	173.50	335.25	52
1896	917.51	1,015.25	90	142.40	310.28	46
1901	952.68	1,083.15	88	138.85	412.21	34
1906	971.73	1,232.40	79	140.98	491.53	29
1911	990.83	1,544.04	64	176.35	504.91	35

Table 5.2 French and U.S. military pensions compared. Adults defined as fifteen years of age or older. (For further discussion, see note on page 228.)

of its national wealth to pay veterans' pensions to about 1 percent of its population, while it had no old-age pension system comparable to that of the French. No wonder, then, that advocates of social insurance complained in the 1910s about the U.S. pension system, which had come later and paid less than the European example on which it was modeled, and which served as a poor substitute—if indeed it could be said to serve as a substitute at all—for a pensions system that paid the elderly simply to survive their declining years with dignity. After all, the most likely recipients of a U.S. military pension in the 1910s were native-born white Americans living in the northeastern part of the country—people far less likely to be needy than their fellow countrymen who were black, foreign-born, or southern.[69]

Thus even the most expensive lasting legacy of American war in the nineteenth century reflected the distinctive circumstances of the United States. The basic assumption that war was an occasional and even surprising circumstance requiring ad hoc expense programs, rather than an ongoing and normal cost of national power, remained untouched even as Americans paid over decades the price of their Civil War.

Little changed once empire became explicit. Even after the brief and successful war against the traditional imperial power of Spain in 1898 put the United States in possession of the Philippines, against the wishes of a significant number of Filipinos, American attitudes toward the army stayed essentially the same. Some thousands of Filipinos soon began expressing their discontent at occupation through organized rebellion. Despite the immediate and increasing importance of fighting this insurgency, the army and the U.S. government remained confused and ambivalent about their intentions in the archipelago. The war there expanded slowly, and without guidance or interest from Washington. Manpower began to be and remained a vexing issue for commanders who did not have enough soldiers to maintain order, who felt themselves abused by troop-rotation policies, and who tried to win a war with fewer men than they needed and less equipment than they wanted while keeping a nervous eye on the electoral returns at home.[70] Even though most of the men who fought the Philippine-American War had only a tenuous connection with the men who a generation earlier had fought the Indians, they shared with them the experience of fighting an important war that nevertheless remained on the edge of political awareness, a fact that neither their military commanders nor their civilian representatives had much intention of changing. Nobody, not even Secretary of War Elihu Root, who was busily modernizing the U.S. Army, planned to make the Pacific garrison over into a permanent colonial force. More soldiers and better planning might sooner have stopped what the army called simply "the Insurrection," which dragged on for years of ugly fighting after its official end in 1902.[71] But as with the Indian Wars, so with the Philippine War: the U.S. Army stayed a small "skeleton army," just about adequate to the task at hand. Allegedly ready to expand at a moment's notice into a force commensurate with European legions, it nevertheless spent most of its time and energy, during a meantime that lasted decades, doing the difficult work of policing an empire without the explicit authority or numbers to do it.[72]

Thus, despite three years of bloodshed on the western front, despite decades of talk about modernizing the American state to prepare it for war, despite the devastation the U.S. Army had already learned firsthand that an organized army could wreak, and despite even the efforts of Elihu Root, the U.S. Army entered World War I looking much like the frontier force it had been for a half century. On the eve of the Great War, the U.S. Army still faced west, wrangling with the problems of expansion and immigration as they arose. In 1913, as in 1907, Californians succumbed to "yellow peril" fever over the possibility that Japanese investors might buy real estate, and the passage of further discriminatory legislation and another diplomatic crisis led to a war scare and the fortification of the Corregidor garrison in the Philippines. During the first few years of the Great War, these westernmost island outposts accounted for slightly more than 10 percent of the army's entire strength.[73]

So habitual had this minimal military commitment grown since Appomattox that the creation during World War I of a more normal government felt like a wrenching aberration to the majority of Americans, who did not spend their time studying the policies of other countries. Even though in its one almost full year of war in 1918 the United States spent half as much per person on defense as Germany and less than one-third as much as France, the experience of giving up its distinctive character, even for a year, asked more of Americans than they were willing to give for long. (See table 5.3.) And even though the postwar world looked nothing like the one in which they had built their exceptional form of government, they wanted nothing more than to return to their peacetime ways, whatever the cost to the world they thought they had saved.

Country	Military Expenditure (USD) Per Capita, 1918
France	234.79
United Kingdom	187.96
Germany	131.40
United States	67.96
Austria-Hungary	39.25
Sweden	14.87
Greece	8.63
Spain	6.49
Italy	6.31
Norway	5.94

Table 5.3 Top ten countries by military expenditure per capita for 1918, measured in U.S. dollars.

6
Americanness on Trial

Early in 1915, Woodrow Wilson reminded an audience of his fellow Democrats that as a former professor he was capable of "speaking as a historian," and he went on to offer his view of where recent events left America with respect to the other nations of the earth:

> Half the world is on fire. Only America among the great powers of the world is free to govern her own life. . . . Look abroad in the troubled world! Only America at peace! Among all the great powers of the world, only America saving her power for her own people. Only America using her great character and her great strength in the interest of peace and prosperity. . . . Think of the reservoir of hope, the reservoir of energy, the reservoir of sustenance that there is in this great land of plenty. May we look forward to the time when we shall be called blessed among the nations because we succored the nations of the world in their time of distress and dismay?[1]

In Wilson's retrospective analysis, the modern era had produced an America proudly apart, unique—and blessedly so—among the nations of the earth. Even when, two years later, he sent an army of his constituents into the global conflagration, he kept the ideal of American distinctiveness high on his list of war aims. Even though the war would require that the United States develop, and quickly, something approaching the kind of state power typical of other countries, Wilson would make sure this deviation did not last, and that the country would enter the 1920s already well on its way back to what his successor would call "normalcy."[2] That the rest of the world failed to return to its normal behavior—the behavior that till then had so handsomely benefited the United States and encouraged Americans to preserve their eccentric practices—put the American way to a difficult test. America's unique habits would have to survive, without evolving, in a newly hostile environment.

THE WITHERING AWAY OF THE STATE

The war emergency almost succeeded where decades of globalization had failed, as the needs of mobilization forced the United States to build a powerful national state with the capacity for making economic policy. Reformers who had long wanted the United States to modernize its ability to make national policy seized the opportunities the war gave them, hoping to make their country over into a nation at least as capable of guiding its people through the crises endemic to modern economies as European nations.

Early in 1918, Paul Warburg and two of his fellow Federal Reserve Board members met to discuss how, in the interest of aiding the war effort, they might make it difficult for anyone but the U.S. government to borrow money. They named themselves the Capital Issues Committee, like the similar body in London, and designated themselves the choke point for the country's capital. All bids to borrow more than one hundred thousand dollars from the open markets had to get past them.[3] They believed that the U.S. government in time of war ought to have first call on credit, and that "nobody should draw upon the credit resources of the country except to finance transactions which are essential for a nation at war."[4]

These appointed experts at the apex of the American banking system thus put themselves in an unprecedented position. By determining whether to approve a bond issue, their committee would tell businesses, cities, counties, and states what did and did not qualify as worthwhile public spending. So unusual were the committee's activities, so out of tune with American tradition, that even though Congress finally authorized its work, the legislators avoided mentioning exactly what the committee was doing. "Congress did not in express terms refer to States, counties, or municipalities. The reason for this omission is presumed to be because Congress did not wish even indirectly to regulate the affairs of the sovereign States," the official *Federal Reserve Bulletin* noted.[5] Yet unless the committee reached into the affairs of the sovereign states, down even to the most local level, it could not do what was required of it. Under the authority of Federal Reserve Board member and Treasury Secretary William McAdoo, the committee operated as an official agency of the U.S. government, and yet it would decide whether Nashville, Tennessee, could build a police station or whether Lima, Ohio, might dig sewers.[6] If it had not done so, it would have been unable to protect the federal government's access to capital, because taken together the cities and states normally were much bigger borrowers than the federal government.[7]

Moreover, the committee soon moved beyond its initial purpose. Regulating the allocation of capital meant saying where there would and would not be new jobs. This implied regulating the allocation of labor. So the committee began working with representatives of the Department of Labor and the American Federation of Labor "to secure a scientific distribution of labor fitted to prevailing conditions."[8]

And though the committee had no actual power to compel businesses and municipalities to comply with its rulings, and indeed repeatedly congratulated itself on receiving the "voluntary cooperation" of would-be borrowers, it used less-voluntary language in communicating with the public. As its local representatives in Dallas wrote to Texas cities and businesses, "This is a government requirement . . . there are no exceptions to it, and . . . the Capital Issues Committee at Washington has instructed our committee to immediately report to them the name and address of any concern that is found to be offering its securities without authority from this committee."[9] Likewise, however sternly the committee insisted that its approval simply meant that a measure was not inconsistent with the national interest and did not in any way constitute endorsement of the security's actual worth, its stamp of authorization provided an imposing gloss for borrowers advertising their securities to the public.[10] Carter Glass, who by the end of the year had succeeded McAdoo at Treasury, lauded the committee for its role in "protecting the public investor against the flood of worthless or doubtful securities."[11]

Nor did its members envision the committee as simply a wartime imposition to be lightly endured until peace broke out: "In some rare cases the unfortunate attitude had been taken by certain prospective applicants of heeding peace propaganda and looking upon the committee's work as a temporary expedient that would soon become obsolete upon the declaration of a not very distant peace. The chairman emphasized the obvious fallacy of such belief."[12] As the war ground to a close, not quite a year after the committee had begun its work, the committee suggested its continued usefulness in peacetime: "So long as [the U.S. government's] borrowings are intended for the maintenance of the national integrity, there can be no doubt that the policy to be adopted must be one which should subordinate all other considerations to that of success of national finance."[13]

The Capital Issues Committee was only the most basic of the federal government's wartime innovations in regulatory policy. At the War Industries Board, administrators drew up priority lists for the use of raw materials and ventured into the realm of price-fixing in an effort to curb war-induced inflation. The WIB's activities encouraged some reformers to think beyond the war as well. As Robert Brookings, one of the businessmen serving on the board, wrote to President Wilson, inflation was "probably our most important economic problem," and suggested that the president use the WIB's capacity "to establish a more or less basic relation between the cost of living and the scale of wages, in preparation for the inevitable competition between nations after the war."[14]

Establishing the rate of inflation with sufficient accuracy to set policy by it had required the government to develop, swiftly, the capacity to collect and report good data on prices and wages. The WIB's Central Bureau of Planning and Statistics, under Edwin F. Gay, volunteered itself to serve as the clearinghouse for data in the summer of 1918, and by the time of the Armistice, in November, it had almost cemented itself in this role.[15] In addition, its Price Section had produced estimates of commodity prices. At the close of the war, the economist Wesley Clair Mitchell pored over these estimates with evident enthusiasm, writing that "an indefinite number of correlations" suggested themselves to his expert eye as he perused the tables, and he urged that "the collection of prices should never stop." Mitchell recorded a palpable sense of thwarted expectation when the war work came to an end: "To trace the rise of prices during the war and to break off when peace returned, is to rouse an eager interest and then disappoint it."[16]

Yet those promising activities all stopped with breathtaking speed after the Armistice on November 11, 1918, with even businessmen who little loved government scratching their heads. "Persons acquainted with Washington at the time," wrote two economists assessing the war effort, "will remember that the activity of some units ceased so abruptly that unit chiefs had to lend money to their stenographers for transportation home."[17]

That the purely military elements of the wartime state should not last made sense to almost everyone. Strategists took from the war the lesson that they ought to have at hand a plan for mass mobilization if it should ever again prove necessary. But beyond laying plans, the military establishment soon returned to its prewar norms. The army would remain a small professional force that would serve, in case of emergency, as the nucleus for a larger citizens' army. Talk of universal military training, to ensure that the citizens would stand ready for a call to arms, quickly faded.[18] And military spending dropped steeply from its brief wartime peak to prewar levels. For the postwar decade of 1921–1930, Americans spent no larger share of their resources on readiness for war than they had during the prewar decade 1901–1910.[19]

The nonmilitary elements of the state disappeared with equal speed. Despite the advice of Federal Reserve bank presidents and private bankers such as J. P. Morgan, Jr., the Capital Issues Committee shut its doors by year's end.[20] The War Industries Board lifted its regulations, and its Statistics Division stopped collecting data. Going into the 1920s, the U.S. government did not ordinarily monitor unemployment or wholesale or retail sales; it had no figures on gross national product. It later used income figures from a single one-time study in 1926. On the heels of the war effort, the U.S. government had in many cases actively worked to stop inquiry into commercial processes so that it could remain wholly innocent of the workings of the world's greatest economy.[21]

No reasonable person asked that the entire extraordinary wartime apparatus of the state endure indefinitely. But it was easy to find important people who thought it should have lasted a little longer, simply to wind down the wartime commitments with a degree of grace, if not elegance. At the least, the complete and abrupt shaking-up that the war had occasioned provided an opportunity to reassess the country's economic policies. After all, the government had grown enough to run a veritable command economy. The least it could do was let go of the reins with a degree of decorum.

And some people thought that a few of the government's wartime activities—particularly those relating simply to the gathering of information—should have endured indefinitely. Certainly within a generation such work would become normal for the U.S. government—but not before a disastrous interim had interposed itself.

The decision to end the government's wartime efforts toward a more normal statehood rested with Woodrow Wilson. Despite the urgings of businessmen, bankers, and other reformers, Wilson resisted with a fine indifference the calls for a plan of "reconstruction." When the Reconstruction Congress of American Industries met in November 1918, he declined their invitation to appear by saying, "You may be sure that I would send a message to the meeting . . . if I knew what message to send, but frankly I do not."[22] Toward the end of that month, Wilson's advisors assured him that "reconstruction would take care of itself."[23] Early in December, Wilson told Congress that his agencies could not "direct [reconstruction] any better than it will direct itself. The American business man is of quick initiative."[24]

In truth, it was partly Wilson's confidence in the businessman's quick initiative that made him so leery of preserving any part of the wartime government, which necessarily offered corporate chieftains access to the levers of power. From the beginning, Wilson had fretted over the damage the war effort might do to the United States, not because he thought war would militarize the nation but because he thought it would corporatize it. He worried that mobilization would require him to let businessmen gain back the authority in Washington he believed he had wrested from them: "The people we have unhorsed will inevitably come into control of the country for we shall be dependent upon the steel, oil and financial magnates."[25] Given these fears, Wilson's willingness to wash his hands of any schemes that had J. P. Morgan's approval makes perfect sense.

By the end of 1918, Wilson's reluctance to guide reconstruction had set the country on its return to normalcy. That winter, as men left the army and their war work for the job market, which itself had been deranged by war demands, a deep recession occurred. An ensuing boom in 1919–1920 soon collapsed into another bust. In 1921, at President Warren Harding's Conference on Unemployment, the participants naturally wanted to know how many Americans were out of work. None of the assembled experts knew of a reliable figure. So the men guessed, took a vote on their guesses, and put that number in their report.[26] The country had returned to the point where it had been at the start of the war, when nobody in Washington even knew how to frame an economic problem with any degree of specificity, let alone propose an informed solution. The decision to end even the collection of data banished the most ambitious social scientists back to their universities. They returned to the status of highly regarded sages, occasionally consulted (especially in crisis) but, in the normal course of policymaking, safely ignored.

POLICY WITHOUT KNOWLEDGE

Without those elements of the wartime state that might have let Americans regulate their economy in a less unusual fashion, the United States returned in the 1920s to the kinds of policies it had developed to deal with the circumstances of the era of globalization. Like sluice gates, these mechanisms directed or diverted the irrigating flow of resources into the country. Washington set such policies in response to internal pressures, with little thought for what they might do to the rest of the world. After all, the rest of the world had taken care of itself till now. But whereas before the war the United States had occupied a special position on the periphery of the global system, it now stood in the center and bore responsibilities it had never before considered. American policies that, as recently as a decade before, might have done no harm and perhaps even a little good, now edged the entire earth ever closer to disaster.[27]

The swift and thoughtless whisking away of the wartime state amounted, as two observers wrote, to "laissez faire with a vengeance; the Government created the disturbance in the economic system, then ignored its results."[28] The results included the 1921 downturn. After President Harding's panel of guest experts tried to determine the scale and scope of the crisis by sticking their moistened fingers into the wind, the government fell back on its time-honored method of dealing with economic squeezes: shifting the flow of international trade.

Throughout the early part of American history, American producers in both countryside and city lobbied for relief from recessions by asking that their representatives raise a tax on imports, which let them price their goods without regard for foreign competition. American leaders going back to Alexander Hamilton had argued that if the United States wished to become a great power, it needed to protect its manufacturing sector from more-developed countries: Americans sheltered from foreign competition would perfect their methods and mature to their potential strength. Whatever the merit of this "infant industry" argument for factories, whenever any industry won such protection it became easier for others to ask for similar benefits from the federal government. By the late 1800s, haggling among various interests over what goods would go on the tariff schedule, and at what rate of protection, had become a periodic ritual among congressmen. The juggling of sectional and economic interests when devising the tariff schedule presented legislators with a problem whose successful solution was vital to their continued victory at the polls. As new western states afflicted by the effects of globalization came into the Union, the shape of the tariff compromise shifted in favor of protecting the interest of agricultural producers as well as manufacturers.

In keeping with this tradition, Congress in 1921 began debating an Emergency Tariff bill as a response to the recession. The bill began by seeking to block imports of agricultural goods and thus relieve pressure on American farm producers. Opening the tariff to revision for some producers let others lobby for similar protection from foreign competition. Congress ended by passing, at the end of the summer of 1922, the Fordney-McCumber Tariff, which raised tariff rates on some critical crops and ores to their highest levels ever.[29] The bill won widespread support from the newer states in the West and represented a wedding of northeastern and western wishes for protection.[30]

The tariff's domestic success paled beside its international failure.

For the United States to keep tariffs high in the nineteenth century had done little damage then.[31] Before the war, other countries had no special need to sell goods to Americans and thereby earn dollars. But after the war, the situation had changed dramatically.

In the nineteenth century the major creditor nation, Great Britain, lent money to developing countries for railroads and other enterprises that pushed out their frontiers. These investments allowed debtor nations to produce more goods and export some of them to Britain, which favored free trade. The pounds sterling they earned they could then use to clear their balance with British creditors. Observers at the time appreciated the mutually reinforcing character of this system, as one British economist wrote in 1909:

> This growth of our trade and prosperity is largely the result of our investment of capital in other countries. By building railways for the world, and especially for the young countries, we have enabled the world to increase its production of wealth at a rate never previously witnessed and to produce those things which this country is specially desirous of purchasing—foodstuffs and raw materials. Moreover, by assisting other countries to increase their output of the commodities they were specially fitted to produce, our investors have helped those countries to secure the means of producing the goods that Great Britain manufactures. Thus by the investment of capital in other lands we have, first, provided the borrowing countries with the credit which gave them the power to purchase the goods needed for their development, and secondly, enabled them to increase their own productions so largely that they have been able to pay us the interest and profits upon our capital and also to purchase greatly increased quantities of British goods.[32]

For all the occasional crises of the nineteenth century, including depressions and short wars, the era appeared to have produced a durable, self-perpetuating, and generally profitable system. British money went into productive investment around the world and returned with the increment of interest, only to go out once more.

This system ceased its operation when the war came. Britain stopped spending its money on building railroads and started spending it on blowing up the other belligerent nations. When it ran through its own money, it borrowed from the United States. The war made the United States into the world's great creditor, but unlike British investment of the last century, American investment went into destructive rather than productive enterprise. The war loans, serving their intended purpose, made the world a poorer place, as the armies they funded systematically laid waste to the riches of their enemies. Yet Americans, like any lender, would have their money back in due course, whether their borrowers were enjoying a prosperous season or not.

The finely woven web of lines representing back-and-forth flows of capital and labor that characterized the prewar world thus gave way to the bolder lines of war reparations and war debt that the peace settlement made. (See figure 6.1.) All arrows led ultimately to the United States. As the *New York Times* noted in 1926, this map meant the country had long "outgrown" the tariff as policy. Continuing it now plainly meant disaster for other countries and ultimately for the United States.

> It needs no political economist to see that our situation in the world of trade has been radically altered by the events following 1914. A fiscal policy which might have been defensible before that year has since gone hopelessly awry. Our immense and increasing investments abroad cannot indefinitely be paid for unless we are willing to take what our foreign debtors can offer us. To put artificial obstacles in the way of their paying us is to hurt us more than it does them.[33]

Yet American leaders resisted seeing this system as their responsibility. The tariff suited them as a tool for dealing with domestic

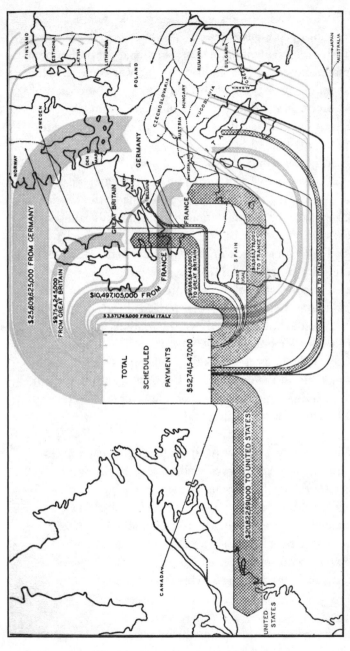

Figure 6.1 The system of debt after World War I. Originally printed in color, the map has been altered to preserve the contrast between money owing and money owed.

issues, irrespective of its effect elsewhere. Britain's world of free trade gave way to America's world of protectionism. Other countries reacted in indignation and dismay, and ultimately concluded that their only defense was to adopt tariffs of their own.[34]

Just as U.S. trade policy prevented the resumption of the currents that typified the prewar global economy, so too did U.S. immigration policy. And just as trade policy reflected domestic concerns irrespective of international implications, so too did immigration policy. The literacy test, over which Americans had wrangled for so long, did not keep nearly enough immigrants out of the country to satisfy restrictionist constituencies. Border officials disqualified almost fifteen hundred would-be immigrants in 1920–1921 on the basis of illiteracy, in a year that saw eight hundred thousand come into the country.[35]

Meanwhile, the war contributed to a much less selective discrimination against immigrants, providing plenty of opportunities to demonize foreigners. Politicians of all kinds enthusiastically participated in this patriotic pastime. President Wilson himself, who worried little about the wartime threat to civil liberties, sometimes savored, quite visibly, his opportunities to quell dissent and step on ethnic minorities. "The sinister intrigue is being . . . actively conducted in this country. . . . The false betray themselves always in every accent," he told this nation of immigrants on Flag Day, 1917. "Woe be to the man or group of men that seeks to stand in our way."[36] The Bolshevik Revolution also made Americans leery of European subversives. Unable so far to keep a satisfactory number of immigrants out, officials turned their energies to getting rid of those already in their midst. Deportations ran into the thousands in 1919, and rose into the tens of thousands in the late 1920s and early 1930s.[37]

The combined effects of economic uncertainty, war fever, and red scares raised support for another emergency antiglobalization law, the Emergency Immigration Restriction Act of 1921.[38] For the first time, Congress set an upper cap on the overall number of immigrants who could enter the country. A further law in 1924 divided the world, in the spirit of the 1917 "Asiatic barred zone," into countries from which immigrants were more desirable and those from which they were less so. Although immigration into the United States did continue, it was cut almost in half after 1924.[39] And just as the trade-blocking tariff of 1921 encouraged other countries to block trade as well, so did the immigration-blocking law of 1921 spur other countries to block immigration, so that by the end of the decade the golden doors to each of the New World countries had swung almost completely shut.[40]

Before the war, immigration increased the availability of cheap labor in the United States, as native-born and foreign-born competed for jobs. At the same time, the departure of workers from Europe brought wages up in the old countries. Unsurprisingly then, the reduction of immigration in the United States in the 1920s saw the opposite effect. Throughout the decade, unemployment in the United States remained exceptionally low, while in the former labor-exporting countries of Europe it stayed high.[41] The prewar global labor market had let people move from countries where jobs were scarce to countries where jobs were plentiful, but as immigration restriction increased, this market could not operate, inhibiting productivity in those debtor countries that desperately needed to increase it.[42]

Thus, with respect both to goods and people, the United States contributed to the continued closure of international channels. Americans continued to act as if they could rely on the world to take care of itself, as if they could go on using the tools that had suited them when they stood in a fortunate place at the edge of world commerce. The same held true even for the major economic regulatory mechanism of the U.S. economy, the Federal Reserve Board, whose hands cradled the trigger switch for the ultimate crisis.

The bankers who staffed the Federal Reserve knew enough about the international system of finance to seek some cooperation with their counterparts across the water. But as Benjamin Strong, head of New York's Federal Reserve Bank, put it to Montagu Norman, head of the Bank of England, Americans and British might "cooperate where our respective interests made it possible."[43] Which was to say, as Strong implied, their respective interests would take precedent over cooperation when a conflict arose. In consequence, Federal Reserve Board policy focused principally on keeping American consumers and voters happy in the short term and not on sustaining the global circulation of capital. After all, the Federal Reserve System had been designed to reconcile the needs of the new agricultural and mining economies of the West with the manufacturing centers of the East, not to act as banker to the world.

And so the postwar system of finance extracted money in the form of reparations and debt payments from European economies to pay American creditors, while U.S. policies that kept out foreign goods and labor prevented those debtors from improving their economies and paying down their debts. The only solution anyone came up with was to have the United States lend still more money to the limping nations of the earth, money that was then recycled as payment for old debts and reparations. The best the Federal Reserve Board could do was to keep American interest rates low, so that investment capital would flow to countries with higher rates of return on debt. But those investments did not, in the main, take root on productive frontiers and bear productive returns, the way the British loans of the late nineteenth century had done. Instead, they whirled around and around the globe, seeking ever more illusory fertile ground in which to rest.

Finally, in 1928, a Federal Reserve Board increasingly alarmed at speculation on the American stock market tightened its monetary policy, hoping to rein in the irrational enthusiasm of investors. Raising interest rates in the United States made investment in American debt more attractive, and reversed the overseas flow of capital. As the motion of dollars across the ocean slowed, so too did economies around the world. In Europe, Latin America, and the Antipodes, commercial activity ground to a near halt well before the 1929 crash made Americans painfully alert to the crisis they had unwittingly wrought through their optimism and neglect.[44]

Each of America's international economic policies had represented an adequate adaptation to the nineteenth-century world, but proved poorly calibrated to the postwar era. With such a rich stock of natural resources in its internal empire, it needed no external colonies or custom of reliance on international trade. With a mobile labor market including a largely foreign working class, it could use immigration policy rather than social welfare to relieve unemployment. Its relentless, speedy expansion had made it seem unnecessary to manage its economy much, as there was always another opportunity farther West. It appeared to have occurred to fairly few Americans that for such policies, habits, and hopes to remain effective, some government or set of agencies had to perform routine chores to keep the country and the world open to the benefits of global markets.

Had the nation retained, even temporarily as a help to demobilization, some of the regulatory and information-gathering agencies that grew so swiftly during the war, it might have avoided the deep postwar downturn, managing better the return of soldiers and other war workers to the peacetime labor market, and winding down wartime purchasing with greater care.[45] Doing so would have relieved some of the pressure for an emergency tariff and an emergency immigration-restriction bill. Moreover, the nation's ability to weather that depression taught it a spurious lesson: that the old ways were good enough for a new era. Had the country managed its affairs more smoothly, using some of the new regulatory and information-gathering techniques learned in recent years, it might have learned a different lesson—a lesson other countries had already begun learning—about the value to policymakers of such techniques. Had it a more usual set of proto–welfare policies, it might have weathered postwar economic shocks without feeling the need to restrict the flow of foreign goods and labor.

To be fair, we might note that it had taken the British a long time to see the outlines of the nineteenth-century system they themselves had brought about as much by incident as by plan. Moreover, the British investors had benefited from their early experience with the exceptional American borrowers, which despite their occasional embarrassing defaults had presented a continuous series of opportunities.[46] There was no such country in the postwar world to draw investment away from America. There had been, in the recent history of the world, only one such outstanding opportunity among nations, and that country proceeded now, like an indulged child entrusted too soon with the burden of maturity, to keep up its old habits of assuming the world would take care of it.[47]

Conclusion

In the middle of the nineteenth century, as the Irish potato famine and the revolutions brewing across Europe sent migrants streaming across the Atlantic, two visionary economists predicted that globalization would erase the distinctions among nations. Culture, religion, and national peculiarity would yield to the pressures of the market, and anyplace would become indistinguishable from everyplace:

> A constantly expanding market ... must nestle everywhere, settle everywhere, establish connexions everywhere. ... We have intercourse in every direction, universal inter-dependence of nations. ... And as in material, so also in intellectual production. The intellectual creations of individual nations become common property. National one-sidedness and narrow-mindedness become more and more impossible.[1]

About this, as about so much else, Karl Marx and Friedrich Engels proved immensely, if fascinatingly, wrong. So too have their modern heirs among the prophets of globalization. On a blackboard in an introductory economics classroom, where other things can be held equal, global commerce makes us all increasingly alike: but in fact all other things stubbornly refuse to remain equal, and often wreak devastation on the equations.

On the flat and manageable plane of a blackboard, countries with low wages export labor to countries with high wages. As workers leave low-wage countries, labor grows scarcer; relative demand for labor rises, and so therefore do wages. Capital, too, should seek markets where it will garner the highest possible return, until those returns also equilibrate. Then globalization will have worked, making all separate markets into a single market and creating uniform conditions.

If we look away from the blackboard and at the three-dimensional world, a variety of factors interfere with this scenario. Two of them proved especially important in the nineteenth-century era of globalization. First, workers in high-wage countries—which is to say, workers in New World countries—grew understandably upset as the magic of globalization allowed the appearance of millions of immigrants seeking those better wages. Native-born workers suddenly faced the option of losing their jobs or working at lower pay. Countries whose political systems made them responsive to this disgruntlement erected barriers to globalization.[2] Second, countries with expansive and productive frontiers did not necessarily experience the full force of globalization's potential leveling effects. The international investment of capital and labor coupled with the ability to make use of new land allowed wages overall to grow in the United States (even though they might have stagnated or fallen in the jobs particularly affected by immigration).[3] This growth let the majority of Americans keep their belief in limitless opportunities, even while those minority parts of the population most affected by the pressures of global markets mounted protests and demanded redress. So on the whole, globalization reinforced Americans' sense of privileged exemption and gave them reason to resist the growth of state power as it occurred elsewhere. While the American state did grow, it expanded in response to antiglobalization protests. This pattern rendered American institutions ever more peculiar. Where the growth of government might regulate the effects of investment capital on the frontier, where it might seem an appropriate response to immigration, Americans accepted it. The United States did not flatly resist the growth of government, but rather allowed its government to grow in directions that responded specifically to globalization.

Woodrow Wilson, speaking as a historian, thus proved more nearly right than Marx and Engels. Not only had a half-century of globalization failed to make the United States more like other countries, but the operation of global markets had made the country more distinctive, and not merely because Americans continued to think of themselves, in Wilson's phrase, as "blessed among the nations." All peoples believe to one degree or another in their special destiny. The Germans have had their *Sonderweg*, or "special path"; the French have had a *mission civilisatrice*, or "civilizing mission." For the better part of a century the Russians professed to believe that the mechanism of history had given Marx's prediction to them to fulfill. Exceptionalism, as a belief, is not terribly exceptional.

But the workings of history tend to disabuse people of their national myths. Empires fall, missions falter. People look with a sense of humility on the ambition of previous generations. Except for the United States—so far. On the contrary, as we have seen, the workings of world history in the nineteenth century colluded with America by reinforcing its national myth. For a critical phase in both U.S. and world history, the great powers (particularly Britain) served as guarantors of an open world economy that encouraged the free flow of capital and labor to developing economies. So much of each from so many sources went to the United States that it enjoyed a special status among the nations of the earth. The important and peculiar role played by international capital and international labor in developing the U.S. economy indulged Americans in their tendency to think of their government as a referee charged with regulating the influence of such forces in an open and fluid system, rather than as a machine for allocating scarce resources.

The fact of such circumstances matters at least as much as the beliefs they encouraged. Even if it is true that we Americans,

more than most peoples, like to think of ourselves as hardy indi-
viduals without much need for government, we have not lacked
contrary traditions. For example, the U.S. victory in the Civil War
gave rise to a powerful program of what we would now call "big
government," comprising constitutional amendments and legisla-
tive programs meant to increase the power of Washington and
create a national state equipped to pursue policies of economic
development. And again, during the economic crises of the 1890s,
prominent Americans began talking seriously about the end of
America's distinctive destiny and the need for a stronger state.
But both those episodes ended without leaving a lasting legacy
not because big-government proponents were out-argued, but
because circumstances seemed to render their solutions unnecessary.[4] The operations of global markets, supplying the United
States with a range of opportunities of which other peoples could
only dream, gave new life and scope to American peculiarity. The
first modern age of globalization gave Americans reason to believe
that the rest of humankind intended to let the United States fulfill its special wish to have as little government as possible. While
other modern and modernizing countries developed, as Marx and
Engels predicted, common solutions to common problems, the
Americans—experiencing an uncommon set of problems—were
able to develop solutions suited to their special circumstances.
Paying attention to the specific solutions Americans adopted, as
compared to the range of solutions adopted by other countries,
and to the special circumstances under which Americans labored,
as compared to the range of circumstances that beset other peoples, has allowed us to think about the dimensions of Americanness in fairly precise terms. It comprised a degree of divergence
from the path of other nations, which Americans developed as an
adaptation to their discernibly different environment.

The American commitment to a peculiar set of solutions might
not have mattered so much had this commitment not developed
just as the rest of civilization slid into apocalypse. American institutions did no noticeable harm until the special circumstances

that nurtured them changed. World War I made new rules, but Americans preferred not to play by them, and disasters ensued. As a result, Woodrow Wilson would be the last Democratic president for more than seventy years to believe the economy would regulate itself better with the government ignoring it, and after the missteps of the 1920s, Republican leaders were also, for several generations, cautious about asserting an absolute preference for private over public institutions.

Indeed, during the period from the 1920s to the middle 1960s, when globalization was at its low ebb, the United States became less unusual. The effects of the New Deal and war mobilization on the Great Depression alerted Americans to the advantages of having their government manage economic crises. Under restrictionist immigration policies, the number of foreign-born in the United States dwindled, and the power of the labor movement swelled. Within the Democratic Party, which embodied for a time a reigning consensus, a custom of increased social spending developed. Determined to avoid the errors of the last peace, when the United States failed utterly to restore the nineteenth-century global economy, American leaders of the 1940s embedded the United States within a web of international institutions designed to resuscitate and then preserve global commerce. The Bretton Woods system, the European Recovery Program, the United Nations, the North Atlantic Treaty Organization, and other similar institutions all pledged Americans to the support of other nations' economies to an extent unimagined a generation before.

As a result, the powerful United States succeeded after World War II where it had failed after World War I, ultimately reproducing something like the globalization of the nineteenth century. Other countries regained prosperity as they had not in the 1920s, and the developing world came, at least partially, into this global system. By coordinating policy with other countries, by distributing resources around the world, by underwriting confidence in international stability, the United States helped to re-create a world economy like that of the nineteenth century, in which—

despite obvious and serious flaws—the world's people have felt a reasonable confidence when moving their resources among nations.[5]

If it seems now that Americans have reason to complain about this system, it is only because it has worked so well. The late-twentieth-century globalization shrank the gap between other advanced countries and the United States. America's unquestioned economic authority began to ebb in the 1960s, when overseas traders took a few runs at the dollar, and vanished completely after poor American fiscal policy and the Vietnam War encouraged President Richard Nixon to end the Bretton Woods system in 1971.

Since then, globalization has begun to work without a guarantor, and America has returned to its older ways. With its return to net debtor status in the 1980s, the country has once again, as a hundred years ago, found itself on the receiving end of significant flows of international investment capital. Moreover, beginning with the liberalization of immigration in the 1960s, the streams of cold war asylum seekers in the 1970s, and the post–cold war opportunity seekers in the 1980s, the United States has once again, as a hundred years ago, found itself on the receiving end of significant flows of international labor. And at the same time, it has abandoned its mid-century experiments with becoming a bit more like other nations.

At a quick glance we can see how this modern-day version of America's distinctive historical habits looks in numerical terms. In 2001, the United States ranked first among recipients of foreign immigration in the world, receiving almost a third of the migrants recorded as crossing borders and more than half as many again as the second most popular destination.[6] The United States presently ranks, as it has for the last two decades, as the foremost recipient of foreign investment, receiving perhaps a great deal more than the second-, third-, and fourth-ranked recipients combined.[7]

Meanwhile, America devotes a disproportionately low share of its resources to social-welfare programs compared with other countries, ranking twenty-sixth out of thirty countries studied by the Organisation for Economic Co-operation and Development.[8] Ironically, other countries seem to have learned the lesson of our historical experience better than we have. Americans now spend so little on public health that, even accounting for other factors, we live shorter and sicker lives than our peers in other rich countries.[9]

In one area we have become an exception of a different kind: not only does the United States no longer rate as a minor military power, but it has become the major military power without peer. Today the United States spends more money on military affairs than any other country, nine times as much as the next largest spender, such that almost half of all money spent on defense in the world comes out of American coffers.[10] Yet it is also true that today, as before World War I, American military potential remains largely untapped. If the United States today were to spend as high a proportion of its money on defense as it did at the height of the peacetime cold war, as in around 1960, it would account for about two-thirds of the money spent on defense around the globe. Moreover, the U.S. military today, as a percentage of the American population, is less than half the size of the U.S. military at 1960, and about two-thirds the size of the British military during the nineteenth century.[11] The American power to fight, as with the American power to fight disease, remains in reserve; and as with the frontier army of the late nineteenth century, the U.S. army today is expected to fight distant, difficult, and even critical battles on imperial frontiers without the mass mobilization and sacrifice of American resources in their support.

Perhaps most important, all that power and all that potential no longer stand behind the system of global openness that Americans built in the 1940s. Since the early 1970s, the United States has been edging away from its commitments to globalization. Under administrations of both major parties, the country has backed away from a variety of international agreements.[12] And acting now more as a consumer than as a saver of financial resources, despite having the world's largest economy, Americans invest in the world more on the level of "a medium-sized European economy."[13] Watching the world market go on working, we have come to rely increasingly on the idea that, as Woodrow Wilson's advisers would have said, the economy can take care of itself. In returning to the philosophy of the 1920s, we have been endangering the international system that gives America its distinctive character and special blessings.

The case of the world crisis of 1914–1945 teaches us that powerful nations must act occasionally, if not continuously, to preserve global openness if it is to last. Globalization will not maintain itself without such intervention. International investors, whether they wish to reap returns on capital or on labor, need to have confidence that the rules and norms protecting their investment enjoy the backing of great powers with an interest in preserving order. If they do not, they will become less eager to invest. People in high-wage countries who feel pushed around by globalization need to have confidence that some safety net will ease their transition to a fully open world economy. If they do not, they will organize and lobby to stop globalization.

Looking at American history through the lens of globalization, we can see that an especially lucky country on the periphery of a global system, with no special responsibility for its maintenance, might harmlessly sustain the illusion that the world economy will right and regulate itself without government action. But we can also see that a country at the center of such a system cannot afford to indulge in such myths.

Yet it seems that now, as a hundred years ago, the habit of being unusual is leading Americans into unfortunate fallacies. Almost a century ago, President Wilson encouraged his fellow Americans to believe that they derived their blessed status from God's approval combined with the business community's reliable competence, rather than from the particular circumstances of peaceable commerce that prevailed before the war. Wilson and his successors further supposed that what God and business had brought America, God and business would in due course bring to other countries. They ignored (and banished from their presence

those few who had not ignored) the role of governments in promoting the free flow of the world economy's blessings. In consequence, God and business failed to act as their promoters had
prophesied.

We find ourselves in a similar position today. Having enjoyed
several decades of globalization's special blessings, we are little
inclined to believe the warnings we have had that without government action to prop it up, the beneficial aspects of the system will
fail. Whether in the midst of this bout of globalization Americans
will repeat the mistakes of the 1920s or remember the lessons of
the 1940s depends on whether we see ourselves as the recipients
of the blessings of Providence or as the trustees of the invested
hope and confidence of the world's people.

■ Appendix

Factors Affecting Per Capita Spending in Health and Sanitation	Coefficient	t
Municipal woman suffrage	0.27	3.01
Population (natural log)	0.25	6.19
Mean SEI	0.02	1.27
Standard deviation of SEI	–0.06	–2.15
Share of foreign-born in the population	2.76	5.86
Share of black citizens	1.06	1.82
Share of new immigrants from Italy, Austria-Hungary, and Russia	–2.36	–3.28
Share of black migrants from the South	4.63	2.42
City in a Southern state	0.29	1.52
Date of state's entry to the Union	–0.01	–4.46
Share of manufacturing jobs in the workforce	–0.98	–2.81

Appendix Table For further discussion, see note on page 228.

■ A Note on Motive, Method, and Metaphor

This book began with a conversation, when Desmond King (an analyst of immigration history and policy, who later read and critiqued what I've said here about migrations) asked if I would explain, to a group of academics more eminent than I, why the United States, in the age of industrialization, had something called progressivism instead of a more usual kind of European or Antipodean social democracy. This was an excellent example of an apparently simple question of the kind that one should answer carefully, if at all. I suggested that students of U.S. history traditionally see progressivism as a movement toward social democracy that commenced from a different starting point than most other countries' similar movements, and that never in the end quite got where it was going. Whereupon the distinguished company politely persuaded me that this was a poor way to think about progress. An eminent evolutionary biologist ended the lesson by arguing that the word *progress* made sense only if defined as increasingly complex adaptations to environment, which meant that although you might progress from somewhere, you were never progressing toward anywhere in particular.*

With this chastening in mind, I began thinking about the development of the modern United States as a set of better or worse adaptations to

---

*I learned afterward that Richard Dawkins had earlier described this idea of progress in print: see "Human Chauvinism and Evolutionary Progress" in *A Devil's Chaplain: Reflections on Hope, Lies, Science, and Love* (Boston: Houghton Mifflin, 2003), 206–17.

environment. In this book I've tried to depict American development in this fashion, judging it as neither especially good nor especially bad in itself, just as suitable or unsuitable to circumstances. In the course of seeking to render my tone as neutral as possible, I benefited from the efforts of Glenn Altschuler, Roger Daniels, Ari Kelman, Kathy Olmsted, and Louis Warren (all of whom kindly read and critiqued the book) to alert me to where even my most mellow efforts at avoiding the judgmental note had sometimes failed. Nevertheless, I hope the reader will appreciate that I am not saying American pecularities are good or bad; as I have elsewhere pointed out, a biologist does not regard an elephant's trunk as good or bad, but she does of necessity see it as belonging peculiarly to the elephant.

In identifying the influential elements of the nineteenth-century environment, I followed traditional economic analyses by looking at the impact of capital and labor, and I let the voices of historical figures and later scholars guide me to the important international aspects of these subjects. Further conversations with my next-door neighbor at the office, Peter Lindert (who read and critiqued what I've said here about welfare policy and capital investment), followed; I benefited immensely from his generosity and wide-ranging interests. Alan M. Taylor (a historian of international capital movement, who kindly read and critiqued what I've said here about capital) urged on me more international comparisons than I had already supplied, and Alan S. Taylor (who knows about many New World frontiers) kindly spoke to me about the Canadian example. Jay Sexton (an expert on the role of the United States in dealing with foreign debt, who kindly read what I've said here about default and credit) pressed me to consider the critical role of warfare in defining credit. As I worked on what I had to say about warfare, I benefited further from the excellent counsel and lively conversation of the military historian David Silbey, who generously read and commented on what I've said here about American defense capacity. For the French case, Ted Margadant and Chazz Hammond assisted me; for Russia, Dan Brower and Doug Northrop. In our time, many valuable scholarly conversations are carried on over the Internet, and through such communications I have received generous assistance from people on whom I have never laid eyes; on many occasions they have unfogged my beclouded mind. I am especially grateful to Dora Costa and Jacob Vigdor for helping an unseen if not quite unmet inquirer.

In outlining the social character of the United States in the early twentieth century, I learned to lean carefully, but constantly, on the U.S. census and the samples from it collected and made comparable in the truly marvelous Integrated Public Use Microdata Series (IPUMS) project at the

University of Minnesota.* The census of this era did what contemporaries sometimes described as a flawed, even corrupted, job of counting Americans. Even disregarding the political pressures on enumerators, they were still likely to miss the poor, the foreign-born, and people in motion—in short, the people on whom this book focuses for its discussion of labor. Estimates of the undercounts range from 6 percent nationwide to more than 20 percent in some communities.† Moreover, excellent as IPUMS is (and it is truly excellent), like all samples it is subject to sampling error. I have taken what care I could think to take, comparing my observations with those of others, checking my sums against those of others, and treating no estimate as too precise a number. In chapter 1 I urged readers to remember the excellent advice of John Coatsworth (see note 10 on page 183), who kindly took time out of a casual conversation to talk over the problems of rough data with me—as did Angus Maddison, who explained some of his methods of making estimates. But as both they and the economic historian William Summerhill (who also kindly read and critiqued this book) note, having taken these cautions, we must go ahead and say what we see, with due circumspection. That we will nevertheless make mistakes is an inevitable, if regrettable, result of our innate fallibility. I tried to avoid errors not only by double- and triple-checking on my own, but also by enlisting the help of others, especially including Dana Sherry and Peter Hohn, to check my figures. Any errors remaining, if discovered, will be corrected in future editions.

The growth of government amid great social and economic transformations is a complex and abstract process, and it can be rendered comprehensible only by selecting examples and generalizing about trends. Normally this means choosing metaphors. In addition to the process of adaptation, I have employed two major metaphors: the lens, to describe the interpretive

---

*See Steven Ruggles and Russell R. Menard, "The Minnesota Historical Census Projects," *Historical Methods* 28, no. 1 (Winter 1995): 6–10; Steven Ruggles, J. David Hacker, and Matthew Sobek, "General Design of the Integrated Public Use Microdata Series," *Historical Methods* 28, no. 1 (Winter 1995): 33–39; and Michael A. Strong, Samuel H. Preston, and Mark C. Howard, "An Introduction to the Public Use Sample of the 1910 U.S. Census of Population," *Historical Methods* 22, no. 2 (Spring 1989): 34–36.

†Miriam L. King and Diana Magnuson, "Perspectives on Historical U.S. Census Undercounts," *Social Science History* 19, no. 4. (Winter 1995): 455–66. Also Susan B. Carter and Richard Sutch, "Fixing the Facts: Editing of the 1880 U.S. Census of Occupations with Implications for Long-Term Trends and the Sociology of Official Statistics," National Bureau of Economic Research (NBER) Historical Working Paper no. 74 (1995): 1–51.

process itself (a meta-metaphor, then) and the fluid/irrigation image, to describe the resources of a world in motion and the ways different peoples adapted to the varying availability of fluid resources. Metaphors, of course, are a gift to unfriendly critics: it is easy to take the offer of a lens and say it renders the world out of focus, or to say that the hydraulic analogy is "all wet." But if metaphors are consistently used and accurately applied, they can indicate the salient features of otherwise undistinguished masses of words and data. To the extent that these metaphors remain unmixed and the message comes through clearly, I owe a great debt to the editorial staff of Hill and Wang/Farrar, Straus and Giroux, headed by Thomas LeBien.

The foregoing indicates my immense authorial debt to others, as do the notes in this book; and in truth that debt is greater still. Participants in the Cambridge one-day colloquium on Progressivism, in the United Nations University/World Institute for Development Economics Research meeting on Institutions and Economic Development, in the British American Nineteenth Century Historians' meeting on the Gilded Age and Progressive Era, in the Oxford U.S. history seminar series, and in the University of Virginia's Miller Center for Public Affairs colloquium have all heard versions or parts of this book and provided thoughtful comments. So, too, have my colleagues here at the University of California, Davis—especially the economic historians, the Institute for Governmental Affairs, and the history department, all of whom asked to hear these ideas expounded in seminar talks. To the extent that this book addresses scholarly debates with any vigor and cogency, it owes a great debt to all such interlocutors. In addition, and perhaps more so, I hope to appeal to active citizens outside the academy, such as those who comprise the Chancellor's Club of UC Davis, who generously supported my research and listened to me talk about it afterward. I hope it will make a small repayment on that debt by making a good contribution to further discussions.

It is never possible to thank everyone who helped, but I hope I have not left out anyone who helped conspicuously, and apologize if I have. The book's dedication is to those who have helped me most.

■ Notes

Introduction

1. Readers interested in pursuing the Fortinbras problem in its original Shakespearean version may wish to begin with William Witherie Lawrence, "Hamlet and Fortinbras," *PMLA* 61, no. 3 (September 1946): 673–98.

Chapter 1: Globalization and America

1. As I hope will prove clear from what follows, I neither cheer for nor jeer at what scholars know as American exceptionalism, nor am I even especially interested in it. I am interested in discernible degrees of difference in the impact of world systems and the extent to which they appear to have mattered in American national development.

2. "Transcript of Reagan's Farewell Address to the American People," *New York Times*, January 12, 1989, B8.

3. John Winthrop, "A Modell of Christian Charity," in *The American Intellectual Tradition*, ed. Charles Capper and David Hollinger (New York: Oxford University Press, 2001), 1:15.

4. Scholars studying the impact of American constitutionalism abroad find a general interest in American ideas but much less imitation of key institutions. "[T]he impact is thus segmented and fragmented": Carl J. Friedrich, *The Impact of American Constitutionalism Abroad* (Boston: Boston University Press, 1967), 8. Also Albert P. Blaustein, *The Influence of the United States Constitution Abroad* (Washington, D.C.: Washington Institute, 1986); Stephen Randall and Roger Gib-

bins, eds., *Federalism and the New World Order* (Calgary: University of Calgary Press, 1994).

5. Classic texts emphasizing values and institutions include Louis Hartz, *The Liberal Tradition in America: An Interpretation of American Political Thought Since the Revolution* (1955; reprint, San Diego: Harcourt Brace Jovanovich, 1991); and Richard Hofstadter, *The American Political Tradition and the Men Who Made It* (New York: Alfred A. Knopf, 1948). Perhaps the best-known argument for the influence of environment on values is Frederick Jackson Turner, *The Significance of the Frontier in American History* (1893; reprint, New York: Frederick Ungar, 1963). For a useful summary of such arguments see Michael Kammen, "The Problem of American Exceptionalism: A Reconsideration," *American Quarterly* 45, no. 1 (1993): 1–43. For a critique see Daniel T. Rodgers, "Exceptionalism," in *Imagined Histories*, ed. Anthony Molho and Gordon S. Wood (Princeton, N.J.: Princeton University Press, 1998). For a comparison of values and political traditions with a skeptical eye on the differentness of American institutions, see John Gerring, *Party Ideologies in America, 1828–1996* (Cambridge: Cambridge University Press, 2001), 22–54.

6. See the discussion in Carl N. Degler, "In Pursuit of an American History," *American Historical Review* 92, no. 1 (1987): 1–12.

7. Alexis de Tocqueville, *Democracy in America*, ed. Francis Bowen, trans. Henry Reeve, 3d ed., 2 vols. (Cambridge, Mass.: Sever and Francis, 1862), 2:42.

8. Data from *The Economist, Pocket World in Figures* (London: Profile, 2004).

9. Data from Angus Maddison, *The World Economy: Historical Statistics* (Paris: Organisation for Economic Co-operation and Development, 2003), 259, table 8b. Maddison has the U.S. GDP as $98 billion in 1870 and $517 billion in 1913, in constant 1990 dollars, for an increase in size of 5.3 times and of $419 billion. During the same period, the world GDP went from $1.112 trillion to $2.73 trillion, for an increase of $1.62 billion, of which the U.S. growth was 25.9 percent. At 1913, the U.S. GDP was slightly more than twice the size of any of China, Germany, Russia, or the United Kingdom. As to involvement in the war, both China and Russia were allies at one part of the war or another, which the United States, an "associated power," never was. The only country accounting for more than 1 percent of the world's 1913 GDP to remain neutral throughout the war was Spain.

10. "Spurious precision infects all, or nearly all, quantitative work. Margins of error are necessarily large. . . . All of the numbers . . . are, without exception, inaccurate; however, that is not a valid argument against their use. Literary estimates typically contain fewer errors (we all know that Mexico was 'poorer' than its northern neighbor), but only because they specify a ridiculously wide range of values." John H. Coatsworth, "Obstacles to Economic Growth in Nineteenth-Century Mexico," *American Historical Review* 83, no. 1 (1978): 80–100, esp. 80–81. On degrees of difference, see George M. Fredrickson, "From Exceptionalism to Variability," in *The Comparative Imagination: On the History of Racism, Nationalism, and Social Movements* (Berkeley: University of California Press, 1997); Kammen, "Problem."

11. Eric Hobsbawm, *The Age of Empire, 1875–1914* (New York: Vintage, 1989).

12. The tradition of regarding America's western territories as a peculiar kind of empire has a long history and one that I will honor in later chapters. See also Patricia Nelson Limerick, "Going West and Ending Up Global," *Western Historical Quarterly* 32, no. 1 (2001): 5–24; Patricia Nelson Limerick, *The Legacy of Conquest: The Unbroken Past of the American West* (New York: W. W. Norton & Co., 1988), 79–96.

13. Social spending figures as in Peter H. Lindert, "The Rise of Social Spending, 1880–1930," *Explorations in Economic History* 31 (1994): 1–37, 10, table 1A. See also Peter H. Lindert, *Growing Public: Social Spending and Economic Growth Since the Eighteenth Century* (Cambridge: Cambridge University Press, 2004).

14. Walter Bagehot, *Lombard Street: A Description of the Money Market*, ed. Hartley Withers (London: Smith, Elder & Co., 1910), 50–53.

15. On the unlikeness of the original Federal Reserve to a central bank, see the opening chapters of Allan H. Meltzer, *A History of the Federal Reserve, 1913–1951* (Chicago: University of Chicago Press, 2003).

16. On army size, see Correlates of War Project, *National Material Capabilities Data Version 3.01* (2004); available from http://www.correlatesof war.org (accessed January 12, 2005). National Material Capabilities Data based on J. David Singer, Stuart Bremer, and John Stuckey, "Capability Distribution, Uncertainty, and Major Power War, 1820–1965," in *Peace, War, and Numbers*, ed. Bruce Russett (Beverly Hills, Calif.: Sage, 1972). On state expenditure relative to GDP see Angus Maddison, *Monitoring the World Economy, 1820–1992* (Paris: Development Centre of the Organisation for Economic Co-operation and

Development, 1995), 65, table 3.5. On socialism, see Seymour Martin Lipset and Gary Wolfe Marks, *It Didn't Happen Here: Why Socialism Failed in the United States* (New York: W. W. Norton & Co., 2000), 188, table 5.1.

17. On globalization and convergence of conditions, see Kevin H. O'Rourke and Jeffrey G. Williamson, *Globalization and History: The Evolution of a Nineteenth-Century Atlantic Economy* (Cambridge, Mass.: MIT Press, 1999). On the factors encouraging common policy solutions, see Lindert, *Growing Public*, and Lindert, "The Rise of Social Spending." On the global traffic in ideas about solutions to industrial problems, see Daniel T. Rodgers, *Atlantic Crossings: Social Politics in a Progressive Age* (Cambridge, Mass.: Belknap Press of Harvard University Press, 1998).

18. B. R. Mitchell, *International Historical Statistics: The Americas, 1750–2000*, 5th ed. (New York: Palgrave Macmillan, 2003), 539–41, series F1. Mitchell gives length of U.S. railway line open as 85,170 kilometers in 1870 and 401,977 kilometers in 1913, for an increase of 4.7 times.

19. This is not to quarrel with Robert Fogel but simply to say, as Fogel does, "Cheap inland transportation was a necessary condition for economic growth," and that investment in such transportation was likewise necessary. See Robert William Fogel, *Railroads and American Economic Growth: Essays in Econometric History* (Baltimore: Johns Hopkins Press, 1964), 237. Also Lance Edwin Davis and Robert E. Gallman, *Evolving Financial Markets and International Capital Flows: Britain, the Americas, and Australia, 1870–1914* (Cambridge: Cambridge University Press, 2001), 333n543.

20. O'Rourke and Williamson, *Globalization and History*, 4.

21. Niall Ferguson, *Empire: The Rise and Demise of the British World Order and the Lessons for Global Power* (New York: Basic Books, 2003), xxii–xxix.

22. Timothy J. Hatton and Jeffrey G. Williamson, *The Age of Mass Migration: Causes and Economic Impact* (New York: Oxford University Press, 1998), 123.

23. See cumulative tables in Irving Stone, *The Global Export of Capital from Great Britain, 1865–1914: A Statistical Survey* (New York: St. Martin's, 1999). Also the chapter "Capital" in this book.

24. Arizona and New Mexico became the last of the continental states in 1912. Noncontiguous territories, including Alaska, Hawaii, Puerto

Rico, Midway, the Philippines, and other islands, played an important role in American ambition but did not affect the politics of the early twentieth century so significantly as the inland empire did. See also in this book the chapter "Warfare."

25. William Cronon, *Nature's Metropolis: Chicago and the Great West* (New York: W. W. Norton & Co., 1991), xv.

26. On "free security," see C. Vann Woodward, "The Age of Reinterpretation," *American Historical Review* 66, no. 1 (October 1960): 1–19, 2.

27. Mark Twain, *The Innocents Abroad, or the New Pilgrim's Progress* (1869; reprint, New York: Thistle Press, 1962), 290. For recent scholarly comparisons between Russian and American expansions, see, inter alia, Daniel Brower, *Turkestan and the Fate of the Russian Empire* (London: Routledge Curzon, 2003), esp. 126–51; Kate Brown, "Gridded Lives: Why Kazakhstan and Montana Are Nearly the Same Place," *American Historical Review* 106, no. 1 (2001): 17–48; Dominic Lieven, *Empire: The Russian Empire and Its Rivals* (New Haven, Conn.: Yale University Press, 2000), esp. 206–30; Willard Sunderland, *Taming the Wild Field: Colonization and Empire on the Russian Steppe* (Ithaca, N.Y.: Cornell University Press, 2004); John C. Weaver, *The Great Land Rush and the Making of the Modern World, 1650–1900* (Montreal: McGill-Queen's University Press, 2003), esp. 41–45.

28. In Russian Turkestan in the 1890s, there were about five million people, of which about one hundred thousand were part of "the colonial machinery of Russian autocracy in Turkistan [*sic*]": Nadira A. Abdurakhimova, "The Colonial System of Power in Turkistan," *International Journal of Middle East Studies* 34, no. 2 (2002): 239–62, 242. In Arizona, Dakota, Idaho, Montana, New Mexico, Utah, Washington, and Wyoming there were about 1.6 million people (including reservation Indians and "persons with Indians"), of which about 3,000 were employees of all levels of government and a further 10,000 were officers or men in the military—this according to the 1890 census, within a year of statehood for Idaho, Montana, the Dakotas, Washington and Wyoming. (Earlier territorial estimates, as in the governors' reports of 1889, allege significantly different, usually larger, populations.) This set of territories excludes Alaska, Indian Territory, and Oklahoma. On general population: U.S. Census, *Report on the Population of the United States at the Eleventh Census, 1890*, vol. 1, pt. 1 (Washington, D.C.: Government Printing Office, 1895), 2, table 1.

On government employees: U.S. Census, *Report on the Population of the United States at the Eleventh Census, 1890*, vol. 1, pt. 2 (Washington, D.C.: Government Printing Office, 1897), 306, table 79. On American Indian population, U.S. Census, *Report on Indians Taxed and Indians Not Taxed in the United States (except Alaska)*, vol. 17 (Washington, D.C.: Government Printing Office, 1894), 81.

29. Cited in Brower, *Turkestan*, 166.

30. This was true to such an extent that the colonial government armed the settlers, and indeed such that the defining feature of the colony was the Turkmen's revolt. See ibid., 130–75.

31. To further prove this point, the territory with the highest ratio both of civilian officials to settler population, at .26 percent, and of total government employees (including military) to total population, at 2.4 percent, was Arizona, which also had the highest ratio of indigenous to settler population, with 48 percent. On the relation between agents and objects of empire, see Limerick, *Legacy*.

32. Richard White, *"It's Your Misfortune and None of My Own": A New History of the American West* (Norman: University of Oklahoma Press, 1991), 58.

33. Thanks to the 1884 establishment of the Naval War College at Newport, Rhode Island had a higher percentage of military people among its workforce than any state except Arizona or Wyoming; see U.S. Census, *Twelfth Census of the United States, Taken in the Year 1900*, vol. 2, pt. 2 (Washington, D.C.: Government Printing Office, 1902), table 93. In the IPUMS sample for 1880, about 30 percent of the U.S. military was stationed in the terrritories that would enter the Union as states after the Civil War; in the 1900 census, only about half that; by 1920 the percentage had fallen to below 10. By 1920 New Jersey, Virginia, Maryland, and Kentucky were among the top ten states for per capita military presence. Steven Ruggles, Matthew Sobek, et al., *Integrated Public Use Microdata Series: Version 3.0* (Minneapolis: Population Center, 2004), available from http://www.ipums.org.

34. Donald Meinig, "American Wests: Preface to a Geographical Interpretation," *Annals of the Association of American Geographers* 62, no. 2 (1972): 159–84, 181.

35. The western states probably enjoyed more control over their affairs than India and less than the white settler colonies such as Canada or Australia. They had a greater role in shaping metropolitan policy than either. In terms of the various kinds of colonial administration, the United States spent far more effort on assimilating aboriginal peoples

and negotiating the autonomy of white settlers than it did on administering an established, conquered people with no real intention of assimilation (which it did try in the Philippines).

36. On the wildness of the West as a manifestation of anticolonial feeling, see Richard Maxwell Brown, *No Duty to Retreat: Violence and Values in American History and Society* (Norman: University of Oklahoma Press, 1994).

37. Nebraska (1867), Colorado (1876), North and South Dakota, Montana, and Washington (1889), Idaho and Wyoming (1890), Utah (1897), Oklahoma (1907), Arizona and New Mexico (1912).

38. Lindert, *Growing Public*; Lindert, "Rise of Social Spending."

39. On the near-total absence of American socialism, see Lipset and Marks, *It Didn't Happen Here.* On the importance of agrarian protest in shaping the growth of the American state, see Elizabeth Sanders, *Roots of Reform: Farmers, Workers, and the American State, 1877–1917* (Chicago: University of Chicago Press, 1999).

40. Hatton and Williamson, *Age of Mass Migration,* 168–69. Also Hope T. Eldridge and Dorothy Swaine Thomas, *Demographic Analyses and Interrelations,* ed. Simon Kuznets, vol. 3, *Population Redistribution and Economic Growth* (Philadelphia: American Philosophical Society, 1964), 71–75; Carter Goodrich et al., *Migration and Economic Opportunity: The Report of the Study of Population Redistribution* (Philadelphia: University of Pennsylvania Press, 1936), 679–85.

41. Imre Ferenczi and Walter Francis Willcox, *International Migrations,* 2 vols. (New York: National Bureau of Economic Research, 1929), 1:81, 1:215–23.

42. In the 1920 IPUMS sample, 37 percent of urban laborers were foreign-born, and of them 33 percent had come since 1910; in 1910, 49 percent were foreign-born, and of them 60 percent had come since 1901; in 1900, 41 percent were foreign-born and 33 percent had come since 1890. *Urban* areas are those with a population over 2,500, and laborers are those whose occupational codes on the 1950 basis range between 910 and 970 inclusive, covering fishermen, garage workers, gardeners and groundskeepers, longshoremen and stevedores, lumbermen, teamsters, and otherwise unspecified laborers. In each sample, laborers represent about 13 percent of the urban workforce. Ruggles et al., *IPUMS.*

43. Between the two major sources on real wages for the *Historical Statistics of the United States,* Paul Douglas found them falling for manufacturing workers, and Albert Rees found them rising gradually. Both

believed these wages were depressed owing to immigration, with Rees reasoning that they were depressed from the level to which they would otherwise have risen. Claudia Goldin finds immigration lowering real wages in local markets, and Timothy Hatton and Jeffrey Williamson find immigration depressing the economy-wide rise in such wages. Kevin O'Rourke and Jeffrey Williamson, like Douglas, found real-wage inequalities occurring during the period. Susan Carter and Richard Sutch emphasize the continuing overall rise in real wages through the period of highest immigration.

The supportable *economic* conclusion is probably that in particular urban labor markets, the impact of immigration lowered real wages noticeably, an effect that would have eased as those immigrants were assimilated into the labor force. But the supportable *political* conclusion is that such impacts, even if they were soon alleviated, created lasting and unhappy impressions on American workers.

Susan B. Carter, Scott Sigmund Gartner, et al., *Historical Statistics of the United States on CD-ROM, Colonial Times to 1970*, Bicentennial ed. (Cambridge: Cambridge University Press, 1997); Susan B. Carter and Richard Sutch, "Historical Background to Current Immigration Issues," in *The Immigration Debate: Studies on the Economic, Demographic, and Fiscal Effects of Immigration*, ed. James P. Smith and Barry Edmonston (Washington, D.C.: National Academy Press, 1998); Paul H. Douglas, *Real Wages in the United States, 1890–1926* (Boston: Houghton Mifflin, 1930); Claudia Goldin, "The Political Economy of Immigration Restriction in the United States, 1890–1921," in *The Regulated Economy: A Historical Approach to Political Economy*, ed. Claudia Goldin and Gary D. Libecap (Chicago: University of Chicago Press, 1994) 223–57; Hatton and Williamson, *Age of Mass Migration*; O'Rourke and Williamson, *Globalization and History*; Albert Rees, *Real Wages in Manufacturing, 1890–1914* (Princeton, N.J.: Princeton University Press, 1961).

44. On immigration and inequality, see O'Rourke and Williamson, *Globalization and History*, 173–80. Peter Lindert finds that across countries and time periods, greater inequality means less social spending. He calls this the "Robin Hood paradox": Peter H. Lindert, "Toward a Comparative History of Income and Wealth Inequality," in *Income Distribution in Historical Perspective*, ed. Y. S. Brenner, Hartmut Kaelble, and Mark Thomas (Cambridge: Cambridge University Press, 1991), 226. Lindert finds also that wider gaps between middle and

poor quintiles of income hold down transfer of wealth through social policy: Lindert, *Growing Public*, 186–88.

45. Ruggles et al., *IPUMS*. These numbers are supported in, e.g., the 1910 census population and occupation tables, in which 31 percent of all workers in manufacturing industries were foreign-born, while 38 percent of general laborers in manufacturing were foreign-born; and in Niles Carpenter's study in which 31 percent of all manufacturing workers over the age of ten years were foreign-born in 1910 and 28 percent were in 1920. Niles Carpenter, *Immigrants and Their Children, 1920* (Washington, D.C.: Government Printing Office, 1927), 273–74; U.S. Census, *Thirteenth Census of the United States, Taken in the Year 1910*, vol. 4 (Washington, D.C.: Government Printing Office, 1914), 312–410; table vi.

46. Lipset and Marks, *It Didn't Happen Here*, 125–66.

Chapter 2: Capital

1. Committee on Public Information, *National Service Handbook* (Washington, D.C.: Government Printing Office, 1917), 253.

2. Richard H. Timberlake, *Monetary Policy in the United States: An Intellectual and Institutional History* (Chicago: University of Chicago Press, 1993), 220.

3. Robert J. Bulkley, "The Federal Farm-Loan Act," *Journal of Political Economy* 25, no. 2 (1917): 129–47, 135–36.

4. Harold U. Faulkner, *The Decline of Laissez Faire, 1897–1917*, vol. 7, *The Economic History of the United States* (New York: Rinehart and Company, 1951), 363–65; Elizabeth Sanders, *Roots of Reform: Farmers, Workers, and the American State, 1877–1917* (Chicago: University of Chicago Press, 1999), 236–59. The Land Banks financed under 9 percent of farm mortgages up to the New Deal. See Milton Friedman and Anna Jacobson Schwartz, *A Monetary History of the United States, 1867–1960* (Princeton, N.J.: Princeton University Press, 1963), 244n.

5. Eagle reportedly said this to Charles Hamlin. See John J. Broesamle, *William Gibbs McAdoo: A Passion for Change, 1863–1917* (Port Washington, N.Y.: Kennikat, 1973), 122 and 248 n12.

6. Maurice Obstfeld and Alan M. Taylor, "Globalization and Capital Markets," (National Bureau of Economic Research, 2002), NBER Working Paper no. 8846, 1–69, 25.

7. Debt was the most common form of foreign investment, but interna-

tional holdings extended commonly (30 percent of foreign capital invested) to equity shares as well. British investment declined from a peak of around 80 percent of world foreign investment to around 40 percent at 1914. See ibid., 21 and 24, figure 3; Irving Stone, *The Global Export of Capital from Great Britain, 1865–1914: A Statistical Survey* (New York: St. Martin's Press, 1999), 6–7; Mira T. Wilkins, *The History of Foreign Investment in the United States to 1914* (Cambridge, Mass.: Harvard University Press, 1989), 145, table 5.3.

8. All figures are at best approximate: "The large number of estimates notwithstanding, no one knows how much money was invested in the United States from abroad in the years 1875–1914." Wilkins, *History of Foreign Investment to 1914*, 144–45.

9. Stone, *Global Export*, 393, table 45. See also assessments cited in Wilkins, *History of Foreign Investment to 1914*, 157.

10. Lance Edwin Davis and Robert Gallman, *Evolving Financial Markets and International Capital Flows: Britain, the Americas, and Australia, 1870–1914* (Cambridge: Cambridge University Press, 2001), 234.

11. Canada had also become an international creditor at 1914, and had lent out perhaps 5 percent as much as it borrowed. See Obstfeld and Taylor, "Globalization," 22, table 2; Wilkins, *History of Foreign Investment to 1914*, 145, table 5.3.

12. Mira T. Wilkins, *The History of Foreign Investment in the United States, 1914–1945* (Cambridge, Mass.: Harvard University Press, 2004), 60.

13. This includes the United States and the nations that received the next most capital from Britain: in descending order, Canada, Argentina, Australia, India, South Africa, and Brazil. Stone, *Global Export*, 42–111, tables 1–7.

14. Davis Rich Dewey, *Financial History of the United States*, 5th ed. (New York: Longmans, Green, and Co., 1915), 89–96.

15. Michael D. Bordo and Carlos A. Vegh, "What If Alexander Hamilton Had Been Argentinean? A Comparison of the Early Monetary Experiences of Argentina and the United States," (National Bureau of Economic Research, 1998), NBER Working Paper no. 6862, 1–56.

16. John Lauritz Larson, "'Bind the Republic Together': The National Union and the Struggle for a System of Internal Improvements," *Journal of American History* 74, no. 2 (1987): 363–87; Joel H. Silbey, *The American Political Nation, 1838–1893* (Stanford, Calif.: Stanford University Press, 1991), 85, 161–62, 277n39. Also Carter Goodrich, "National Planning of Internal Improvements," *Political Science Quarterly* 63, no. 1 (1948): 16–44; Carter Goodrich, "The Gallatin

Plan After One Hundred and Fifty Years," *Proceedings of the American Philosophical Society* 102, no. 5 (1958): 436–41.

17. Leland Hamilton Jenks, *The Migration of British Capital to 1875* (London: Nelson, 1963), 74.

18. On the pattern of the initial crash, part recovery, and mixed implications of the crises of 1837–1843, see John Joseph Wallis, Richard E. Sylla, and Arthur Grinath, III, "Sovereign Debt and Repudiation: The Emerging-Market Debt Crisis in the U.S. States, 1839–1843" (National Bureau of Economic Research, 2004), NBER Working Paper no. 10753, 1–50.

19. See ibid., 12; Wilkins, *History of Foreign Investment to 1914*, 66–71.

20. "Veto Message of Governor M'nutt, of Mississippi," *U.S. Commercial and Statistical Register*, May 5, 1841, 276. The Rothschilds did not establish a lending relationship with Turkey until 1854; the rumor that they had acquired or wished to acquire Jerusalem was an anti-Semitic myth of long standing in the U.S. press. See Niall Ferguson, *The World's Banker: The History of the House of Rothschild* (London: Weidenfeld and Nicolson, 1998), 584 and 419–20.

21. Cited in Jay Sexton, *Debtor Diplomacy: Finance and American Foreign Relations in the Civil War Era, 1837–1873* (Oxford: Clarendon Press of Oxford University Press, 2005), 27.

22. Jeffrey G. Williamson, *American Growth and the Balance of Payments, 1820–1913: A Study of the Long Swing* (Chapel Hill: University of North Carolina Press, 1964), 106.

23. Davis and Gallman, *Evolving Financial Markets*, 204–9.

24. Wallis, Sylla, and Grinath, "Sovereign Debt," 23.

25. Sydney Smith, *Letters on American Debts* (London: Longman, Brown, Green and Longmans, 1843), 9, 14.

26. Ibid., 9, 14, 20.

27. "Mr. Charles Dickens' 'Reading,'" *New York Times*, July 22, 1857, 2.

28. Charles Dickens, *Christmas Stories*, 2 vols. (Philadelphia: T. B. Peterson, 1857), 1:47.

29. "Debts of the States," *North American Review* 58 (1844): 109–57, 109, 157.

30. On Barings and the campaign for American fiscal responsibility, see Sexton, *Debtor Diplomacy*, 40–45. The successful Mexican War brought some restoration of credit, but the ensuing sectional crisis damaged it again so that by 1859, U.S. bonds dropped below par. Sexton, *Debtor Diplomacy*, 78.

31. Sexton, *Debtor Diplomacy*, 87.
32. Ibid., 117–19. Mississippi stayed in default. Wilkins, *History of Foreign Investment to 1914*, 609.
33. Although the Confederacy was able to place one London loan in 1863, most of its funding had to come from domestic sources. Wilkins, *History of Foreign Investment to 1914*, 103. The placing of the loan, Jay Sexton notes, was supposed to serve political and diplomatic purposes, strengthening the Confederacy's position. In this it failed: "The mismanagement of the loan and its depreciating bonds discouraged future investment in Confederate securities and contributed to the South's long-term financial troubles abroad." Sexton, *Debtor Diplomacy*, 164–74.
34. Vincent P. Carosso, *Investment Banking in America* (Cambridge, Mass.: Harvard University Press, 1970), 15–17; Heather Cox Richardson, *The Greatest Nation of the Earth: Republican Economic Policies During the Civil War* (Cambridge, Mass.: Harvard University Press, 1997), 44.
35. Sexton, *Debtor Diplomacy*, 251–52.
36. Cleona Lewis and Karl T. Schlotterbeck, *America's Stake in International Investments* (Washington, D.C.: The Brookings Institution, 1938), 59. For conversion to modern money, Louis Johnston and Samuel H. Williamson, *The Annual Real and Nominal GDP for the United States, 1789–Present* (Economic History Services, March 2004); available from http://www.eh.net/hmit/gdp/ (accessed August 17, 2005).
37. On the rise of investment banks with the Civil War and their development of cooperative techniques, see Carosso, *Investment Banking in America*, 13–23, 52–53.
38. Davis and Gallman, *Evolving Financial Markets*, 759–61, 786–87, 793–800. Also, on Australia, see Victor S. Clark, "Australian Economic Problems. I. The Railways," *Quarterly Journal of Economics* 27, no. 3 (May 1908): 399–451.
39. The parenthetical question mark appears in the original. So do the capital letters. H. L. Loucks, *The Great Conspiracy of the House of Morgan, and How to Defeat It* (1916; reprint, New York: Arno, 1975), 57.
40. "An Act to aid in the Construction of a Railroad and Telegraph Line from the Missouri River to the Pacific Ocean, and to secure to the Government the Use of the same for Postal, Military, and Other Pur-

poses," July 1, 1862, 12 Stat. 489. Also David Haward Bain, *Empire Express: Building the First Transcontinental Railroad* (New York: Viking, 1999), 104–18; Richardson, *Greatest Nation*, 175–87.

41. Lloyd J. Mercer, "Taxpayers or Investors: Who Paid for the Land-Grant Railroads?," *Business History Review* 46, no. 3 (1972): 279–94. Mercer finds that in the case of other land-grant railroads the government made a "substantial contribution," though not by any means all or even most. One-third could be a larger estimate than warranted: see also Albert Fishlow, *American Railroads and the Transformation of the Antebellum Economy* (Cambridge, Mass.: Harvard University Press, 1965). But for the purposes of biasing the estimate against the argument in this book, we should consider the Union Pacific to be as heavily subsidized as plausible.

42. Mercer, "Taxpayers or Investors," 293.

43. J. Lorne McDougall, *Canadian Pacific: A Brief History* (Montreal: McGill University Press, 1968), 68. McDougall gives CP mileage in 1885 as 3,998 miles and in 1896 as 6,476 miles; in both cases this is about 40 percent of total mileage then open—10,273 and 16,270, respectively. B. R. Mitchell, *International Historical Statistics: The Americas, 1750–2000*, 5th ed. (New York: Palgrave Macmillan, 2003), series F1. For the United States see Lewis Henry Haney, *A Congressional History of Railways in the United States, 1850–1887* (Madison: University of Wisconsin, 1910), 14. Haney gives land-grant construction at 1886 as 17,724 miles, about 13.46 percent of the 131,649 miles then open, as noted in Mitchell, *International Historical Statistics: The Americas, 1750–2000*, series F1.

44. See also William S. Greever, "A Comparison of Railroad Land-Grant Policies," *Agricultural History* 25, no. 2 (1951): 83–90.

45. Other countries saw other patterns. In Australia governments made little use of land grants and either took over or simply built and ran railways themselves. Argentina guaranteed rates of return on railways securities. See Davis and Gallman, *Evolving Financial Markets*, 361, 483, 608, 720.

46. John Moody and George Kibbe Turner, "Morgan: The Great Trustee," *McClure's* 36 (1910): 3–25, 16.

47. See Ferguson, *World's Banker*, 763ff.

48. Priscilla Roberts, "The American 'Eastern Establishment' and World War I: The Emergence of a Foreign Policy Tradition" (Ph.D. dissertation, University of Cambridge, 1981), 32.

49. Peter Louis Galison, *Einstein's Clocks, Poincaré's Maps: Empires of Time* (New York: W. W. Norton, 2003); Neal Stephenson, "Mother Earth Mother Board," *Wired* 4, no. 12 (1996): 97–160, 98.
50. Cited in Arthur Charles Clarke, *How the World Was One: Beyond the Global Village* (New York: Bantam Books, 1992), 48.
51. J. Bradford DeLong, "Did J. P. Morgan's Men Add Value? A Historical Perspective on Financial Capitalism" (National Bureau of Economic Research, 1990), NBER Working Paper no. 3426, 1–37, 18–20; J. Bradford DeLong, "J. P. Morgan and His Money Trust," (1992), paper given at Harvard University, August 1992, 1–33, 17.
52. On building railroads ahead of demand, see Fishlow, *American Railroads*; Robert William Fogel, *The Union Pacific Railroad: A Case in Premature Enterprise* (Baltimore, Md.: Johns Hopkins University Press, 1960); Lloyd J. Mercer, "Buiding Ahead of Demand: Some Evidence for the Land Grant Railroads," *Journal of Economic History* 34, no. 2 (1974): 492–500.
53. Charles Francis Adams, Jr., "The Granger Movement," *North American Review* 120, no. 247 (1875): 394–424, 397–400.
54. Moody and Turner, "Morgan," 17.
55. Cited in Davis and Gallman, *Evolving Financial Markets*, 787.
56. Lance Edwin Davis and Robert J. Cull, *International Capital Markets and American Economic Growth, 1820–1914* (Cambridge: Cambridge University Press, 1994), 61; Jean Strouse, *Morgan: American Financier* (New York: Random House, 1999), 248–49.
57. "One Opinion," *The Wall Street Journal*, October 29, 1889, 2. On "the embryo," see Strouse, *Morgan*, 249.
58. Moody and Turner, "Morgan," 17.
59. Ibid.
60. Cited in Anthony Perl, "Public Enterprise as an Expression of Sovereignty: Reconsidering the Origin of Canadian National Railways," *Canadian Journal of Political Science* 27, no. 1 (1994): 23–52, 42. On the comparability of Canadian protest politics to American protest politics, see J. F. Conway, "Populism in the United States, Russia, and Canada: Explaining the Roots of Canada's Third Parties," *Canadian Journal of Political Science* 11, no. 1 (1978): 99–124.
61. H.G.J. Aitken, "Defensive Expansion: The State and Economic Growth in Canada," in *Approaches to Canadian Economic History*, ed. W. T. Easterbrook and M. H. Watkins (Toronto: McClelland and Stewart, 1967), 181–221.
62. Raymond H. Polley, "The Railroad and Argentine National Develop-

ment, 1852–1914," *The Americas* 23, no. 1 (July 1966): 63–75; Winthrop R. Wright, "Foreign-Owned Railways in Argentina: A Case Study of Economic Nationalism," *Business History Review* 41, no. 1 (Spring 1967): 62–93.

63. William R. Summerhill, "Market Intervention in a Backward Economy: Railway Subsidy in Brazil, 1854–1913," *Economic History Review* 51, no. 3 (August 1998): 542–68, esp. 562–63.

64. Support for nationalization remained a minority position in the United States. See Thomas Frank, "The Leviathan with Tentacles of Steel: Railroads in the Minds of Kansas Populists," *Western Historical Quarterly* 20, no. 1 (1989): 37–54.

65. Henry Adams, *The Education of Henry Adams*, ed. Ernest Samuels and Jayne N. Samuels, *Novels, Mont Saint Michel, The Education* (New York: Literary Classics of the United States, 1983), 940.

66. On the politics of the new states, see Nolan McCarty, Keith T. Poole, and Howard Rosenthal, "Congress and the Territorial Expansion of the United States," in *Party, Process, and Political Change in Congress: New Perspectives on the History of Congress*, ed. David W. Brady and Mathew D. McCubbins (Stanford, Calif.: Stanford University Press, 2002), 392–451; Charles Stewart, III, and Barry R. Weingast, "Stacking the Senate, Changing the Nation: Republican Rotten Boroughs, Statehood Politics, and American Political Development," *Studies in American Political Development* 6 (1992): 223–71.

67. John Franklin Crowell, "Railway Receiverships in the United States," *Yale Review* 7, no. 3 (1898): 319–30, 323.

68. W. H. Harvey, *Coin on Money, Trusts, and Imperialism* (1899; reprint, Westport, Conn.: Hyperion Press, 1975), 80–82.

69. Strouse, *Morgan*, 680–81.

70. Allan H. Meltzer, *A History of the Federal Reserve, 1913–1951* (Chicago: University of Chicago Press, 2003), 74.

71. "Wilson Fighting to Retain Warburg," *New York Times*, July 8, 1914, 1.

72. Charles Austin Beard and William Beard, *American Leviathan: The Republic in the Machine Age* (New York: Macmillan, 1930), 365.

73. Paul M. Warburg, "The Owen-Glass Bill as Submitted to the Democratic Caucus: Some Criticisms and Suggestions," in *The Federal Reserve System: Its Origin and Growth* (New York: Macmillan, 1930), 251–67.

74. Faulkner, *Decline*, 170. See also Strouse, *Morgan*, 469–70.

75. "Jones Rejected by Committee," *New York Times*, July 10, 1914, 1.

76. See, e.g., "Federal Reserve Board Nominations in Muddle," *Nevada State Journal*, July 8, 1914; "If Foxes Were Hounds," *Atlanta Constitution*, July 12, 1914; "Opposing Senators Are Seeking Full Publicity," *Wichita Daily Times*, July 12, 1914; "President Wilson Praised for Appointments to Board," *Atlanta Constitution*, May 10, 1914; "Warburg Asks to Be Withdrawn," *New York Times*, July 7, 1914; "Wilson Fighting to Retain Warburg."

77. "Let It All Be Told," *Washington Post*, July 12, 1914, 1.

78. "Warburg's Replies Satisfy Senators," *New York Times*, August 2, 1914, 11.

Chapter 3: Labor

1. Timothy J. Hatton and Jeffrey G. Williamson, *The Age of Mass Migration: Causes and Economic Impact* (New York: Oxford University Press, 1998), 7. A much smaller number of Asians and Africans came also. But because New World nations had adopted racially restrictive laws and because the great push for emigration relied on modern economic and technological factors that did not exist in Asia or Africa, fewer migrants came from those continents than from Europe.

2. John Bodnar, *The Transplanted: A History of Immigrants in Urban America* (1985; reprint, Bloomington: Indiana University Press, 1987).

3. Hatton and Williamson, *Age of Mass Migration*, 7.

4. Bodnar, *Transplanted*, 60; Herbert S. Klein, "The Integration of Italian Immigrants into the United States and Argentina: A Comparative Analysis," *American Historical Review* 88, no. 2 (1983): 306–29. Although this difference in intent and region of origin is evident, there is no point exaggerating it, either: on the whole, Italians who went to Argentina returned home almost as often as those who went to the United States. See Jeremy Adelman, *Frontier Development: Land, Labour, and Capital on the Wheatlands of Argentina and Canada, 1890–1914* (Oxford: Clarendon Press of Oxford University Press, 1994), 112–13.

5. Mark Wyman, *Round-Trip to America: The Immigrants Return to Europe, 1880–1930* (Ithaca, N.Y.: Cornell University Press, 1993), 9–12.

6. On Australia, see B. R. Mitchell, *International Historical Statistics: Africa, Asia and Oceania, 1750–2000*, 4th ed. (New York: Palgrave Macmillan, 2003), 87, table A8. Also David Pope and Glenn Withers, "Do Migrants Rob Jobs? Lessons of Australian History, 1861–1991," *Journal of Economic History* 53, no. 4 (1993): 719–42. On Canada,

see Duncan M. McDougall, "Immigration into Canada, 1851–1920," *Canadian Journal of Economics and Political Science* 27, no. 2 (1961): 162–75. On Argentina, see A. G. Ford, "British Investment in Argentina and Long Swings, 1880–1914," *Journal of Economic History* 31, no. 3 (1971): 650–63. On Canada and Argentina compared, see Adelman, *Frontier Development*. For the United States, see Bernard Axelrod, "Historical Studies of Emigration from the United States," *International Migration Review* 6, no. 1 (1972): 32–49; Campbell Gibson, "The Contribution of Immigration to the Growth and Ethnic Diversity of the American Population," *Proceedings of the American Philosophical Society* 136, no. 2 (1992): 157–75; Campbell Gibson, "The Contribution of Immigration to United States Population Growth: 1790–1970," *International Migration Review* 9, no. 2 (1975): 157–77.

7. Adelman, *Frontier Development*, 109–10.

8. Imre Ferenczi and Walter Francis Willcox, *International Migrations*, 2 vols. (New York: National Bureau of Economic Research, 1929), table 13, 1:267–70.

9. Todd DePastino, *Citizen Hobo: How a Century of Homelessness Shaped America* (Chicago: University of Chicago Press, 2003), 67.

10. Steven Ruggles, Matthew Sobek, et al., *Integrated Public Use Microdata Series: Version 3.0* (Minneapolis: Population Center, 2004), available from http://www.ipums.org. The IPUMS sample shows the rural/urban ratio of internal migrants in the 1880 census as 74:26 at a time when the population as a whole was 71:29, whereas the rural/urban ratio of internal migrants in the 1910 census was 52:48 at a time when the population as a whole was 54:46.

11. Ibid. Immigrants in the 1880 sample appear as 44:55 rural/urban, and in 1910 as 28:72. The shift in character of immigrants is illustrated in the 1910 sample because there the immigrants who came after 1890 appear as 25:75 rural/urban, whereas immigrants who came before 1890 split 34:66.

12. Ibid.

13. Hatton and Williamson, *Age of Mass Migration*, 11. The figures are 76 percent aged 15–40 among migrants as against 45 percent of the U.S. population at 1910; 64 percent of migrants were men as against 52 percent of the U.S. population at 1910. U.S. figures from Ruggles et al., *IPUMS*.

14. Walter Augustus Wyckoff, *The Workers, an Experiment in Reality: The East* (1897; reprint, New York: Charles Scribner's Sons, 1903);

Walter Augustus Wyckoff, *The Workers, an Experiment in Reality: The West* (1898; reprint, New York: Charles Scribner's Sons, 1900).

15. Wyckoff, *Workers: East*; Wyckoff, *Workers: West*.

16. Wyckoff, *Workers: East*, 55.

17. Lipset and Marks, *It Didn't Happen Here*, 129.

18. Israel Zangwill, *The Melting Pot: Drama in Four Acts*, new and rev. ed. (New York: Macmillan, 1914), afterword, 215.

19. Figures from B. R. Mitchell, *International Historical Statistics: The Americas, 1750–2000*, 5th ed. (New York: Palgrave Macmillan, 2003), tables A1 (population in enumeration years) and A8 (international migrations).

20. Zangwill, *Melting Pot*, 215.

21. Randolph Silliman Bourne, "Trans-National America," in *War and the Intellectuals: Collected Essays, 1915–1919*, ed. Carl Resek (New York: Harper, 1964), 109.

22. Hatton and Williamson, *Age of Mass Migration*, 32–74, 130–53.

23. See, e.g., Henry B. Leonard, "Ethnic Cleavage and Industrial Conflict in Late Nineteenth-Century America: The Cleveland Rolling Mill Company Strikes of 1882 and 1885," *Labor History* 20, no. 4 (1979): 524–48, 42; Ronald T. Takaki, *Strangers from a Different Shore: A History of Asian Americans* (New York: Penguin Books, 1990).

24. Philip S. Foner, *History of the Labor Movement in the United States*, 7 vols. (New York: International Publishers, 1955), 364.

25. Lipset and Marks, *It Didn't Happen Here*, 134.

26. Henry George, "Labor in Pennsylvania," *North American Review* 143, no. 359 (1886): 360–71, 360–61.

27. Henry George, "England and Ireland," *North American Review* 142, no. 351 (1886): 185–93, 186.

28. Lance Edwin Davis, Richard A. Easterlin, et al., *American Economic Growth: An Economist's History of the United States* (New York: Harper & Row, 1972), 138, table 5.7; Ruggles et al., *IPUMS*.

29. These observations derived by tabulating the nativity of people by occupation code and the birthplaces of the foreign-born in the iron and steel industries in the 1910 census sample. Ruggles et al., *IPUMS*.

30. Wyckoff, *Workers: West*, 168.

31. Ibid., 132–33.

32. Nels Anderson, *The Hobo: The Sociology of the Homeless Man* (Chicago: University of Chicago Press, 1923), 87.

33. Hatton and Williamson, *Age of Mass Migration*, 168. Also Hope T. Eldridge and Dorothy Swaine Thomas, *Demographic Analyses and Interrelations*, ed. Simon Kuznets, vol. 3, *Population Redistribution and Economic Growth* (Philadelphia: American Philosophical Society, 1964), 71–75; Carter Goodrich et al., *Migration and Economic Opportunity: The Report of the Study of Population Redistribution* (Philadelphia: University of Pennsylvania Press, 1936), 679–85.

34. For the classic dissent from Turner's "safety valve" thesis, see Carter Goodrich and Sol Davidson, "The Wage-Earner in the Westward Movement I," *Political Science Quarterly* 50, no. 2 (June 1935): 161–85, and "The Wage-Earner in the Westward Movement II," *Political Science Quarterly* 51, no. 1 (March 1936): 61–116. Goodrich and Davidson dispute Turner's idea that factory workers settled western lands. They do not, they note, address the question of whether "the growing industries of the Middle West recruited their labor supply from eastern wage-earners," and indeed they confirm that "the abundance of western land drew away many thousands of *potential* wage-earners who might otherwise have crowded into the factories." Goodrich and Davidson, "Wage-Earner II," 115; emphasis in the original.

Drawing on this analysis, Richard C. Overton noted that "the factory worker, despite his hardships, stayed with his trade however much he shifted his scene of operations," and that "the growing industrial importance of the Pacific Coast after 1910 offered a fresh start to the discontented Eastern or foreign laborer who could move. To the extent that he availed himself of this opportunity he fed the stream of westward expansion." Richard C. Overton, "Westward Expansion Since the Homestead Act," 342–78, in Harold F. Williamson, ed., *The Growth of the American Economy: An Introduction to the Economic History of the United States* (New York: Prentice-Hall, 1946), 360.

But beyond this, it is worth noting that Joseph P. Ferrie has more recently discovered a relationship between geographic and occupational mobility in the nineteenth-century United States, for both laborers and more-skilled workers, and resurrected a version of the safety-valve thesis, critiquing what he calls Goodrich and Davidson's "anecdotal" methods. See Joseph P. Ferrie, "Up and Out or Down and Out? Immigrant Mobility in the Antebellum United States," *Journal of Interdisciplinary History* 26, no. 1 (Summer 1995): 33–55; Jason Long and Joseph Ferrie, "A Tale of Two Labor Markets: Intergenerational Occupational Mobility in Britain and the U.S. Since 1850," (National Bureau of Economic Research, 2005) NBER Working Paper no. 11253; and Joseph P. Ferrie, "The End of American Exceptionalism: Mobility in the U.S. Since 1850," (National Bureau of Economic Research, 2005), NBER Working Paper no. 11324.

35. DePastino, *Citizen Hobo*, 13–15.

36. See, e.g., Hatton and Williamson, *Age of Mass Migration*, 169.

37. Roger Daniels points out that this language rather dehumanizes immigrants. But it is often unavoidable when describing the patterns made by the movements of great numbers of people. See Roger Daniels and Otis L. Graham, *Debating American Immigration, 1882–Present* (Lanham, Md.: Rowman & Littlefield, 2001), 7.

38. On appropriations of Xenophon see Tim Rood, *The Sea! The Sea!: The Shout of the Ten Thousand in the Modern Imagination* (London: Duckworth Overlook, 2005).

39. This includes those living in New Mexico and Arizona, which were still territories at 1910. Ruggles et al., *IPUMS*.

40. People of Mexican birth were 39 percent of the post-1890 immigrant population in the former Confederacy at 1910. The next-largest new immigrant ethnicity was Italian, at 12 percent, and the largest part of them—40 percent—lived in Louisiana. Ibid.

41. Ibid. In the 1920 census, the proportion of African Americans from the South in those states rose to almost 44 percent. On the isolation of the South from the national and international markets of the nineteenth century, see principally Gavin Wright, *Old South, New South: Revolutions in the Southern Economy Since the Civil War* (New York: Basic, 1986). Also see David F. Good, "Uneven Development in the Nineteenth Century: A Comparison of the Habsburg Empire and the United States," *Journal of Economic History* 46, no. 1 (1986): 137–51; Joshua L. Rosenbloom, "One Market or Many? Labor Market Integration in the Late Nineteenth-Century United States," *Journal of Economic History* 50, no. 1 (1990): 85–07.

42. Remarks of Congressman Robert Switzer, Republican of Ohio. *Congressional Record*, 63d Cong., 3d Sess., v. 52, pt. 3 (February 4, 1915), p. 3034.

43. An Act to Make Provision for Certain Immigrants, no. 39 of 1855, Parliament of Victoria; available from http://www.foundingdocs.gov .au/places/vic/vic4.htm#description (accessed March 11, 2005). See Robert A. Huttenback, *Racism and Empire: White Settlers and Col-*

ored Immigrants in the British Self-Governing Colonies, 1830–1910 (Ithaca, N.Y.: Cornell University Press, 1976), 62.

44. A. H. Charteris, "Australian Immigration Policy," *International Conciliation* 235 (1927): 515–46, 522–23; Huttenback, *Racism and Empire*, 69. Through the 1860s and 1870s some legislatures repealed such laws only to adopt them again. See Huttenback, *Racism and Empire*, 62–125.

45. The "Asiatic barred zone" covered the continent of Asia west of longitude 110° east (thus sweeping in the Indo-Chinese peninsula), east of longitude 50° east (roughly, those countries east of the Caspian Sea), and south of latitude 50° north, so including Turkestan southward. The zone included a cutout rectangle exempting Persia, which was covered under a separate arrangement, and did not include Japan or China, also covered under separate arrangements, and under the 1917 law's specification that "no alien now in any way excluded from, or prevented from entering, the United States shall be admitted." The law also specified a further, oceanic excluded zone south of latitude 20° north, west of longitude 160° east, and north of latitude 10° south, barring natives of islands that were not U.S. territories. 39 Stat. 874, 876. See also "Meets Japan's Objections," *New York Times*, May 17, 1916, 3.

46. U.S. Department of Labor (Bureau of Immigration), *Annual Report of the Commissioner General of Immigration to the Secretary of Labor* (Washington, D.C.: Government Printing Office, 1917), xx.

47. *Congressional Record*, 64th Cong., 2d Sess., 54, pt. 3: 2619.

48. Veto message of President Wilson, dated January 29, 1917, in *Congressional Record*, 64th Cong., 2d Sess., 54, pt. 3: 2443.

49. Michael Perman, *Struggle for Mastery: Disfranchisement in the South, 1888–1908* (Chapel Hill: University of North Carolina Press, 2001), 85.

50. Huttenback, *Racism and Empire*, 141.

51. "An act to place certain restrictions on Immigration and provide for the removal from the Commonwealth of prohibited Immigrants (no. 17 of 1901)," Attorney General's Department, reference A1559, 1901/17, National Archives of Australia, and "Dictation test passages—draft," from 1925, Department of Home and Territories, reference A1, 1935/704, National Archives of Australia. Both available through "Virtual Reading Room," National Archives of Australia, http://www.xpoint.com.au/vrroom/ (accessed May 25, 2005). See also Charteris, "Australian Immigration Policy."

52. "An Act to Regulate the Immigration of Aliens to, and the Residence of Aliens in, the United States," 39 Stat. 874, 877.
53. Veto message of President Wilson.
54. "The Labor Exclusion Bill," New York Times, January 20, 1917, 10.
55. Congressional Record, 63d Cong., 3d Sess., 52, pt. 4: 3014–15.
56. Ruggles et al., IPUMS. This is for the 1910 sample, including as literate only those who could both read and write (i.e., with the answer "Yes, literate").
57. Claudia Goldin, "The Political Economy of Immigration Restriction in the United States, 1890–1921," in The Regulated Economy, ed. Claudia Goldin and Gary D. Libecap (Chicago: University of Chicago Press, 1994), 223–57.
58. Congressional Record, 64th Cong., 2d Sess., 54, pt. 3: 2450.
59. Roll call on overturning the president's veto of the immigration restriction bill (literacy test), House, Congressional Record, 64th Cong, 2d Sess., 54, pt. 3: 2456–57. Of 106 "no" votes, only 6 came from states of the former Confederacy and 5 from the post–Civil War states.
60. Cited in Rowland T. Berthoff, "Southern Attitudes Toward Immigration, 1865–1914," Journal of Southern History 17, no. 3 (1951): 328–60, 330–31.
61. Goldin, "Political Economy."
62. U.S. Department of Labor (Bureau of Immigration), Annual Report of the Commissioner General of Immigration to the Secretary of Labor (Washington, D.C.: Government Printing Office, 1919), 15.

Chapter 4: Welfare

1. Harold Wilensky, cited in Peter H. Lindert, "The Rise of Social Spending, 1880–1930," Explorations in Economic History 31 (1994): 1–37, 2.
2. Great Britain Inter-departmental Committee on Social Insurance and Allied Services and William Henry Beveridge, Social Insurance and Allied Services, American ed. (New York: Macmillan, 1942), 170.
3. Andrew Roth in The Nation, cited in Daniel T. Rodgers, Atlantic Crossings: Social Politics in a Progressive Age (Cambridge, Mass.: Belknap Press of Harvard University Press, 1998), 501.
4. The original version of the much-borrowed and -abused phrase that serves as the title to this section is the question, which rested on an inaccurate premise, "Why is there no socialism in the United States?," from the 1906 book by the German economist Werner Sombart, Warum Gibt Es in Den Vereinigten Staaten Keinen Sozialismus? (Tübingen: J.C.B. Mohr [Paul Siebeck], 1906).

5. And indeed why the United States never had a proper welfare state with the philosophical apparatus characteristic of other countries. See Seymour Martin Lipset and Gary Wolfe Marks, *It Didn't Happen Here: Why Socialism Failed in the United States* (New York: W. W. Norton, 2000), 284–92.

6. Otto Pflanze, *Bismarck and the Development of Germany*, 2d ed., 3 vols. (Princeton, N.J.: Princeton University Press, 1990), 3:156.

7. For models of *how* welfare states grew, see Peter Flora and Arnold J. Heidenheimer, *The Development of Welfare States in Europe and America* (New Brunswick, N.J.: Transaction, 1981), esp. 17–121. For a subsequent reconsideration of *why* they grew, see Peter H. Lindert, *Growing Public: Social Spending and Economic Growth Since the Eighteenth Century* (Cambridge: Cambridge University Press, 2004).

8. Debs cited in Sari Bennett, "The Geography of American Socialism: Continuity and Change, 1900–1912," *Social Science History* 7, no. 3 (1983): 267–88, 282; see also analysis on 282–84.

9. Cited in Lipset and Marks, *It Didn't Happen Here*, 157.

10. *Congressional Record*, 63d Cong., 3d Sess., 52, pt. 3: 3028.

11. Jeffery A. Jenkins, Eric Schickler, and Jamie L. Carson, "Constituency Cleavages and Congressional Parties: Measuring Homogeneity and Polarization, 1857–1913," *Social Science History* 28, no. 4 (2004): 537–73, 551–52. Some presidential voting patterns are similarly suggestive. The general pattern holds at the state level over a number of elections as well. Eric Rauchway, "The New Electorate and Progressive Policies, 1884–1917," paper presented at Organization of American Historians Annual Meeting, Boston, 2004.

12. See also Lipset and Marks, *It Didn't Happen Here*, 145–54; Gerald Rosenblum, *Immigrant Workers: Their Impact on American Labor Radicalism* (New York: Basic Books, 1973).

13. Cited in Nick Salvatore, *Eugene V. Debs: Citizen and Socialist* (Urbana: University of Illinois Press, 1982), 245. See also Ira Kipnis, *The American Socialist Movement, 1897–1912* (New York: Columbia University Press, 1952), 276–88.

14. Robert F. Hoxie, "The Socialist Party in the November Elections," *Journal of Political Economy* 20, no. 3 (1912): 205–23, 215–16n.

15. Salvatore, *Debs*, 198.

16. Hoxie, "Socialist Party," 215n.

17. On the geographic, non-class basis of American socialism, see Robert F. Hoxie, "'The Rising Tide of Socialism': A Study," *Journal of Political Economy* 19, no. 8 (1911): 609–31. Also see Bennett, "Geography."

18. This relationship changed in the later twentieth century. Lindert, "Rise of Social Spending," 22–23.

19. Lindert, *Growing Public*, 179–88; Lindert, "Rise of Social Spending," 16–24.

20. B. R. Mitchell, *International Historical Statistics: Africa, Asia and Oceania, 1750–2000*, 4th ed. (New York: Palgrave Macmillan, 2003), tables A1 and A2; B. R. Mitchell, *International Historical Statistics: Europe, 1750–2000*, 5th ed. (New York: Palgrave Macmillan, 2003), tables A1 and A2; B. R. Mitchell, *International Historical Statistics: The Americas, 1750–2000*, 5th ed. (New York: Palgrave Macmillan, 2003), tables A1 and A2.

21. Peter H. Lindert, "The Rise of Social Spending, 1880–1930," University of California–Davis Agricultural History Center Working Paper no. 68 (1992), 90–94.

22. Kevin H. O'Rourke and Jeffrey G. Williamson, *Globalization and History: The Evolution of a Nineteenth-Century Atlantic Economy* (Cambridge, Mass.: MIT Press, 1999), 175–76.

23. The United States remains within the predictions of Lindert's model until the decade of the 1920s, when it spends considerably less than the model would predict. Lindert, "Rise of Social Spending."

24. Taliesin Evans, *American Citizenship and the Right of Suffrage in the United States* (Oakland, Calif.: Tribune Print, 1892), 143–44.

25. Alexander Keyssar, *The Right to Vote: The Contested History of Democracy in the United States* (New York: Basic Books, 2000), 136–41. Also Ronald Hayduk, "Noncitizen Voting Rights: Shifts in Immigrant Political Status During the Progressive Era," (Boston: Annual Meeting of the American Political Science Association, 2002), 1–28.

26. James T. Kloppenberg, *Uncertain Victory: Social Democracy and Progressivism in European and American Thought, 1870–1920* (New York: Oxford University Press, 1986).

27. Jane Addams in 1912, cited in Rodgers, *Atlantic Crossings*, 74.

28. This is a major argument in ibid.

29. Charles Austin Beard, *American City Government: A Survey of Newer Tendencies* (New York: Century, 1912), 19–20. Beard could also be classed as a historian or a reformer, depending on the context.

30. Ibid., 22–24.

31. Certainly such factors seem to characterize modern discussions of welfare policies, so that the more a policy benefits a group of people defined as culturally or racially different, the less popular it is. See

Lindert, *Growing Public*, 186–88. Also Alberto Alesina and Edward L. Glaeser, *Fighting Poverty in the U.S. and Europe: A World of Difference* (New York: Oxford University Press, 2004), 133–81.

32. R. A. Musgrave and J. M. Culbertson, "The Growth of Public Expenditures in the United States, 1890–1948," *National Tax Journal* 6, no. 2 (1953): 97–115, 113, appendix table III. Local government spending on health and sanitation increased from $30.6 million to $91.8 million between 1902 and 1913, and to $303.4 million in 1923. In 1902, local spending on assistance was $42.8 million, and it had increased only to $63.7 million by 1913. The excess of spending on health over assistance persisted until, probably, the Depression: local poor relief almost tripled from 1923 to 1932, while spending on health and sanitation stayed almost level.

33. Beard, *American City Government*, 262.

34. For the purposes of this discussion, the universe of major cities means the 198 cities of over 30,000 population found in both the 1910 IPUMS sample and in U.S. Census, *Wealth, Debt, and Taxation: 1913*, vol. II, pt. 8 (Washington, D.C.: Government Printing Office, 1915). Everett, Washington, appears in *Wealth, Debt, and Taxation*, but it had only just crested 30,000 population as of the 1913 estimate, and it does not appear in the 1910 IPUMS sample. Ruggles et al., *IPUMS*.

35. Cited in Charles E. Rosenberg, *The Cholera Years: The United States in 1832, 1849, and 1866*, with a new afterword (Chicago: University of Chicago Press, 1987), 215.

36. Werner Troesken, *Water, Race, and Disease* (Cambridge, Mass.: MIT Press, 2004), 65–73.

37. Cited in Martin V. Melosi, *The Sanitary City: Urban Infrastructure in America from Colonial Times to the Present* (Baltimore, Md.: Johns Hopkins University Press, 2000), 112.

38. Louis P. Cain and Elyce J. Rotella, "Death and Spending: Urban Mortality and Municipal Expenditure on Sanitation," *Annales de Démographie Historique* (2001): 139–54, 139. This is over the years 1902 to 1929.

39. Michael R. Haines, "The Urban Mortality Transition in the United States, 1800–1940," *Annales de Démographie Historique* (2001): 33–64, 47. Haines finds that, by the 1920s, white infant mortality was the same in the cities as in the countryside, and that overall the rural/urban gap disappeared by 1940.

40. Cited in Cain and Rotella, "Death and Spending," 139.
41. Ibid., 146.
42. Beard, *American City Government*, 25–26.
43. Per capita spending on schools in 1913 averaged $4.45 nationwide among 196 cities with populations over 30,000 for which there is data. In the 167 cities outside the former Confederacy, the mean per capita spending on schools was $4.76. In the 29 cities in the former Confederacy, it was $2.68. U.S. Census, *Wealth, Debt, and Taxation: 1913*. The influence of the factors mentioned here holds up when accounting for the influence of other factors; see appendix table.
44. Per capita spending on health and sanitation in 1913 averaged $1.28 nationwide among 198 cities for which there is data. In the 167 cities outside the former Confederacy, the mean per capita spending on health and sanitation was $1.25. In the 31 cities in the former Confederacy, it was $1.47. Ibid.
45. Werner Troesken, "The Limits of Jim Crow: Race and the Provision of Water and Sewerage Services in American Cities, 1880–1925," *Journal of Economic History* 62, no. 3 (2002): 734–72, 741.
46. Michael Perman, *Struggle for Mastery: Disfranchisement in the South, 1888–1908* (Chapel Hill: University of North Carolina Press, 2001), 264–68.
47. David M. Cutler, Edward L. Glaeser, and Jacob L. Vigdor, "The Rise and Decline of the American Ghetto," *Journal of Political Economy* 107, no. 3 (1999): 455–506.
48. Cited in Stuart Galishoff, "Germs Know No Color Line: Black Health and Public Policy in Atlanta, 1900–1918," *Journal of the History of Medicine and Allied Sciences* 40, no. 1 (1985): 22–41, 29.
49. Streetcar companies and blacks resisted streetcar segregation, which finally went into effect in the South by 1906. Perman, *Struggle for Mastery*, 266.
50. Nationwide, the 104 cities with a below-average percentage of foreign-born spent $1.15 per capita, while the 94 cities with above-average concentrations spent $1.43, or 24 percent more. Essentially the same difference obtained among non-southern cities. Dora Costa and Matthew Kahn find these results, and those for African Americans, consistent over the early twentieth century in a working paper. See Dora L. Costa and Matthew E. Kahn, "Public Health and Mortality: What Can We Learn from the Past?" (Berkeley, Calif.: Symposium on Poverty, December 2003).
51. Cited in Susan Craddock, *City of Plagues: Disease, Poverty, and*

Deviance in San Francisco (Minneapolis: University of Minnesota Press, 2000), 82.

52. At 1913, San Francisco spent $1.50 per capita on health and sanitation, 17 percent above the national average. U.S. Census, *Wealth, Debt, and Taxation: 1913.*

53. Cited in Nayan Shah, *Contagious Divides: Epidemics and Race in San Francisco's Chinatown* (Berkeley: University of California Press, 2001), 53.

54. Among the 94 cities with above-average shares of foreign-born, those with below-average concentrations of new immigrants spent $1.47 per capita on health and sanitation, while those with above-average concentrations spent $1.35, or 8 percent less. In non-southern states alone, the figures were $1.45 and $1.35, for a difference of 7.4 percent.

55. Cited in Galishoff, "Germs Know No Color Line," 29.

56. Troesken, "Limits of Jim Crow," 739–41.

57. David M. Cutler, Edward L. Glaeser, and Jacob L. Vigdor, "Ghettos and the Transmission of Ethnic Capital," in *Ethnicity, Social Mobility and Public Policy,* ed. Glenn C. Loury, Tariq Modood, and Steven M. Teles, 204–21 (Cambridge: Cambridge University Press, 2005), 206. Also Stanley Lieberson, *Ethnic Patterns in American Cities* (New York: Free Press of Glencoe, 1963), 65–73.

58. Cited in Howard Markel, *Quarantine! East European Jewish Immigrants and the New York City Epidemics of 1892* (Baltimore, Md.: Johns Hopkins University Press, 1997), 34.

59. The largest share (about 38 percent) of new immigrants employed as factory operatives in major cities were working in the apparel industry. Ruggles et al., *IPUMS.*

60. See, e.g., the description of Down Neck, or Ironbound, the neighborhood near the iron foundries of Newark, in Stuart Galishoff, *Newark: The Nation's Unhealthiest City, 1832–1895* (New Brunswick, N.J.: Rutgers University Press, 1988), 65.

61. This said, segregation is not the same as isolation, as the example of Chinatown suggests. The Chinese were concentrated in a community separate from other San Franciscans, but that community was highly visible, given its location. The different locations of different ethnic ghettos, as well as the different work interactions with other Americans, might have had differing effects. In addition, immigrant communities sometimes resisted health laws for cultural reasons, and also paid the price for doing so. See ibid., 103, 191–92; Alan M. Kraut, "Southern Italian Immigration to the United States at the Turn of the

Century and the Perennial Problem of Medicalised Prejudice," in *Migrants, Minorities, and Health: Historical and Contemporary Studies*, ed. Lara Marks and Michael Worboys (London: Routledge, 1997), 228–49; Judith Walzer Leavitt, *The Healthiest City: Milwaukee and the Politics of Health Reform* (Princeton, N.J.: Princeton University Press, 1982), 83–84.

62. Jane Addams, *Newer Ideals of Peace* (New York: Macmillan, 1907), 14.

63. Steven P. Erie, *Rainbow's End: Irish-Americans and the Dilemmas of Urban Machine Politics, 1840–1985* (Berkeley: University of California Press, 1988); Terrence J. McDonald, *The Parameters of Urban Fiscal Policy: Socioeconomic Change and Political Culture in San Francisco, 1860–1906* (Berkeley: University of California Press, 1986).

64. E. P. Hutchinson, *Immigrants and Their Children, 1850–1950* (New York: John Wiley & Sons, 1956), 59–60, 276.

65. Beard, *American City Government*, 262–63.

66. R. B. Haldane, *Report of the Machinery of Government Committee* (London: H.M. Stationery Office, 1918), 59.

67. Melosi, *Sanitary City*, 109. On the growth of state power at the local level, see also Michael Willrich, *City of Courts: Socializing Justice in Progressive Era Chicago* (Cambridge: Cambridge University Press, 2003).

68. Reuben A. Kessel, "The A.M.A. and the Supply of Physicians," *Law and Contemporary Problems* 35, no. 2 (1970): 267–83, 270; Charles E. Rosenberg, *The Care of Strangers: The Rise of America's Hospital System* (New York: Free Press, 1987), 209–11.

69. Spending on education at the local level in the United States increased from $175.5 million in 1902 to $375.6 million in 1913 and $1,242.5 million in 1923. The United States was an early international leader in public schooling, and Americans' interest in public schooling is often attributed to their desire to Americanize immigrants. See Musgrave and Culbertson, "The Growth of Public Expenditures," appendix table III; Lindert, *Growing Public*, 87–127; and Michael B. Katz, "The Origins of Public Education: A Reassessment," *History of Education Quarterly* 16, no. 4 (1976): 381–407, esp. 394.

70. Committee on Public Information, *National Service Handbook*, (Washington, D.C.: Government Printing Office, 1917), 3–4.

71. Ibid., 4.

72. Theodore Roosevelt, *An Autobiography*, ed. Hermann Hagedorn, national ed., 20 vols., vol. 20, *Works of Theodore Roosevelt* (New

York: Charles Scribner's Sons, 1926), 397; Walter Irving Swanton, *Some Opinions About President Roosevelt* (n.d. [1901–1904?]).
73. Roosevelt, *Autobiography*, 455.
74. Herbert Croly, *The Promise of American Life* (1909; reprint, Boston: Northeastern University Press, 1989), 35.
75. Ibid., 168.
76. Charles Austin Beard, *Contemporary American History, 1877–1913* (New York: Macmillan, 1914), 254.
77. Although the U.S. Constitution created the District of Columbia, it had been made the City of Washington in the early nineteenth century and remained so until the Congress re-created it as a territory in 1871. Legislation of 1874 created the district anew, after which a board of presidentially appointed commissioners governed it. See *United States Government Manual* (Washington, D.C.: Division of Public Inquiries, Office of War Information, 1945), 473–74. The Post Office had previously been treated informally as a cabinet post. The Department of Education, created in 1867, was demoted to an office in 1869, returning to cabinet level in 1979. See Mark Grossman, ed., *Encyclopedia of the United States Cabinet,* 3 vols. (Santa Barbara, Calif.: ABC-CLIO, 2000).
78. Harold T. Pinkett, "The Keep Commission, 1905–1909: A Rooseveltian Effort for Administrative Reform," *Journal of American History* 52, no. 2 (1965): 297–312, 310.
79. *U.S. Government Manual,* 612–13.
80. The taxonomy of functions is that of Haldane, *Report of the Machinery of Government Committee.*
81. See Eric Rauchway, "The High Cost of Living in the Progressives' Economy," *Journal of American History* 88, no. 3 (2001): 898–924.
82. See Kriste Lindenmeyer, *A Right to Childhood: The U.S. Children's Bureau and Child Welfare, 1912–46* (Urbana: University of Illinois Press, 1997).
83. See Steven R. Weisman, *The Great Tax Wars: Lincoln to Wilson* (New York: Simon & Schuster, 2002), 281–308.
84. *Employers' Liability Cases,* 207 U.S. 463, 498 (1908).
85. "Various Opinions," *Wall Street Journal,* November 23, 1889, 2. But see Paul Kens, "The Source of a Myth: Police Powers of the States and Laissez Faire Constitutionalism, 1900–1937," *American Journal of Legal History* 35, no. 1 (1991): 70–98; William J. Novak, "Public Economy and the Well-Ordered Market: Law and Economic

Regulation in 19th-Century America," *Law & Social Inquiry* 18, no. 1 (1993): 1–32.

86. Flora and Heidenheimer, *Development of Welfare States*, 51.
87. Lindert, *Growing Public*, 20–21.
88. Charles Stewart III and Barry R. Weingast, "Stacking the Senate, Changing the Nation: Republican Rotten Boroughs, Statehood Politics, and American Political Development," *Studies in American Political Development* 6 (1992): 223–71.
89. Elizabeth Sanders, *Roots of Reform: Farmers, Workers and the American State, 1877–1917* (Chicago: University of Chicago Press, 1999), 3.
90. Jacob A. Riis, *How the Other Half Lives* (1890; reprint, New York: Penguin, 1997), 21. Riis was writing of New York.
91. *Congressional Record*, 61st Cong., 2d Sess., 1910, 45, pt. 7: 7742.
92. "Postal Bank Bill Fixed by G.O.P.," *Atlanta Constitution*, June 1, 1910, 1. Also "Republicans Agree on Postal Bank Bill," *New York Times*, June 2, 1910. Southwick was defying the Republican caucus.
93. *Congressional Record*, 61st Cong., 2d Sess., 1910, 45, pt. 7: 7736.
94. Ibid., 7730.
95. See, e.g., comments of Rep. Edward Taylor (D. Colo.), *Congressional Record*, 61st Cong., 2d Sess., 1910, 45, pt. 7: 7736. Also National Monetary Commission, *Notes on the Postal Savings-Bank Systems of the Leading Countries* (Washington, D.C.: Government Printing Office, 1910).
96. Edwin W. Kemmerer, "Six Years of Postal Savings in the United States," *American Economic Review* 7, no. 1 (1917): 46–90, 50–52.
97. Woodrow Wilson, "The Study of Administration," *Political Science Quarterly* 2, no. 2 (1887): 197–222, 218–21. Emphasis in original.
98. Ibid., 209.
99. Randolph Silliman Bourne, "Trans-National America," in *War and the Intellectuals: Collected Essays, 1915–1919*, ed. Carl Resek (New York: Harper, 1964), 115.
100. Rowland T. Berthoff, "Southern Attitudes Toward Immigration, 1865–1914," *Journal of Southern History* 17, no. 3 (1951): 328–60.
101. "Postal Bank Bill Passed by House," *Atlanta Constitution,* June 10, 1910, 1.

Chapter 5: Warfare

1. Harrison Rhodes, "War-Time Washington," *Harper's Monthly*, March 1918, 471.
2. Ibid., 474.

3. For details of the temporary buildings and war workers, see also "Echoes in Lighter Tone from Washington: Some Observations on the Military Salute, the Stenographer, and the Temporary Buildings," *New York Times,* June 16, 1918, 60.

4. Grosvenor Clarkson, *Industrial America in the World War: The Strategy Behind the Line, 1917–1918* (Boston: Houghton Mifflin, 1923), 139. For contemporary reports on economic and human mobilization, see Benedict Crowell and Robert Forrest Wilson, *How America Went to War,* 6 vols. (New Haven, Conn.: Yale University Press, 1921); Wesley Clair Mitchell, *History of Prices During the War: Summary* (Washington, D.C.: Government Printing Office, 1919); United States Provost Marshal General's Bureau, *Second Report of the Provost Marshal General to the Secretary of War on the Operations of the Selective Service System to December 20, 1918* (Washington, D.C.: Government Printing Office, 1919).

5. Committee on Public Information, *National Service Handbook,* 3.

6. "Echoes," 60.

7. Irmgard Steinisch, "Different Path to War: A Comparative Study of Militarism and Imperialism in the United States and Imperial Germany, 1871–1914," in *Anticipating Total War: The German and American Experiences, 1871–1914,* ed. Manfred F. Boemeke, Roger Chickering, and Stig Förster (Cambridge: Cambridge University Press, 1999), 29–53, 33, esp. note 20. On the idea that American character influences strategy of preparedness and fighting, see Russell F. Weigley, *The American Way of War: A History of United States Military Strategy and Policy* (New York: Macmillan, 1973).

8. Cited in Basil Henry Liddell Hart, *A History of the World War, 1914–1918* (London: Faber & Faber, 1934), 49. For the argument that the plans determined the outbreak of war, see A.J.P. Taylor, *War by Time-Table: How the First World War Began* (London: Macdonald & Co., 1969). Even historians who dispute Taylor's larger point concede that the existence of developed plans was a useful lever in forcing decisions on ministers; see Paul Kennedy, "Introduction," in *War Plans of the Great Powers, 1880–1914,* ed. Paul Kennedy (London: Allen & Unwin, 1979), 17.

9. Hew Strachan, *The First World War: To Arms* (Oxford: Oxford University Press, 2001), 104.

10. Richard Cobb, "France and the Coming of War," in *The Coming of the First World War,* ed. Robert J. W. Evans and Hartmut Pogge von Strandmann (Oxford: Clarendon Press, 1988), 133. The numbers

referred to the day in August 1914 on which the citizen would mobilize for war.

11. Cited in David M. Kennedy, *Over Here: The First World War and American Society* (New York: Oxford University Press, 1980), 94.

12. Brian McAllister Linn, *Guardians of Empire: The U.S. Army and the Pacific, 1902–1940* (Chapel Hill: University of North Carolina Press, 1997), 88–89.

13. J.A.S. Grenville, "Diplomacy and War Plans in the United States, 1890–1917," in *The War Plans of the Great Powers, 1880–1914*, ed. Paul Kennedy (London: Allen & Unwin, 1979), 23–38.

14. Cited in Robert D. Cuff, "Organizing for War: Canada and the United States During World War I," *Canadian Historical Association Historical Papers* (1969), 144.

15. See David Silbey, *The British Working Class and Enthusiasm for War, 1914–1916* (London: Frank Cass, 2005), 17–23.

16. Lt. Col. Frank W. Gano, "A Study of Priorities" (Army Industrial College, n.d. [1937–1941?]), 12–13.

17. Clarkson, *Industrial America*, 138–39.

18. Allyn A. Young, "National Statistics in War and Peace," *Publications of the American Statistical Association* 16, no. 121 (1918): 873–85, 873.

19. Wesley C. Mitchell, "Statistics and Government," *Publications of the American Statistical Association* 16, no. 125 (1919): 223–35, 225.

20. Lucy Sprague Mitchell, *Two Lives: The Story of Wesley Clair Mitchell and Myself* (New York: Simon & Schuster, 1953), 298.

21. Mitchell, "Statistics and Government," 226.

22. Ibid., 225.

23. Ibid., 228.

24. United States Secretary of War, "Annual Report" (Washington, D.C.: Government Printing Office), CIS no. 2182, for 1883, 46.

25. W. T. Sherman to Col. A. Beckwith, October 19, 1864, United States War Department, *The War of the Rebellion: A Compilation of Official Records of the Union and Confederate Armies* (Washington, D.C.: Government Printing Office, 1880–1901), series 1, vol. 39, 358.

26. On the demonstrative role of the march, see James M. McPherson, *Battle Cry of Freedom: The Civil War Era* (New York: Ballantine Books, 1989), 808–11; James M. McPherson, "From Limited War to Total War in America," in *On the Road to Total War: The American Civil War and the German Wars of Unification, 1861–1871*, ed. Stig

Förster and Jörg Nagler (Cambridge: Cambridge University Press, 1997), 295–309, esp. 307.

27. McPherson, "From Limited War to Total War," 308.

28. It might, that is, if accompanying decisions had been made about the logistics of moving and provisioning such a force, and if the new rail lines had been built with that purpose in mind.

29. Size of the overall army in 1866 was 57,072 officers and men, and in 1871 was 29,115. Susan B. Carter, Scott Sigmund Gartner et al., *Historical Statistics of the United States on CD-ROM, Colonial Times to 1970,* Bicentennial ed. (Cambridge: Cambridge University Press, 1997), series Y905.

30. On southern resistance, see Michael Perman, *Reunion Without Compromise: The South and Reconstruction, 1865–1868* (Cambridge: Cambridge University Press, 1973).

31. On the army's lacking an occupation strategy, see James E. Sefton, *The United States Army and Reconstruction, 1865–1877* (Baton Rouge: Louisiana State University Press, 1967).

32. United States Secretary of War, "Annual Report," CIS no. 1367, for 1868, and United States Secretary of War, "Annual Report," CIS no. 1558, for 1872.

33. General George Meade, cited in Sefton, *Army and Reconstruction*, 8.

34. Cited in Sherry L. Smith, *The View from Officer's Row: Army Perception of Western Indians* (Tucson: University of Arizona Press, 1990), 106.

35. United States Secretary of War, "Annual Report," CIS no. 2369, for 1885, 62.

36. Smith, *View from Officer's Row*, 92–138; United States Secretary of War, "Annual Report," CIS no. 1843, for 1878, 6.

37. Cited in Smith, *View from Officer's Row*, 7.

38. Cited in Robert M. Utley, *Frontier Regulars: The United States Army and the Indian, 1866–1891* (Lincoln: University of Nebraska Press, Bison Books ed., 1984), 60.

39. United States House of Representatives. Subcommittee of the Committee on Military Affairs, "Reorganization of the Army" (Washington, D.C.: Government Printing Office, 1878), CIS no. 1818, 45th Cong., 2d Sess., H. Misdoc 56, 5.

40. United States Secretary of War, "Annual Report," CIS no. 2277, for 1884, 45.

41. United States House of Representatives Subcommittee of the Committee on Military Affairs, "Reorganization of the Army," 5.

42. Robert M. Utley, "Total War on the Indian Frontier," in *Anticipating Total War: The German and American Experiences, 1871–1914*, ed. Manfred F. Boemeke, Roger Chickering, and Stig Förster (Cambridge: Cambridge University Press, 1999), 399–414.

43. United States Secretary of War, "Annual Report," CIS 2010, for 1881, 35.

44. Ibid., CIS no. 2182, for 1883, 46.

45. David Adams, "Internal Military Intervention in the United States," *Journal of Peace Research* 32, no. 2 (1995): 197–211, 201, and 203. One estimate puts the total number of labor-related deployments in the post–Civil War decades at more than three hundred. Russell F. Weigley, *History of the United States Army* (New York: Macmillan, 1967), 281. The 1877 strike is, as well, usually regarded as the occasion for modernizing the National Guard, which went out on such occasions at the behest of state governors more frequently than and before the regular army.

46. United States Secretary of War, "Annual Report," CIS no. 3295, for 1894, 57–59.

47. "Central Labor Union Acts," *New York Times*, July 2, 1894, 2.

48. In fairness to the official's judgment, these strikers had assembled weapons for use against potential strikebreakers. "Cannon Made of Gas Pipe," *New York Times*, July 4, 1894, 1.

49. "The Result of Immigration," *New York Times*, July 16, 1894, 2.

50. "The Chautauquans," *Los Angeles Times*, July 25, 1894, 5.

51. "News of the Railroads," *New York Times*, July 31, 1894, 2.

52. "Echoes of the Strike," *Los Angeles Times*, July 19, 1894, 4.

53. United States Secretary of War, "Annual Report," CIS no. 3206, for 1893, 19.

54. Ibid., CIS no. 3084, for 1892, 22.

55. United States Senate Committee on Military Affairs, "Regulating Enlistments in the Army of the United States" (Washington, D.C.: Government Printing Office, 1894), CIS no. 3179, 53d Cong., 2d Sess., S.Rpt 151, 3. Another factor may have been the increasing number of war scares in this era of jingoism, but these scares were also, Bruce White notes, tied to immigrant and ethnic divisions within the United States. See Bruce White, "War Preparations and Ethnic and Racial Relations in the United States," in Boemeke, Chickering, and Förster, eds. *Anticipating Total War*, 97–124.

56. United States House of Representatives Committee on Military

Affairs, "Regulating Enlistments in the Army" (Washington, D.C.: Government Printing Office, 1894), CIS no. 3269, 53d Cong., 2d Sess., H. Rpt 339, 2.

57. "An Act to Regulate Enlistments in the Army of the United States," *United States Statutes at Large* 28, no. 179 (1894): 216.

58. White, "War Preparations and Ethnic and Racial Relations in the United States," 107.

59. Edward S. Miller, *War Plan Orange: The U.S. Strategy to Defeat Japan, 1897–1945* (Annapolis, Md.: Naval Institute Press, 1991), 21–22.

60. Authorizing legislation for such surveillance was adopted in 1910. Joan M. Jensen, *Army Surveillance in America, 1775–1980* (New Haven, Conn.: Yale University Press, 1991), 113–15.

61. George B. Duncan, "Reasons for Increasing the Regular Army," *North American Review* 166, no. 497 (1898): 448–60, 451–53. The latter quotation is Duncan's citation of another, unnamed, expert.

62. On Upton, see Stephen E. Ambrose, "Emory Upton and the Armies of Asia and Europe," *Military Affairs* 28, no. 1 (1964): 27–32; Richard C. Brown, "General Emory Upton—The Army's Mahan," *Military Affairs* 17, no. 3 (1953): 125–31; Weigley, *History of the United States Army*, 281.

63. On the survival of French civic republicanism into the Restoration and empire, see Stéphane Audoin-Rouzeau, "French Public Opinion in 1870–71 and the Emergence of Total War," in *On the Road to Total War: The American Civil War and the German Wars of Unification, 1861–1871*, ed. Stig Förster and Jörg Nagler (Cambridge: Cambridge University Press, 1997), 393–411. On the U.S. survey of other countries' pension systems and the French system, see Edward T. Devine and Lilian Brandt, *Disabled Soldiers and Sailors: Pensions and Training* (New York: Oxford University Press, 1919), 25 and 98ff.; Antoine Prost, *Les anciens combattants et la Société Française 1914–1939*, 3 vols. (Paris: Presses de la Fondation nationale des sciences politiques, 1977), 1:14–15. As Prost points out, the various amendments, elaborations, and stratifications of this system made it unsuitable to the conditions of 1914–1918, but it had survived until then.

64. William Henry Glasson, *Federal Military Pensions in the United States* (New York: Oxford University Press, 1918), 99.

65. *Congressional Globe*, 37th Cong., 2d Sess., 2105.

66. Remarks of Richard Almgill Harrison (Unionist of Ohio), *Congressional Globe*, 37th Cong., 2d Sess., 2105.

67. R. A. Musgrave and J. M. Culbertson, "The Growth of Public Expenditure in the United States, 1890–1948," *National Tax Journal* 6, no. 2 (1953): 97–115.

68. French assistance to the elderly and infirm in 1910 went to about 571,000 people. Peter H. Lindert, "The Rise of Social Spending" (Davis, Calif.: University of California Agricultural History Center Working Paper no. 68, 1992), 75.

69. For contemporary criticism of the U.S. pension system for poorly serving the role of an old-age social-insurance program, see, e.g., I. M. Rubinow, *Social Insurance, with Special Reference to American Conditions* (New York: Henry Holt, 1913), 404–8. The program was also criticized for paying fraudulent claims; see, e.g., Douglas C. McMurtrie, *The Disabled Soldier* (New York: Macmillan, 1919), 24. Later historians have argued similar cases in retrospect, emphasizing the perceived expense and corruption of veterans' pensions in the . United States; see, e.g., Theda Skocpol, "America's First Social Security System: The Expansion of Benefits for Civil War Veterans," *Political Science Quarterly* 108, no. 1 (1993): 85–116; Theda Skocpol, *Protecting Soldiers and Mothers: The Political Origins of Social Policy in the United States* (Cambridge, Mass.: Belknap Press of Harvard University Press, 1992). On the pensions as a valuable retirement support for those who could get them, see Dora L. Costa, *The Evolution of Retirement: An American Economic History, 1880–1990* (Chicago: University of Chicago Press, 1998).

70. Brian McAllister Linn, *The Philippine War, 1899–1902* (Lawrence: University Press of Kansas, 2000), on early confusion, 6; on insufficient soldiers, 325 and throughout; on equipment, 143; on elections, 213.

71. Edward M. Coffman, *The Regulars: The American Army, 1898–1941* (Cambridge, Mass.: Belknap Press of Harvard University Press, 2004), 35.

72. Linn, *Guardians of Empire*, 52–53. The extent to which the Root reforms mark a true break in the history of the old army is subject to interpretation. Linn holds that they do so only when viewed through the perhaps more transformative experience of the First World War; Coffman holds otherwise. See also Brian McAllister Linn, "The Long Twilight of the Frontier Army," *Western Historical Quarterly* 27, no. 2 (1996): 141–67, esp. 164.

73. Walter LaFeber, *The Clash: U.S.-Japanese Relations Throughout History* (New York: W. W. Norton, 1997), 104–6; Linn, *Guardians of Empire*, 107 and 253.

Chapter 6: Americanness on Trial

1. "President Wilson's Speech," *New York Times*, January 9, 1915, 4. I am grateful to Kathy Olmsted for directing me to this speech.

2. Harding is sometimes incorrectly credited with coining this term. On the Wilson administration's anticipation of Harding's normalcy, see Burl Noggle, *Into the Twenties: The United States from Armistice to Normalcy* (Urbana: University of Illinois Press, 1974).

3. The municipal limit was originally $250,000, but the committee lowered it in February. *Federal Reserve Bulletin* 4, no. 2 (1918): 168–69.

4. *Federal Reserve Bulletin* 4, no. 1 (1918): 2.

5. *Federal Reserve Bulletin* 4, no. 7 (1918): 628.

6. Woodbury Willoughby, *The Capital Issues Committee and War Finance Corporation* (Baltimore, Md.: Johns Hopkins University Press, 1934), 19. Also "Officials Meet with Bankers in Big Conference," *Lima* (Ohio) *Daily News*, April 25, 1918, 4.

7. State and local government debt outstanding at the end of 1913 was $4.4 billion while federal debt was $1.2 billion, or slightly more than a quarter of state and local borrowing. The war changed this relationship; in 1922 the federal government had more than twice as much debt outstanding as states and localities. Carter, *HSUS*, Series Y601 (federal) and Y680 (state and local).

8. *Federal Reserve Bulletin* 4, no. 5 (1918), 400.

9. "Rules Governing Stock Companies and Stock Sales," *Wichita* (Wichita Falls, Texas) *Daily Times*, October 10, 1918, 6. Also *Federal Reserve Bulletin* 4, no. 1 (1918): 1; *Federal Reserve Bulletin* 4, no. 2 (1918): 74; *Federal Reserve Bulletin* 4, no. 3 (1918): 171; *Federal Reserve Bulletin* 4, no. 8 (1918): 705.

10. See, e.g., Kimbley Oil and Refining, "Advertisement," *Wichita Daily Times*, February 9, 1919, 3.

11. "Legislation Wanted to Protect Investors," *Wall Street Journal*, December 27, 1918, 7. At this point the committee had only suspended operation. It continued nominally to exist into the next year. Paul Warburg later agreed that certifying the basic worth of securities had been a valuable function of the committee, a function that should continue into peacetime. See Paul Warburg, "Some Phases of Financial Reconstruction," *Annals of the American Academy of Political and Social Science* 82 (1919): 347–73, esp. 353.

12. *Federal Reserve Bulletin* 4, no. 2 (1918): 171.

13. Ibid., 1164.

14. Cited in Robert D. Cuff, *The War Industries Board: Business-*

Government Relations During World War I (Baltimore, Md.: Johns Hopkins University Press, 1973), 233.

15. Joseph W. Duncan and William C. Shelton, *Revolution in United States Government Statistics, 1926–1976* (Washington, D.C.: Government Printing Office, 1978), 9.

16. Wesley Clair Mitchell, *History of Prices During the War: Summary* (Washington, D.C.: Government Printing Office, 1919), 94. Mitchell's *History* has a military analogue in Leonard P. Ayres, *The War with Germany: A Statistical Summary* (Washington, D.C.: Government Printing Office, 1919). Ayres was chief of the Statistical Branch of the General Staff. On this general disappointment, see William J. Breen, "Foundations, Statistics, and State-Building: Leonard P. Ayres, the Russell Sage Foundation, and U.S. Government Statistics in the First World War," *Business History Review* 68, no. 4 (1994): 451–82; Robert D. Cuff, "Creating Control Systems: Edwin F. Gay and the Central Bureau of Planning and Statistics, 1917–1919," *Business History Review* 63, no. 3 (1989): 588–613. There were other important aspects to the wartime government; on these, see Frederic L. Paxson, "The American War Government, 1917–1918," *American Historical Review* 26, no. 1 (1920): 54–76. On the railroad controls, see Robert D. Cuff, "United States Mobilization and Railroad Transportation: Lessons in Coordination and Control, 1917–1945," *Journal of Military History* 53, no. 1 (1989): 33–50.

17. Paul A. Samuelson and Everett E. Hagen, *After the War, 1918–1920: Military and Economic Demobilization of the United States* (Washington, D.C.: Government Printing Office, 1943), 6–7.

18. Russell F. Weigley, *History of the United States Army* (New York: Macmillan, 1967), 399–408.

19. For 1921–1930, average spending on the army and navy as an annual share of GDP was 1 percent; for 1901–1910 it was .96 percent. Between the Civil War and the Spanish-American War it averaged .75 percent. Spending on army and navy from Carter, *HSUS*, Series Y458 and Y459. GDP from Louis Johnston and Samuel H. Williamson, *The Annual Real and Nominal GDP for the United States, 1789–Present* (Economic History Services, March 2004), available from http://www.eh.net/hmit (accessed August 17, 2005).

20. "Bankers Would Retain War Credit Board," *New York Times*, November 20, 1918, 10.

21. Duncan and Shelton, *Revolution*, 13–20, esp. 15.

22. Cited in Samuelson and Hagen, *After the War*, 6.

23. Cuff, *War Industries Board*, 259.

24. "Text of the President's Address to Congress," *New York Times*, December 3, 1918, 3.

25. Cited in Jerold S. Auerbach, "Woodrow Wilson's 'Prediction' to Frank Cobb: Words Historians Should Doubt Ever Got Spoken," *Journal of American History* 54, no. 3 (1967): 608–17, 612; Arthur S. Link, "That Cobb Interview," *Journal of American History* 72, no. 1 (1985): 7–17, 12.

26. Ewan Clague, *The Bureau of Labor Statistics* (New York: Praeger, 1968), 44.

27. The contribution of American policies to the Great Depression and the relation of such policies to international factors has produced a vast and unsettled literature. The account here has most in common with those of Barry Eichengreen, *Golden Fetters: The Gold Standard and the Great Depression, 1919–1939* (New York: Oxford University Press, 1992); Charles Poor Kindleberger, *The World in Depression, 1929–1939* (London: Allen Lane, 1973); and Brinley Thomas, *Migration and Economic Growth: A Study of Great Britain and the Atlantic Economy*, 2d ed. (Cambridge: Cambridge University Press, 1973). All emphasize the contribution of American policies to the construction of a global system quite likely to propagate economic shocks. Historians differ as to the nature and size of the shock required. See also Milton Friedman and Anna Jacobson Schwartz, *A Monetary History of the United States, 1867–1960* (Princeton: Princeton University Press, 1963); Allan H. Meltzer, *A History of the Federal Reserve, 1913–1951* (Chicago: University of Chicago Press, 2003); Christina D. Romer, "The Nation in Depression," *Journal of Economic Perspectives* 7, no. 2 (1993): 19–39; Peter Temin, *Lessons from the Great Depression* (Cambridge, Mass.: MIT Press, 1989).

28. Samuelson and Hagen, *After the War*, 8.

29. Rates compared with Underwood-Simmons and Payne-Aldrich tariffs appear in "Final Tariff Rates Reported to House; Vote Is Due Today," *New York Times*, September 13, 1922, 1.

30. Richard Franklin Bensel, *Sectionalism and American Political Development, 1880–1980* (Madison: University of Wisconsin Press, 1984), 71, table 3.2.

31. But it appears to have done little good, either. See Douglas A. Irwin, "Could the U.S. Iron Industry Have Survived Free Trade after the Civil War?," (National Bureau of Economic Research, 2000), NBER Working Paper no. 7640; Douglas A. Irwin, "Did Late Nineteenth Century U.S. Tariffs Promote Infant Industries? Evidence from the Tinplate Industry," (National Bureau of Economic Research, 1998), NBER Working

Paper no. 6835; Douglas A. Irwin, "Higher Tariffs, Lower Revenues? Analyzing the Fiscal Aspects of 'The Great Tariff Debate of 1888,'" *Journal of Economic History* 58, no. 1 (1998): 59–72; Douglas A. Irwin, "Tariffs and Growth in Late Nineteenth Century America" (Washington, D.C.: National Bureau of Economic Research, 2000), NBER Working Paper no. 7639. Also, for the later period, Edward S. Kaplan, *American Trade Policy, 1923–1995* (Westport, Conn.: Greenwood, 1996).

32. George Paish, "Great Britain's Capital Investments in Other Lands," *Journal of the Royal Statistical Society* 72, no. 3 (1909): 465–95, 480.

33. "The Outgrown Tariff," *New York Times*, August 25, 1926, 20.

34. Barry Eichengreen, "The Political Economy of the Smoot-Hawley Tariff," *Research in Economic History* 12 (1989): 1–43, 32; Kindleberger, *The World in Depression, 1929–1939*, 77.

35. Roger Daniels, *Guarding the Golden Door: American Immigration Policy and Immigrants Since 1882* (New York: Hill and Wang, 2004), 46.

36. "Wilson Declares Berlin Is Seeking Deceitful Peace," *New York Times*, June 15, 1917, 1.

37. Daniels, *Guarding*, 274n52.

38. See, e.g., "Immigration Bill Discussed in House," *New York Times*, December 10, 1920; "Immigration Bill Passed," *New York Times*, May 14, 1921.

39. Daniels, *Guarding*, 46–55 and 274n52. Total immigrants 1921–1925 numbered 2.6 million and for 1926–1930, 1.5 million. Carter, *HSUS*, series C89.

40. Ashley S. Timmer and Jeffrey G. Williamson, "Immigration Policy Prior to the 1930s: Labor Markets, Policy Interactions, and Globalization Backlash," *Population and Development Review* 24, no. 4 (1998): 739–71.

41. The unemployment rate in Britain stayed mainly over 10 percent, and in Germany over 6.8 percent, while in the United States it fell below 3 percent. Barry Eichengreen, "The Origins and Nature of the Great Slump Revisited," *Economic History Review* 45, no. 2 (1992): 213–39, esp. 216–17.

42. Thomas, *Migration*, 200. Thomas goes even further, arguing that immigration restriction, by increasing the availability of cheap labor in Europe, attracted U.S. speculative investment to the Old World, which increased after 1924. Eichengreen attributes this effect to the Dawes Plan, also of 1924. Barry Eichengreen, "The U.S. Capital Mar-

ket and Foreign Lending, 1920–1955," in *Developing Country Debt and Economic Performance*, ed. Jeffrey D. Sachs, 1:107–155 (Chicago: University of Chicago Press, 1989).

43. Cited in Meltzer, *History of the Federal Reserve*, 174n53.

44. Eichengreen, *Golden Fetters*, 216–30. Eichengreen's view is widely though not universally shared. See also Meltzer, *History of the Federal Reserve*.

45. Even in the revised, less volatile series of Christina Romer, the unemployment rate rose from 2.95 percent in 1919 to 5.16 percent in 1920 and 8.73 percent in 1921. See Christina D. Romer, "Spurious Volatility in Historical Unemployment Data," *Journal of Political Economy* 94, no. 1 (1986): 1–37, 31, table 9.

46. Albert Fishlow, "Lessons from the Past: Capital Markets During the 19th Century and the Interwar Period," *International Organization* 39, no. 3 (1985): 383–439, 397.

47. See also Barry Eichengreen and Peter B. Kenen, "Managing the World Economy under the Bretton Woods System: An Overview," in *Managing the World Economy: Fifty Years After Bretton Woods*, ed. Peter B. Kenen (Washington, D.C.: Institute for International Economics, 1994), 3–57, esp. 9–10.

Conclusion

1. Karl Marx and Friedrich Engels, *The Communist Manifesto*, trans. Samuel Moore, 1888 ed. (reprint, Oxford: Oxford University Press, 1998), 6–7.

2. Globalization's contribution to its own demise is a major theme of Kevin H. O'Rourke and Jeffrey G. Williamson, *Globalization and History: The Evolution of a Nineteenth-Century Atlantic Economy* (Cambridge, Mass.: MIT Press, 1999).

3. Timothy J. Hatton and Jeffrey G. Williamson, *The Age of Mass Migration: Causes and Economic Impact* (New York: Oxford University Press, 1998), 277.

4. The worldwide inflation in gold alleviated the depression of the 1890s without requiring political action from the U.S. administration. Milton Friedman and Anna Jacobson Schwartz, *Monetary History*, 135.

5. Eichengreen and Kenen, "Managing the World Economy . . . Overview"; John Williamson, "On the System in Bretton Woods," *American Economic Review* 75, no. 2 (1985): 74–79.

6. Organisation for Economic Co-operation and Development,

"Trends in International Migration" (OECD, 2003), Series A.1.1 and B.1.1.

7. Although the OECD cautions against thinking this with any degree of certitude. Organisation for Economic Co-operation and Development, "Trends and Recent Developments in Foreign Direct Investment: 2005" (OECD, 2005), 9.

8. Organisation for Economic Co-operation and Development, "Social Expenditure Database (SOCX), 1980–2001" (OECD, 2004).

9. Peter H. Lindert, *Growing Public: Social Spending and Economic Growth Since the Eighteenth Century* (Cambridge: Cambridge University Press, 2004), 257–63.

10. In 2003, the United States spent between 3 and 4 percent of its GDP on defense, for a total spending of $417 billion. Stockholm International Peace Research Institute, *SIPRI Data on Military Expenditure* (2004); available from http://www.sipri.org (accessed January 12, 2005).

11. The U.S. military has lately amounted to about 1.4 million, or about .5 percent of a population of almost 280 million. In 1960, the United States had 2.3 million men under arms of a population of about 181 million, or about 1.3 percent. In 1860, the British had about 278,000 men under arms of a population of about 37 million, or about .75 percent. For historical data on military sizes, see Correlates of War Project, *National Material Capabilities Data,* Version 3.01 (2004); available from http://correlatesofwar.org (accessed January 12, 2005). Proposals considered in 2004 to increase the size of the military would take it to perhaps 1.47 million. See Edward F. Bruner, *Military Forces: What Is the Appropriate Size for the United States?* (Congressional Research Service, 2004); available from http://www.fas.org/man/crs/RS21754.pdf (accessed January 12, 2005).

12. Philippe Sands, *Lawless World: America and the Making and Breaking of Global Rules from FDR's Atlantic Charter to George W. Bush's Illegal War* (London: Penguin, 2005).

13. Organisation for Economic Co-operation and Development, "Trends and Recent Developments," 9.

Notes and Sources for Figures and Tables

Figure 1.1. Eighty percent of the U.S. territorial empire given in the figure represents Alaska, without which the American colonies would appear vanishingly small. Countries with zero colonial territory are excluded; otherwise there would be a cluster of unreadable dots and text around the origin. Countries included are "advanced capitalist countries," defined as in Angus Maddison, *Monitoring the World Economy, 1820–1992* (Paris: Development Centre of the Organisation for Economic Co-operation and Development, 1995). Effectively, these are countries that were rich in both absolute and per capita terms owing to their modern economies. *Sources:* Colonial territory as in Grover Clark, *The Balance Sheets of Imperialism: Facts and Figures on Colonies* (New York: Columbia University Press, 1936), 23–28, table I. GDP as in Angus Maddison, *The World Economy: Historical Statistics* (Paris: Development Centre of the Organisation for Economic Co-operation and Development, 2003).

Figure 1.2. "Social spending" here includes spending at all levels of government on public housing, health, pensions for the elderly, and assistance to the poor. Regarding per capita GDP, the United States would be closer to trend but still below the line. As in figure 1.1, countries with zero social spending are excluded. *Sources:* Social-spending figures as in Peter H. Lindert, "The Rise of Social Spending, 1880–1930," in *Explorations in Economic History* 31 (1994): 1–37, 10, table 1A. Social spending for Germany is an estimate based on Lindert's 1900 figure. GDP as in Maddison, *The World Economy.*

Figure 1.3. In keeping with Charles Goodhart's argument, the later date is given for the establishment of Sweden's Riksbank as a central bank; see sources below. As in previous figures, countries with no central bank are excluded. *Sources:* Age of central banks from Charles Goodhart, *The Evolution of Central Banks* (Cambridge, Mass.: MIT Press, 1988); also from Web sites of various banks and from European Association for Banking History, *Inventory of Central Banks* (2004); available from http://www.bankinghistory.de (accessed January 12, 2005). GDP as in Angus Maddison, *The World Economy.*

Table 1.1. From Steven Ruggles, Matthew Sobek, et al., *Integrated Public Use Microdata Series: Version 3.0* (Minneapolis: Population Center, 2004), available from http://www.ipums.org. *Urban* is defined as an incorporated place with more than 2,500 residents. The *manufacturing* workforce here includes people employed in an industry that on the 1950 classification basis fell under the heading of manufacturing; i.e., that in IPUMS has a value of between 306 and 499 inclusive, covering both durable and nondurable goods. The *professional* workforce here includes people employed in an industry that on the 1950 classification basis fell under the heading of professional and related services; i.e., that in IPUMS has a value of between 868 and 899 inclusive, covering medical, legal, educational, welfare, religious, nonprofit, engineering, and architectural services. *Recent immigrants* are defined as those recorded as having arrived since the last census year. In each case, the IPUMS sample finds a number for recent immigrants that is only a fraction of those recorded arriving at ports of entry (the fraction ranges between 60 and 70 percent of the figure in Susan B. Carter, Scott Sigmund Gartner, et al., *Historical Statistics of the United States on CD-ROM, Colonial Times to 1970,* Bicentennial ed. (Cambridge: Cambridge University Press, 1997), C89. This is consistent with the usual estimate that about a third of immigrants who arrived in the United States in this period subsequently left; it is also consistent with census undercounting of migrants, on which point see note on undercounts on page 179.

Figure 2.1. *Source:* U.S. Committee on Public Information, *National Service Handbook* (Washington, D.C.: Government Printing Office, 1917), 253 (foldout page).

Figure 2.2. *Source:* From Lawrence Martin, "Maps Showing Territorial Changes Since the World War, the Transfer of German Cables and the League of Nations in 1923," *International Conciliation* 198 (May 1924): 119–41; map on 132. Altered for clarity.

Figure 2.3. *Source:* William H. "Coin" Harvey, from *Coin's Financial School* (1895), 215.

Figure 2.4. *Sources:* Flow of British capital from Lance Edwin Davis and

Robert J. Cull, *International Capital Markets and American Economic Growth, 1820–1914* (Cambridge: Cambridge University Press, 1994), 39, table 2.8b, column 9. Miles added to the railway system from Jeffrey G. Williamson, *American Growth and the Balance of Payments: A Study of the Long Swing* (Chapel Hill: University of North Carolina Press, 1964), 274, table b-13.

Figure 2.5. *Source:* Harvey, *Coin's Financial School,* 213.

Figure 3.1. *Sources:* Immigrant arrival figures from B. R. Mitchell, *International Historical Statistics: The Americas, 1750–2000,* 5th ed. (New York: Palgrave Macmillan, 2003), 94–95, table A8. Miles added to the railway system from Williamson, *American Growth and the Balance of Payments,* 274, table b-13.

Figure 3.2. The category "Others" includes as many as a couple of dozen other source nations, none of which accounts for more than 2 percent of the total migration stream to the receiving country. The definition of an immigrant varies from country to country, but the general proportions are still informative. *Source:* Imre Ferenczi and Walter Francis Willcox, *International Migrations,* 2 vols. (New York: National Bureau of Economic Research, 1929), 1:267–70, table 13.

Figure 3.3. For 1880, $n=1,027$; for 1910, $n=2,775$. For the 1910 graph, "New immigrants" refers to those arriving between 1891 and 1910, "Old immigrants" to those arriving up to and including 1890. These proportions were obtained by finding entries for workers whose industrial classification by the 1950 system (IND1950 variable) was either 336 ("Blast furnaces, steel works, and rolling mills") or 337 ("Other primary iron and steel industries").

In the published report of the 1910 census, the categories of "blast furnaces and rolling mills" and "other iron and steel factories" were both top-ten employers of manufacturing workers (nos. 5 and 2, respectively; workers in "other iron and steel" were fewer only than workers in the catchall category of "building and hand trades"). Together they accounted for about 9 percent of manufacturing workers in the census. (The "building and hand trades" accounted for about 31 percent.) Of all workers in "other iron and steel factories," 32.4 percent were foreign-born; of all workers in "blast furnaces and rolling mills," 50.5 percent were foreign-born. The percentages were higher among people classed as general laborers in these industries: 52.5 and 69.9 percent, respectively. These were not the most or least foreign-born industries among the major manufacturing sectors. The building and hand trades were about 25 percent foreign-born. People employed making suits, coats, cloaks, and overalls were about 66 percent foreign-born. People employed in turpentine distilleries were only 1 percent foreign-born. The average manufacturing subsector employed 32.6 percent foreign-born, and overall the manufacturing sector employed 31.2 percent foreign-born. See U.S. Census, *Thirteenth Census of the United States, taken in the year 1910,* vol. IV, *Population: Occupation Statistics* (Washington, D.C.: Government Printing Office, 1914), 312–410, table VI.

Because this report classifies workers by industry, it counts people in management and service positions within the industry as well as general laborers, although laborers and operatives are the most numerous category of employee. This method of identifying workers in the iron and steel industries captures fewer people in the 1880 census and more people in the 1910 census than appear in *Historical Statistics of the United States,* series D176. The lower number found for 1880 here may be due to the fact that census enumerators did not record industry as a variable in 1880, leaving it to the judgment of later statisticians as to which industrial category embraces a given entry. The higher number found for 1910 here may be due to the fact that series D176 seeks to count only "primary wage earners," while this method should find all participants in the iron and steel industries. But discrepancies in numbers may also result from errors in the published reports. See Susan B. Carter and Richard Sutch, "Fixing the Facts: Editing of the 1880 Census of Occupations with Implications for Long-Term Trends and the Sociology of Official Statistics" (National Bureau of Economic Research, 1995).

Figure 3.4. *Source:* IPUMS, Carter Goodrich et al., *Migration and Economic Opportunity: The Report of the Study of Population Redistribution* (Philadelphia: University of Pennsylvania Press, 1936), plate VI-A, between pages 686 and 687.

Table 3.1. *Source:* IPUMS.

Figure 4.1. *Source:* Seymour Martin Lipset and Gary Wolfe Marks, *It Didn't Happen Here: Why Socialism Failed in the United States* (New York: W. W. Norton & Co., 2000), 188, table. 5.1.

Figure 4.2. *Sources:* Internal migrant figures from the 1910 IPUMS sample. Presidential vote percentages from W. Dean Burnham, Jerome Clubb, and William Flanigan, "State-Level Presidential Election Data for the United States, 1824–1972," ICPSR study no. 19. Using the data on estimated net intercensal migration from *Historical Statistics of the United States,* C25-75, reveals essentially the same correlation.

Table 4.1. African Americans were much more likely to be found in jobs that brought them into close contact with native-born whites than new immigrants were. Note, too, that not only were native-born whites less likely to find themselves in the same kind of laboring occupations as blacks or immigrants, they were also less concentrated in such a small variety of jobs. *Source:* IPUMS 1910 sample, frequencies of OCC1950 variable for records for which it was not a "non-occupational response." The sample includes, for cities over 30,000 population, 3,830 African Americans; 6,018 post-1890 immigrants from Austria, Hungary, Italy, or Russia; and 28,898 native-born whites. The total nationwide population of cities over 30,000 in the sample is 108,594, or about 30 percent of the national population.

Figure 4.3. *Source:* U.S. Committee on Public Information, *National Service Handbook,* 248 (foldout page).

Table 4.2. There are, of necessity, some judgments involved in assigning a primary purpose to each of these bureaus. Many of the functions overlap. Few regulatory bureaus try to regulate without first gathering information. In the case of each, I have tried to select what seems to be its major intended function. Likewise with their novelty: there is almost no such thing as a government organization with no predecessor, but the question is whether the federal government was reasonably clearly adding to its living space by creating a new agency or whether it was simply keeping house. *Sources:* For dates of creation, primary purpose, and novelty, see *United States Government Manual,* March 1945 (Washington, D.C.: Office of War Information, 1945), and administrative histories in the National Archives and Records Administrations descriptions. Categories of government functions adapted from R. B. Haldane, *Report of the Machinery of Government Committee* (London: Her Majesty's Stationery Office [HMSO], 1918).

Figure 4.4. *Source:* Edwin W. Kemmerer, "Six Years of Postal Savings in the United States," *American Economic Review* 7, no. 1 (March 1917): 46–90; map on 56.

Table 5.1. Members of the military are those coded as having OCC1950 of 595, "Members of the armed services," in IPUMS. There are 299 in the 1870 sample, 279 in the 1880 sample, 573 in the 1900 sample, and 526 in the 1910 sample, which, owing to the different sample weights, corresponds approximately to 29,900 in 1870, 27,900 in 1880, 114,600 in 1900, and 131,500 in 1910. Citizenship data are not available for the 1880 sample. Microdata are not available for 1890. In these years the question of citizenship was asked only of foreign-born men twenty-one or older, except in 1870, when it was asked of all men twenty-one or older.

Figure 5.1. *Source:* Correlates of War Project, *National Material Capabilities Data,* Version 3.01, http://correlatesofwar.org (accessed January 12, 2005).

Table 5.2. *Sources:* France: military pensions from *Compte général de l'administration des finances rendu pour l'année . . . par le ministre des finance* (Paris: Imprimerie Nationale); GDP and population figures from B. R. Mitchell, *International Historical Statistics,* 5th ed. (New York: Palgrave Macmillan, 2003), tables A2 and J1. United States: military pensions from William Henry Glasson, *Federal Military Pensions in the United States* (New York: Oxford University Press, 1918), 273; GDP from Louis Johnston and Samuel H. Williamson, *The Annual Real and Nominal GDP for the United States 1789–Present* (Economic History Services, March 2004, available from http://www.eh.net/hmit (accessed August 17, 2005). Population figures from HSUS, series A6, A30–31, and A120–122 (percent of adult population estimated by linear fit for 1891 and 1896).

Table 5.3. *Source:* Correlates of War Project, *National Material Capabilities Data,* Version 3.01, http://www.correlatesofwar.org (accessed March 26, 2004).

Figure 6.1. *Source:* Frontispiece from Harold Glenn Moulton and Leo Pasvolsky, *War Debts and World Prosperity* (Washington, D.C.: Brookings Institution, 1932).

Appendix Table. The assumptions are that the factors described in the text, plus some standard ones for progressive reform, should matter: woman suffrage; the size of the population; relative wealth (measured by the mean of the Socio-Economic Index); the distribution of wealth (measured by the standard deviation of the Socio-Economic Index); whether a city is in the South or not; what the date of entry was for the state in which the city is found; the presence of migrants of various kinds and the share of workers employed in manufacturing. Conclusions are as drawn in chapter 4, "Welfare." *Source:* Results of an OLS regression of the per capita spending on health and sanitation, as recorded in *Wealth, Debt, and Taxation* for 1913, on these variables, comprising 198 observations for cities of over 30,000 populations. Overall R-squared is .40.

■ Index

Asia: immigration from, 196*n1*;
    imperialism in, 13, 20
"Asiatic barred zone," 78, 159,
    201*n45*
Atlanta Constitution, 83, 102
Australia, 41, 58, 93, 186*n35*,
    190*n13*, 193*n45*; immigration
    to, 60, 67, 78–80
Austria-Hungary, immigrants from,
    62, 65, 67, 71, 102

Bagehot, Walter, 15
Bank of England, 160
banks, 32, 43–44, 46, 52, 56, 57,
    117–18, 152, 153; British, 8;
    central, 15–16, 54; foreign
    investments of, 39–40;
    monopolies and, 50; private,
    19, 42; regulation of, 53, 116;
    and settlement of West, 19, 23,
    46, 53; during World War I,
    127, 149; *see also* Federal
    Reserve System
Bank of the United States, 36
Barings Bank, 39, 40
Beard, Charles, 95–96, 98–99, 104,
    105, 108, 204*n29*
Berlin, 126, 127
Beveridge, William, 86
Bismarck, Otto von, 14, 88, 96
blacks, *see* African Americans
Bolshevik Revolution, 159
bonds, 40, 117, 149; defaults on,
    36, 37, 52
boom-and-bust cycles, 48, 52, 55,
    75, 135, 153
Boone, Daniel, 73
Borden, Robert, 127
Botanic Garden, U.S., 109
Bourne, Randolph, 67, 120

Brantley, William, 120
Brazil, 13, 51, 58, 190*n13*;
    immigration to, 67
Breckinridge, Joseph, 138
Bretton Woods system, 169, 170
Bristow, Joseph, 57
Britain, 7, 125, 139, 171, 222*n11*;
    foreign investments of, 32, 33,
    35–42, 49, 51, 53, 156–57,
    161, 162, 167, 190*nn7, 13*;
    GDP of, 182*n9*; immigrants
    from, 67, 102; imperial, 8–9,
    19, 20, 23, 80; social spending
    in, 86, 98, 105; trade policy of,
    159–61; unemployment in,
    220*n41*; in World War I, 128
Brookings, Robert, 150–51
Brown Brothers banks, 43
Brown Brothers Harriman, 50
Bulkley, Robert, 31
"bums," 72

California, 115; immigrants in, 70,
    77, 137, 139, 145; internal
    migration to, 73, 76
Caminetti, Anthony, 78
Canada, 20, 38, 41, 43, 51, 58,
    186*n35*, 190*nn11, 13*;
    immigration to, 60, 66–67, 78;
    during World War I, 127–28
Canadian Pacific (CP) Railroad, 43,
    193*n43*
canals, 35, 41
capital: government regulation of,
    30, 161; international flow of,
    4, 12, 18–19, 24, 28, 87, 91,
    160–61, 166, 167 (*see also*
    foreign investment)
Capital Issues Committee, 148–52,
    217*nn3, 11*

South: culture of *(continued)*
plan opposed in, 35;
immigration and, 76–77, 83,
202n59; literacy tests in,
79–81; migration of African
Americans from, 73, 77, 100,
200n41; during
Reconstruction, 120, 131, 132,
135; segregation in, 206n49;
social spending in, 98–100,
206n43; *see also* Civil War;
Confederate States of America
South Africa, 80, 190n13
South Carolina, 40
South Dakota, 23
Southwick, George N., 117
Spain: GDP of, 182n9; immigrants
from, 60, 67, 116
Spanish-American War, 144
"states' rights," 35
steamships, 19, 58, 140
steel industry, foreign-born workers
in, 70–71, 198n29
stock market crash of 1929, 161
Strachan, Hew, 126
streetcars, segregation of, 206n49
strikes, 88, 89, 136–39, 214nn45, 48
Strong, Benjamin, 160–61
submarine warfare, 125
Supreme Court, U.S., 114
Sutch, Richard, 188n43
Swanton, Walter Irving, 108

tariffs, 155–57, 159, 160, 162,
219n29
taxation, 17, 114; class and attitudes
toward, 26; government debts
and, 34, 37; to improve
industrial capacity, 18; for
social spending, 14, 97, 99

Taylor, A.J.P., 211n8
Taylor, Edward T., 118
telegraph lines, 19, 43, 45, 52;
transatlantic, 44
Tennessee, 40
1066 and All That (Sellar and
Yeatman), 7
Texas, 150
Times (London), 44
Tocqueville, Alexis de, 12
total war, 121, 131
trade policy, 155–57, 159, 160, 162,
219n29
tramps, 72
transportation, 35; *see also*
railroads
travel, transoceanic, 19, 58
Treasury Department, U.S., 55
trusts, *see* monopolies
Turkestan, 22, 185n28, 186n30,
201n45
Turkey, 191n20
Turner, Frederick Jackson, 73
Twain, Mark, 21
typhoid, 96

Underwood-Simmons Tariff,
219n29
unemployment, 35, 95, 152,
162, 220n41, 221n45; cyclical,
14, 17; post–World War I,
153–54, 160; social spending
on, 24, 85, 86, 111, 115,
116
unionization, 27, 66, 69, 89, 137
Union Pacific Railroad, 42–43, 65,
73, 193n41
United Nations, 169
Upton, General Emory, 140
Utah, 815n28